OPERATION BIG

OPERATION BIG

The Race to Stop Hitler's Atomic Bomb

COLIN BROWN

AMBERLEY

To Lindy Malone of West Street, Godmanchester,
for telling me the story.

First published 2016
This edition published 2018

Amberley Publishing
The Hill, Stroud
Gloucestershire, GL5 4EP

www.amberley-books.com

British Library Cataloguing in Publication Data.
A catalogue record for this book is available from the British Library.

ISBN 978 1 4456 8285 3 (paperback)
ISBN 978 1 4456 5185 9 (ebook)

Typesetting and Origination by Amberley Publishing.
Printed in the UK.

Contents

Those engaged saw themselves as in a race with the Germans who had a head-start since nuclear fission had been discovered by Hahn in Germany at the end of 1938 ...

Sir Charles Frank, Introduction, *Hitler's Uranium Club*,
University of California Press, 1993

I should say that you might say the whole project, the Manhattan Project, was built on fear: fear that the enemy had the bomb, or would have it before we could develop it. And this they knew to be the case, the scientists did, because they were refugees from Germany, a large number of them, and they had studied under the Germans before the war broke out.

Robert Furman, interview, *Voices of the
Manhattan Project*, Atomic Heritage Foundation,
Washington, 20 February 2008

Seventy years on from the destruction of Hiroshima, we know full well what nuclear weapons do – they kill civilians; they destroy cities.

Our Government plans to waste £100 billion on nuclear weapons over the next 35 years. Weapons much more powerful than those that destroyed Hiroshima.

In the past decade, our Government has bombed Iraq, Afghanistan, Libya and now Syria – leaving behind dead people, chaos and misery. This drift into perpetual warfare is both immoral and dangerous. What happens when our 'interventions' meet their 'interventions'. Will somebody press the button?

CND leaflet to mark Hiroshima Day,
6 August 2015

Foreword

When I first heard the story of Farm Hall, it sounded like a script for a Hollywood movie. It all turned out to be true.

In the dying days of the Second World War, as Hitler's Third Reich collapsed, a small lightly armed US intelligence force made a daring raid across southern Germany in Jeeps and armoured cars. It was named the Alsos mission. Their objective: to capture Hitler's key nuclear physicists known as the *Uranveiren*, the Uranium Club.

The Alsos mission was headed by a Russian-American, Colonel Boris T. Pash, who hunted down the last of Hitler's nuclear scientists in the snow-covered mountains of Bavaria.

Hitler's Uranium Club was rounded up and secretly flown to England, where ten scientists were detained for six months in a corner of England by the rich water meadows of Cambridgeshire at a Georgian mansion called Farm Hall.

They were treated as VIP guests in a five-star country hotel, with their own servants to bring them drinks and chefs to cook their meals. They put on weight, and to try to get some exercise, they played volleyball in the extensive grounds that were put at their disposal. Occasionally, one of them climbed over the garden wall and escaped into the town for a few pints in a pub with the local girls.

In the evenings, they held seminars in the drawing room, listened to the wireless and played cards. Werner Heisenberg, the leader of the group, played Beethoven sonatas on the piano. Unknown to the scientists, every word they uttered was recorded by eavesdroppers for MI6, who were concealed in a nearby barn.

Top-secret reports of their conversations were sent to MI6 chiefs in London as well as General Leslie Groves, the head of the Manhattan Project. These revealed Hitler's Uranium Club were looking forward to cashing in on their atomic secrets after the war by working for the highest bidders in London or Buenos Aires in Argentina.

Their hopes were blown to bits on 6 August 1945 when they heard the news the Americans had exploded an atomic bomb over the Japanese city of Hiroshima. Their response caused outrage among other scientists, and the controversy still rages today. The arguments, though, have been largely academic and written before the Farm Hall transcripts were published. Since then a wealth of new material has come to light.

As Britain faces the renewal of its Trident nuclear weapon system, it seemed a good moment to investigate further the story of Farm Hall and the scientists who were held there ... and to see just how close Hitler's scientists came to beating America and Britain in the race to the atomic bomb.

I have researched Churchill's Cabinet papers on TA (Tube Alloys – the code name for the British atomic bomb project), and the archives of papers from intelligence officers such as R. V. Jones. I have supplemented the highly readable memoirs (now long out of print) of Colonel Pash with over 1,200 separate files from his private papers in the archives at the Hoover Institution Library at Stanford, California, with the help of my US researcher, Camilla Lindan.

I discovered that Farm Hall was not the last scene in the race for the bomb at the end of the Second World War but the start of the arms race that plunged the West into the Cold War against Stalin's Soviet Union, and Pash was to play a controversial role as a Cold War warrior for the CIA.

I followed Pash's journey to the hidden cave beneath a beautiful fairy-tale castle and church on the fringes of the Black Forest where the German nuclear reactor was concealed. But first, I had to go to Farm Hall ...

Colin Brown, Blackheath, 2016.

Timeline

1939

26 January – In Washington, Niels Bohr announces the discovery of uranium fission by Otto Hahn and Fritz Strassman at the Kaiser Wilhelm Institute in Berlin.

24 April – Paul Harteck and his assistant Wilhelm Groth in Hamburg write to Erich Schumann, head of weapons research at the German Army Ordnance Office in Berlin, calling attention to the possibility of an atomic bomb.

2 August – Einstein signs a letter to President Franklin D. Roosevelt warning that an atomic bomb was feasible but would be too big to deliver by plane.

1 September – Hitler's forces invade Poland.

3 September – War declared by France and Britain.

8 September – Hitler's atomic physicists called up.

16 September – First meeting of Hitler's 'Uranium Club'.

19 September – Hitler hints at a 'superweapon' against which 'no defence will avail'.

5 October – Army take over the Kaiser Wilhelm Institute for Physics.

6 December – Heisenberg reports to army on exploiting atomic fission.

1940

29 February – Heisenberg submits second part of a report on the atomic bomb.

9 April – German troops invade Norway.

10 May – Hitler's tanks lead the blitzkrieg into France.

19 May – Frisch and Peierls send a memorandum to the British Government warning that an atomic bomb could contain as little as 1 kg of enriched uranium and *can* be delivered by plane.

26 May – The evacuation of Dunkirk begins, lasting until 4 June.

22 June – France signs an armistice with Germany.

10 July – The Luftwaffe launch the 'Battle of Britain'.

17 July – C. F. von Weizsäcker tells the Ordnance Office that neptunium produced in a reactor could power an atomic bomb.

1941

28 March – American scientists confirm that plutonium could power an atomic bomb.

5 December – Schumann tells the Uranium Club that the Army can continue its support only if 'a certainty exists of attaining an application in the foreseeable future'.

6 December – Americans launch the Manhattan Project to build a bomb.

7 December – Japan attacks Pearl Harbour. America enters the war.

1942

February – Reich Research Council and Army Weapons Bureau jointly sponsor lectures by Hahn, Heisenberg, and Harteck.

4 June – Heisenberg tells Albert Speer a bomb will take a least two years.

9 June – Hitler issues a decree putting head of the Luftwaffe Hermann Goering and Speer in charge of the Reich Research Council.

1 July – Heisenberg becomes the scientific head of the Kaiser Wilhelm Institute for Physics.

July – Kurt Diebner builds reactor using metal cubes of uranium suspended in heavy water, achieving neutron multiplication.

19 November – Operation Freshman Commando raid takes place on the Norsk Hydro heavy water plant.

3 December – Enrico Fermi achieves the world's first atomic sustained chain reaction in a reactor in Chicago.

1943

27/28 February – Operation Gunnerside raid on Norsk Hydro is a success.

Autumn – Kaiser Wilhelm Institute for Physics moves uranium research and labs to secret location in Haigerloch and Hechingen, south Germany, to avoid the heavy bombing of Berlin.

November – US Army Colonel Boris T. Pash is appointed to head a secret mission to seize German atomic scientists, equipment, papers and materiel. It is code-named the Alsos Mission or 'Lightning A'.

1944

6 June – Operation Overlord commences with the Normandy landings.

25 August – The Alsos Mission, headed by Boris T. Pash, is the first American unit to enter Paris.

1945

26 March – Two divisions of US 7th Army cross the Rhine near Worms, followed by the Alsos Mission.

22 April – Pash leads Operation Big into Haigerloch.

3 July – Ten captured German scientists are brought to Farm Hall, Cambridgeshire. They do not know it, but their conversations are bugged.

16 July – 'Trinity' test of world's first atomic bomb using plutonium at Alamogordo, New Mexico.

17 July – The Big Three – Truman, Stalin and Churchill (and later Attlee) – meet at Potsdam.

6 August – Little Boy enriched-uranium bomb dropped on Hiroshima.

9 August – Fat Man plutonium bomb dropped on Nagasaki.

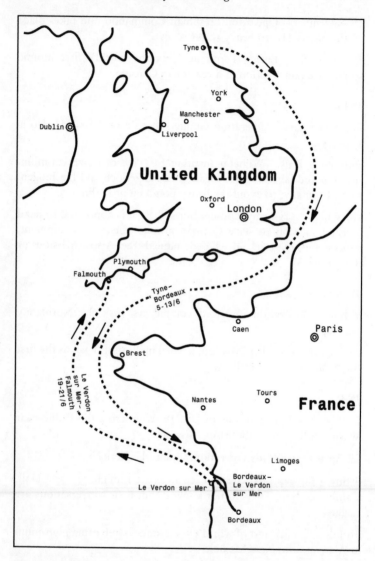

The journey of the SS *Broompark* to rescue the scientists and heavy water from Bordeaux.

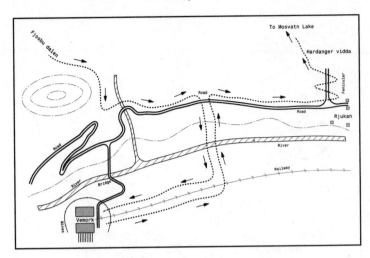

The Rjukan area and the route of the saboteurs.

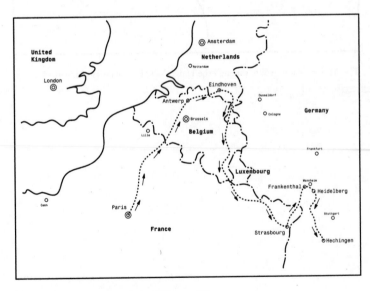

The Alsos mission's route through liberated Europe.

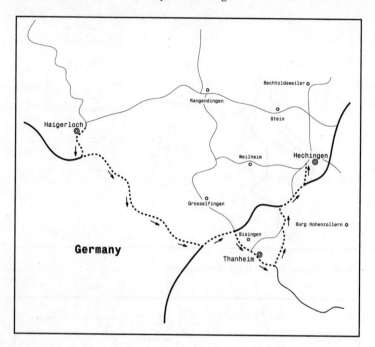

The Alsos mission's route through the Haigerloch/Thanheim/Hechingen area.

1

The House of Secrets

The wires were the clue to Farm Hall's secret past.

Marcial Echenique, a professor of urban planning at Cambridge University, discovered curious wiring when he was renovating his Georgian manor house in Godmanchester, Cambridgeshire, and pulled up the floorboards to take a closer look. In doing so, he also uncovered one of the most extraordinary stories of the Second World War, of how a manor house in a sleepy backwater of the Cambridgeshire fens had played a Top Secret role in the race to stop Hitler acquiring the bomb, and ushered in the Cold War.

The house itself is a classic slice of rural England. It faces onto a water meadow. Cows gently graze by the meandering Ouse as they have done for centuries.

It was near the old coaching route to London from Huntingdon, now the A14, but it remained a backwater to the passage of history. There is nothing to suggest that this was once the home to Hitler's ten most wanted atomic scientists.

After the war in 1947, Farm Hall was sold by the government as surplus to requirements, and was bought by a distinguished architect, Marshall Sisson, who that year was appointed surveyor to the Royal Academy of Art in Piccadilly, a post he held until 1965.

Sisson had been a modernist, but became a passionate admirer of Georgian architecture and a leading light in the Georgian Group that had been formed before the war to protect the nation's Georgian heritage. He bought the house at 24 West Street, called Farm Hall, to stop it suffering the same fate as another nearby Georgian gem called Island Hall, which had been requisitioned for the RAF and the WAAFs, but after the war was turned into flats and badly damaged in a fire.

Island Hall had been rescued by one of his young protégés, Peter Foster, an architect in Sisson's architectural practice – it has since been completely restored and is occasionally open to the public. Sisson wanted to do the same for Farm Hall but almost immediately after acquiring it, he gave Farm Hall to the National Trust to avoid the crippling death duties that had been introduced by the incoming Labour government of Clement Attlee to fund the creation of the modern welfare state.

Under the terms of his gift, Sisson remained a tenant in Farm Hall until his death in 1978; after he died, the National Trust felt it could not afford to maintain a minor Georgian house like Farm Hall, given the many other calls on its finances by much greater houses. The National Trust put Farm Hall up for auction in September 1979. It was advertised in *Country Life* as a desirable country house with no mention of its secret role as an MI6 'safe house' in the Second World War.

Professor Echenique saw Farm Hall in *Country Life* when he returned from a holiday with his family. He had built an experimental Scandinavian-style house on stilts in Cambridge, which today is Grade II listed for preservation because of its unique design, but his young family had outgrown it, and the Chilean-born don wanted a bigger house. Farm Hall appeared perfect and convenient for Cambridge, a twenty-five-minute car drive away.

There is no muck-strewn farmyard, nor lowing cattle in barns. Farm Hall is the redbrick Georgian house of a gentleman farmer. The front door under an elegant stone portico opens onto the lane called West Street that meanders by the Great River Ouse from Godmanchester to St Neots. Dating from 1746 and spread over three storeys on an L-shaped plan, it has a range of airy rooms with five windows across the front, hipped tile roofs hidden behind parapets, a fine staircase, panelling, fireplaces, a kitchen wing added in 1860, and handsome grounds with sweeping lawns, an avenue of limes, a walled kitchen garden and rose garden.

Farm Hall was rebuilt on the site of an older Elizabethan house for Charles Clarke, a Whig Member of Parliament, Recorder of Huntingdon and a Baron of the Exchequer – an ancient title for a court overseeing cases of equity and common pleas. It is thought the core of the house may go back to the mid-1600s when Oliver Cromwell, a local landowner, was leading the

Parliamentary forces in the Civil War. There is a portrait in oil on canvas of Clarke in the library at his alma mater, Corpus Christi College, Cambridge. It was painted by George Beare, a talented portrait artist of the early Georgian middle classes, a year before his house was completed. He was forty-three and clearly at the height of his power, although he was not knighted: he sits in a full wig and red robes looking fat, complacent and severe as though he is about to pronounce a sentence. Charles Clarke became immensely wealthy and was able to rebuild the family house on the same site. Clarke held the post from 1743 until his death in 1750, of a gaol fever, which, according to the History of Parliament, he contracted at the crowded trial of Captain Clark for the killing of a Captain Innes in a duel, at the celebrated 'black sessions' at the Old Bailey.

He had the twenty-three-acre grounds at Farm Hall landscaped, planted an avenue of limes on the meadows at the back of the house, and created an ornamental ha-ha where cattle quietly grazed to protect the shrubs and flowers from their ruminations. Across the lane at the front of his house, Clarke excavated a rectangular 'reflecting pond' like a mirror, framed by two more lines of limes, so that when he strolled with his guests on the bank of the Great River Ouse they could admire a picturesque view of Farm Hall. Little was disturbed over the next three centuries, apart from the bay window on the living room that was probably added by a Victorian owner.

The auction took place at the George Hotel in Huntingdon. Echenique was determined to get it although there was a great deal of interest from property developers who wanted to tear the Georgian mansion apart and convert it into flats. It was nerve-racking for the Cambridge professor. One by one, the other bidders gradually dropped out as the bidding rose, leaving only one rival, a local woman. He dramatically upped his offer for Farm Hall to a round £100,000, a substantial sum at the time.

Professor Echenique told me 'I thought, *I need to scare this lady*. I jumped well above the next step. I think that took her by surprise and I got the house. It was my last bid anyway. I couldn't afford any more than that.'[1] His rival could not match his bid, and the hammer came down. He had bought Farm Hall.

He may have been a professor of urban planning and an expert on architecture but he had no idea what he would discover when he began restoring Farm Hall.

We are sitting in a wood-panelled upstairs room where Professor Echenique lived with his wife and young family while the building was completely renovated around them. After he bought the house at auction, he discovered that the Georgians may have known all about Palladian elegance, but they knew nothing about lead valley gutters. They were cracked, the roof leaked, and there was no central heating. 'It was incredibly cold because there was no heating in the house. Every single room in the house had a fireplace,' he said.

His priority was to fix the roof and design a central heating system that he had built in Sweden before beginning the renovation of the rooms downstairs. It was when the renovation work reached the room that was to be his library, with a bay window overlooking the garden, that he took up the floorboards and uncovered the wires. Professor Echenique realised they were not part of the normal wiring of the house.

'At the time when I was starting work on the main part of the house, we lifted the floorboards in every single room to spray against woodworm and we started to discover all these cables. They were very thin but very well disguised. They were covered by wood, with a wooden cover, like in a pencil case. You slid the cover over the top.'

'So anyone lifting the floorboards would not easily see them?' I asked. 'It would be difficult to notice unless you spotted this fake cover. It was curious,' the professor told me. 'They didn't go to any lamp, no switches or anywhere. I didn't see any microphones. Probably the microphones were taken out when the house was put on the market. I got very curious about that.'

The astonishing truth that emerged was that, in the dying months of the Second World War, the manor house in the sleepy water meadows of Cambridgeshire had been used as a five-star detention centre for ten of Hitler's top nuclear scientists.

American intelligence officers were sent on a Top Secret mission to capture the scientists before they were either shot by Nazi fanatics, or fell into the hands of Josef Stalin who could have exploited the German expertise for the first Soviet nuclear weapon. Working like detectives, the US intelligence team, with British MI6 officers, drew up a detailed target list and raced across Europe in a lightly armed convoy of Jeeps to hunt them down as Hitler's Nazi war machine imploded.

Five years earlier, the conflict had begun with the 'phoney war' when the expected Blitz by Hitler's Luftwaffe in Britain had failed to materialise.

Expecting the worst, the authorities evacuated hundreds of thousands of children from the cities to escape the bombing and requisitioned large houses in the country, such as Farm Hall, to house them. In 1939, Farm Hall became a billet for children evacuated from London.

In the 1920s, Farm Hall had become the home of Alderman Robert Louis Towgood, the mayor of Godmanchester town council and a JP. He had been born in nearby St Neots, then in the former county of Huntingdonshire, on 2 October 1865. He was the son of a paper manufacturer and inherited the family business, with Farm Hall, which he ran for the rest of his life.

He married Annie Geraldine Haughton in 1895. They played the role of Lord and Lady of the manor to perfection. There are photographs of the victorious cricket XI posing with the elderly Robert Towgood, the club president, at Farm Hall with a trophy when they won Cranfield league against Offord in 1933.

The Towgoods, like families all over Britain, listened intently to the wireless broadcast at 11.15 a.m. on 3 September 1939 by the British Prime Minister Neville Chamberlain. The doom-laden words at the start of his broadcast are famous:

> This morning the British Ambassador in Berlin handed the German Government a final Note stating that, unless we heard from them by eleven o'clock that they were prepared at once to withdraw their troops from Poland, a state of war would exist between us. I have to tell you now that no such undertaking has been received, and that consequently this country is at war with Germany.

Less well known are his concluding words:

> The Government have made plans under which it will be possible to carry on the work of the nation in the days of stress and strain that may be ahead. But these plans need your help. You may be taking your part in the fighting services or as a volunteer in one of the branches of Civil Defence. If so you will report for duty in accordance with the instructions you have received ...

The public-spirited Towgoods, like many other owners of large houses in the country, responded to Chamberlain's national appeal by opening Farm Hall to evacuees from London.

The Berry family were also listening to the broadcast in their terraced street in Finsbury Park in the north London borough of Islington. Mrs Berry's resourceful husband had heard London County Council wanted 'evacuation helpers'; this could help get his wife and the kids away from the Blitz that was expected to follow the declaration of war. Mrs Berry applied and was taken on by the council; she was posted to Cambridgeshire to assist with the billeting arrangements for evacuees at Farm Hall in West Street, Godmanchester. She took her young daughter with her, and arrangements were made for her son Ray to be evacuated with the boys, aged eight to eleven years, from his school at Montem Street, Islington.

Ray found his billet on a farm in the village of Warboys in Huntingdonshire, which was close enough to visit his mother in nearby Godmanchester for weekends. Armed with a letter from his mother, he arrived in West Street and stood outside the imposing front door of the handsome mansion. He nervously tugged at the bell and waited. The house was still run as the Towgood's private home with servants on the ground floor, but the upstairs had been turned into dormitories for his two sisters and seven or eight evacuated children.

A young housemaid called Margaret opened the front door in a maid's uniform, a little black dress with a white pinafore, and told him to come inside. She led him to a sweeping staircase and said: 'I'll take you up.'

The walls were lined with Victorian cartoons of bewhiskered members of the House of Commons and peers from the House of Lords. Mrs Berry met him at the top of the stairs where he noticed a sign had been pinned up saying: 'Sweet Berry Lodge'. It had been painted by Mrs Towgood, who had turned over the whole of the first floor to the evacuees from London.

The first floor resembled a large self-contained flat, with a general living room and kitchen attached and several dormitory bedrooms off a long corridor. Mrs Towgood invited Ray to stay for weekends and showed him into a spare room that he could use as his own.

'We used to call this the Blue Room,' Mrs Towgood told Ray. 'But now it's a sealed room. It's safe if we ever have a gas attack.' At that time, it was feared that any attack on Britain might mean that poison gas would be freely used. 'I never really believed that the room could be completely gas-proof,' Ray recalled. 'I imagined

I could feel a draught from either the sealed window or the chimney place, and I reasoned that if a draught could get in, so could the poison gas. But it never worried me. I felt quite proud that I had my "own" room and that it was considered to be the safest in the house.'[2]

Ray's 'sealed room' seemed large; square-shaped, it had a high ceiling, a massive marble fireplace and two shuttered windows that looked out over West Street at the front of the house. It would later become the bedroom of some of Hitler's nuclear physicists.

The former nursery where Mrs Berry and the children spent most of the day was across the corridor almost directly opposite Ray's room. It looked over the gardens with views over the extensive lawns and the avenue of limes.

Ray had the run of the house and the gardens, the flowerbeds, lily pond, a walled rose garden with espalier fruit trees, and a carefully tended vegetable patch where fresh vegetables were grown. He could race through the living rooms where Mrs Towgood and her ailing elderly husband Robert spent their days. Alderman Towgood was an invalid and rarely left his wheelchair. Ray recalls only speaking to him once.

My memories of Farm Hall were of views over the parkland and its stately avenue of huge lime trees, of the walled garden and its rambling roses and fan-shaped fruit trees. I recall my mother's 'family' of evacuee girls acting out their roles as they staged a play in that garden; the lazy coaxing and teasing of the goldfish in the lily-pond and adventure-filled explorations of the stables and tack-rooms which lined the cobbled courtyard at the side of the house.

I remember too the masses of overgrown ivy which smothered the weathered red-bricked rear walls of the house.

Every Saturday, Ray's sister Beryl would join Mrs Towgood in the huge conservatory at the rear of the house to help with the arrangements of flowers that she or her gardener-cum-chauffeur Mr Cook had picked in the garden. When Ray's elder brother Harry got married on a forty-eight-hour pass from the army, Mrs Towgood allowed them to spend their one-night honeymoon at Farm Hall. He was sent off to defend Singapore and was not to see his bride, Gwen, for another three years. He was captured in Singapore, and became a Japanese prisoner of war.

One day in 1942, Ray Berry's mother conspiratorially drew Ray to one side and putting her hand on his shoulder, told her son: 'You must promise me you will never, never tell anyone what I'm about to tell you.'

He promised not to breathe a word of it, and she went on: 'Farm Hall is going to become a spy school. They are going to use the house and grounds to train agents to send across the Channel to fight the Germans. And you must never tell anyone this because if you do, it could mean some of them could die. Spies over here could follow them and give them away.'

Ray remembered the message contained in countless wartime posters issued by the department for propaganda that seemed highly appropriate: 'Be like Dad – Keep Mum.'

2

The Führer's Superweapon

Sixteen days after the start of the war, Adolf Hitler delivered a triumphant speech in the former free city of Danzig that caused alarm in Downing Street.

Hitler postured on the platform with his usual bluster and bombast, but there was one line that caused anxiety when transcripts were circulated around the Foreign Office and Downing Street. Hitler warned Britain that Germany might soon possess a weapon to which Britain had no defence. 'The moment might quickly come,' declared the Führer, 'when we use a weapon which is not yet known and against which no defence would avail ...'

Was this the Nazi 'superweapon' that everyone feared? Chamberlain's officials in Number 10 Downing Street immediately contacted 'C', the head of the British Secret Intelligence Service (SIS), Major General Sir Stewart Menzies, and asked for an urgent report to evaluate the threat. Menzies passed on the urgent request from the Prime Minister's office to Wing Commander F. W. 'Fred' Winterbotham, head of the air component of the Secret Intelligence Service, a post that went under the initials A.I.i (c). Winterbotham had just the man for the task: R. V. Jones, a brilliant scientist, aged twenty-eight, whom he had headhunted a fortnight earlier from the Air Ministry.

Reginald Victor Jones, known universally by his initials, was born on 21 September 1911 in the south London suburb of Herne Hill, the son of a sergeant major in the Grenadier Guards, who had taught him the importance of patriotism and order.[1] He went to the nearby fee-paying Alleyne's School, Dulwich, founded in 1619, and won an open exhibition scholarship to Wadham College, Oxford, where he gained a first in physics. He was encouraged to stay on to gain a doctorate at the Clarendon Laboratory under Professor Frederick Lindemann, Churchill's science guru, later Lord Cherwell, who Churchill called 'Prof'.

Jones had been talent-spotted by the Air Ministry in 1936, when he was carrying out pioneering research on infrared technology to see if it could be used in RAF fighters to detect approaching Luftwaffe bombers by the heat from their engines. Radar would prove superior to infrared detectors for the task, but during the war Jones was to become renowned as a 'wizard' among the 'boffins' developing gizmos to help Britain win the war.

Before the war, he worked for the Royal Aircraft Establishment at Farnborough, and was employed on scientific developments in the relative backwater of the Admiralty Research Laboratory, where he met his future wife, Vera Cain. He was won over by her feisty nature when she chased away a squad of physicists who were trying to dig shelter trenches on her women's hockey pitch.

In May 1939, he received a telephone call from A. E. Woodward-Nutt, Secretary of Sir Henry Tizard's Committee for the Scientific Survey of Air Defence, who asked him whether he was interested in working on intelligence.

Sir Henry was dissatisfied with the intelligence being supplied by the Secret Intelligence Service to the Air Ministry. What they needed was someone with a scientific background to report on what the Germans were up to, particularly on atomic research, and Woodward-Nutt wanted to know whether Jones would be interested.

'This was the main reason that I found myself in my post,' said Jones.[2]

It was agreed that, to give the Admiralty Research Laboratory more time to find a replacement, he would delay the move to the Air Ministry's Directorate of Scientific Research until Friday, 1 September 1939. The same day, Hitler's troops invaded Poland.

Jones had spent Saturday and Sunday, the last weekend of peace, with his fiancée Vera in the blissful surroundings of Hoar Cross Hall, a Victorian mansion in the Jacobean style, deep in the Staffordshire countryside. They were weekend party guests of Colonel and Lady Dorothy Meynell who had adopted Jones almost as a family member since he spent a month tutoring their son Mark, an undergraduate at Christ Church, Oxford. They had gone to the local station on Saturday to organise the billeting of children evacuated to the country from the inner cities.

On Sunday morning, like families all across Britain that morning, the Meynells had gone to the regular Sunday service as usual in their parish church across the parkland. Vera had gone with them, leaving Jones to listen to the Prime Minister's 11:15 a.m. broadcast on the wireless in the hall. They prayed for peace at the Church of the Holy Angels, and returned to find Britain at war.

Hoar Cross Hall, the quintessential English country house, seemed to Jones that morning to symbolise everything that was good about England: weekend parties, tennis and teas on the lawn, the poetry of Rupert Brooke and the quiet sacrifice of men like Scott of the Antarctic. It was, Jones reflected, an England worth fighting for.

Jones did not share the pacifism in vogue among some undergraduates at Oxford and Cambridge, who had voted against serving for king and country in 1933 – a vote that was interpreted by some in Germany and America as confirmation that Britain had become a decadent country. Jones was also a keen shot – he killed a fox on the Hoar Cross estate with his pistol – and was an expert shot with a rifle on the national shooting range at Bisley. He had joined the Oxford Shooting Club and offered to raise a rifle brigade before war broke out.

Jones thought Chamberlain sounded like a decent but ineffectual man let down by a brute. 'It is the evil things that we shall be fighting against,' said Chamberlain. 'Brute force, bad faith, injustice, oppression and persecution – and against them I am certain that the right will prevail.'

Chamberlain's brave words in defence of Poland in his broadcast to the nation that morning quickly turned to ashes. Six German armoured divisions, four light divisions of motorised infantry, and forty infantry divisions – more than 1.5 million men – poured across the Polish border supported by 1,300 war planes, including Hitler's feared Stuka bombers. The flat fields of the Polish plain provided the perfect ground to demonstrate the power of Hitler's Panzer tanks and the Luftwaffe. The German jaws, from Prussia in the east to Silesia in the south, snapped shut.

Vera found R. V. itching to get back to London to 'do his bit'. On Monday 4 September, Jones arrived at the Air Ministry office in Whitehall to find his new colleagues at the Directorate of Scientific Research (D. S. R.) packing their files for evacuation to Harrogate in Yorkshire to avoid the expected bombing by the Luftwaffe.

During a morning of introductions, he met Winterbotham, who immediately asked Jones to join the SIS headquarters staff. It was housed in an anonymous 1920s office block at 54 Broadway, tucked away off Victoria Street in Westminster.

*

54 Broadway Buildings was the unlikely epicentre of Britain's intelligence and espionage. The office block, opposite the St James's Park Underground station in Westminster – immortalised as the 'Circus' in the '*Smiley*' spy novels by John Le Carré – masqueraded behind a brass plaque on the wall by the front door that read *Government Communications Bureau*.

It had been the headquarters of the SIS, better known as MI6, since 1926. There was nothing to betray its true, clandestine use, except for the line of impressive limousines parked outside with civilian number plates and military drivers. MI6 shared the six floors with the Government Code and Cypher School until the codebreakers decamped to Bletchley Park, Buckinghamshire, fifty miles north of London, to avoid the expected Blitz.

The London residence of Sir Stewart Menzies, 'C', was around the corner at 21 Queen Anne's Gate. The smart Georgian house was connected at the rear to Broadway Buildings, enabling 'C' to reach his office in MI6 without stepping into the street. This was probably just as well – the Germans claimed they had a spy disguised as a match-seller in Broadway to watch comings and goings at the MI6 headquarters.

C's residence also housed the London headquarters of the 'Passport Control Office', code for the network of SIS agents posing as passport control officers in cities around the world. Nearby, another fine Georgian house at 16 Old Queen Street became the offices of British Tube Alloys, a front organisation for the embryonic British nuclear programme, staffed by two Imperial Chemical Industries (ICI) employees, Wallace Akers, the director, and his assistant, Michael Perrin.

St Ermin's Hotel near Broadway Buildings served as overspill offices. Suites there were used by SIS for section D, sabotage, and MI (R) research, and rooms were also used for interviewing and briefing agents. The bar at St Ermin's became a popular hangout for intelligence officers, including visiting American agents.

SIS was answerable to the Foreign Office overlooking St James's Park. When a new secret sabotage and resistance organisation, the Special Operations Executive (SOE) was born in 1940, under the auspices of the Ministry of Economic Warfare, it was given offices close to MI6 at 2 Caxton Street, next door to the St Ermin's Hotel. The SOE rapidly expanded and soon moved to Baker Street, the address by which the SOE became generally known.

SIS Air section staff were scattered about in various offices: Mr McArther in charge of pigeons (for agents' messages to England) was in Room 201, C Block, Adastral House; Corporal Pope in charge of packing containers and equipment for air drops was at Princes House; all other equipment was under Captain Atkinson; revolver shooting was organised by Captain Gibson; and parachute training was conducted at Ringway, Manchester, under Captain Burnes.

SIS also had a secret store in Savile Row, the street famous for gentlemen's tailors, offering tailor-made kit to its agents. The stocklist reads like a script for James Bond's fabled quartermaster, 'Q': Sten guns; .455 automatics RAF pattern; .38 revolvers – Army type; torches; MI9 escape equipment including escapers' knives and silk maps; grenades – Bakerlite, Mills, and incendiary; booby trap material – press pull and step-on; automatic handguns for instructing agents in the use of weapons obtained on the Continent; mail pick-up unit equipment; a demonstration Eureka set (directional beacon); luminous balls; Stimsonite reflectors; Heliographs (a mirror for signalling by using the reflection of the sun); signalling lights; sound devices for locating containers in the dark; items for parachuting into water – Mae Wests (buoyancy aids), RAF dinghies, water suits, and water-tight containers. There were also, according to FANYs (the young SOE women who were recruited into the First Aid Nursing Yeomanry), the 'funnies' – ingenious inventions for killing the enemy, such as exploding rats, exploding dung and lethal fountain pens.

*

Winterbotham told Jones to go to Harrogate and read himself into the Directorate of Scientific Research files, but on 19 September he recalled his young scientist to London. He had a job for him. It would be his first big test of the war.

Hitler had swept into Danzig that day in an open-topped Mercedes as a liberator, cheered by thousands of people on the streets. The port city on the Baltic, now known as Gdansk, had been part of Germany before the hated Versailles Treaty had forced Germany to surrender a land corridor to the Polish. It enabled Hitler to raise Aryan hackles about the way they had been unfairly treated in the post-First World War settlement. News reports of his arrival could have been written by Josef Goebbels, Hitler's Nazi propaganda minister: 'Escorted by Generalmajor Rommel, Hitler was first driven through the city, whose streets were lined with thousands of cheering and supportive locals waving swastika-adorned flags.'[3]

The same day that Hitler made his Danzig speech, German troops met up with their Russian allies to carve up Poland. Less than a month before, on 23 August 1939, the Germans had signed the Molotov–Ribbentrop pact – a masterpiece of cynicism – under which the Fascist forces of Nazi Germany became temporary allies of Stalin's Soviet Red Army. It left Poland's army defenceless against the pincer movement.

Listening to the recording of Hitler's Danzig speech today provides a chilling reminder of Hitler's charismatic power as a public speaker, and explains how the odd-looking former Gefreiter (lance corporal) was elected in 1933: his speech combined populist oratory with sinister threats.

First he speaks of the injustice of the Versailles Treaty, which removed the disputed city of Danzig from German control. The Führer tells his adoring audience he had vowed not to step foot in the city until it was returned to the German family: 'Now after twenty years, it returns to the great German *Volksgemeinschaft*. I resolved not to journey to Danzig before this city belonged again to the German Reich. I wished to make my entry into this city as its liberator ...'

The audience bursts into cheering that was clearly orchestrated. They shout: 'We thank our Führer!' Hitler goes on: 'I saw before me the entire German Volk. We need no "hurrah" patriotism. All of us know how terrible war is. Yet we still are determined to bring these developments to a victorious conclusion, come what may.'

Hitler says he tried to avoid war in negotiations with Chamberlain at Munich: 'I still believe that without the British guarantee and the agitation of the warmongers it would have been possible during last August to arrive at an understanding. There was a certain moment when England herself tried to arrange for direct discussions between ourselves and Poland, for which I was quite prepared; the Poles, however, failed to turn up. For two whole days I and my government waited in vain in Berlin.' He assures the world of his peaceful intentions: 'I have no warlike intentions against either England or France. Nor has the German nation any such intentions. Since I have been in office I have endeavoured to re-establish gradually closer relations based on mutual confidence, especially with our opponents in the Great War.' Hitler then casts Churchill as a warmonger and the leader of a 'criminal clique': 'I pointed to the dangers which must arise when, in a country, men can simply get up and freely preach war as a necessity as, for instance, Messrs Churchill, Eden, Duff Cooper etc.'

Finally, as he reaches the fist-thumping climax of his speech, he warns England that Germany may soon possess a wonder weapon. The Foreign Office transcript reported Hitler's chilling threat:

> England possesses one weapon under the umbrella of which it believes it cannot be attacked, namely, its naval forces. And now the English say: 'Because we ourselves cannot be attacked with this weapon, this entitles us to use this weapon not only against the women and children of our enemies, but also against the neutral states, if this should be necessary'. Let them make no mistake here, however. The moment could come very suddenly in which we would employ a weapon to which no defence will avail ...'[4]

Winterbotham told Jones that Downing Street wanted to know what weapon could Hitler possess to which Britain had no defence. He told him to read through the Top Secret files of the SIS to see if he could discover to what Hitler had been referring. Jones spent the next few days at the MI6 headquarters riffling through agents' reports to solve the puzzle, but he could find nothing in the most recent files that amounted to a weapon to which Britain had no defence. After reading through the files, Jones reported to Winterbotham that he had drawn a blank on the current MI6 reports. Winterbotham suggested that he should carry on the investigation by searching for the answer through MI6's pre-war files that had been evacuated with the Government Code and Cipher School to Station X, Bletchley Park.

The house and estate at Bletchley Park had been bought presciently in 1938 by Sir Hugh 'Quex' Sinclair, then head of

SIS – a year before his death from cancer – for the use of the intelligence services to escape the bombing, should war break out. It was extremely handy due to the mainline railway service that ran past Bletchley from London Euston, and also on account of the house's extensive grounds, providing plenty of room in which the organisation could expand. MI6 had grabbed the offices on the first floor of the bay-windowed Victorian mansion overlooking the ornamental lake at Bletchley Park while the codebreakers had to make do with huts in the grounds of the stately home.

Jones shared a room in the mansion at Bletchley Park with a florid-faced RAF officer in the intelligence service, Squadron Leader Cautley Nasmyth-Shaw, who was posted two years later to run Farm Hall as a safe house for MI6 operations in occupied Europe. Jones said Nasmyth-Shaw had a regulation RAF moustache and regulation drawl to match, having been a cavalry officer, but he clearly found him engaging company. Jones knew Nasmyth-Shaw by the nickname of 'Jane' after a ribald rugby song of the day. 'Jane' showed Jones around the huts at Bletchley Park, and the canteen, introducing him to some of the mathematicians and cryptologists who were secretly employed in breaking enemy codes. They included a raconteur on the BBC, A. J. Alan, and some of the 7,000 women, now famous as the 'Bletchley girls', who provided the backbone for the cypher centre, transcribing intercepts, typing transcripts, and helping to break the Enigma codes. Jones made some valuable lifelong contacts at Station X. He was billeted in the home of Sir Kenneth and Lady Macdonald at nearby Winslow along with Commander Edward Travis, Deputy Head of the Government Code and Cypher School, who replaced Commander Alastair Denniston as the head of the school in 1942. Travis discussed with Jones the problem of cracking the code produced by the Enigma machine, which resembled a typewriter but worked like a cyclometer, turning a wheel every time a key was pressed to produce an encoded letter. Travis also introduced Jones to Alan Turing, who led pioneering work on the creation of an electromechanical computer called the Bombe to help decipher German coded messages.

Jones sifted through three years' of SIS top-secret files stretching back to 1936 but the network of spies across Europe had failed to produce any hard intelligence about the nature of Hitler's superweapon. They had been spun along by a Dutch source that claimed he had intelligence about a death ray. Jones discovered it had failed to kill anyone, but it was wonderful at preserving fruit. Jones decided to go back to first principles and to check on precisely what Hitler had said in his speech. To do that, he needed to hear a recording.

The young scientist returned to MI6 headquarters in London and called on Sir Roy Maconachie, the Director of Talks at the BBC, who he had met socially as a fellow weekend party guest at Hoar Cross Hall. He asked if the BBC had a recording of Hitler's Danzig speech. Sir Roy checked and came back to Jones with confirmation that the BBC did indeed possess one. Jones could not speak fluent German, but had an SIS colleague who was a fluent German speaker, and Maconachie arranged for him to listen to the BBC tape.

After listening carefully to the crucial passage, Jones's German-speaking colleague said it had been wrongly translated for the Foreign Office. The key sentence was quite different. Instead of declaring he would soon have a weapon to which 'no defence will avail', Hitler said: 'The moment could come very suddenly in which we would employ a weapon with which we cannot be attacked.'

On 11 November 1939, Jones circulated his conclusions in a secret report on the likely 'superweapons' that Hitler might possess. I found Jones's typed report among his papers at the Churchill Archives, Churchill College, Cambridge. I also found the copy Jones sent to Professor Lindemann at the Air Ministry in the Cherwell Archive at the Nuffield College library, Oxford.[5] Jones concluded:

> The only concrete fact is that the Germans might employ a 'Waffe' with which they could not be attacked. 'Waffe' may be interpreted in many ways, but the best criterion is its relation to the context ... It is reasonably certain that the 'Waffe' which Hitler claims to possess is a 'Waffe' in the sense that describes the British Navy, and is thus a striking force, rather than a specific appliance ...
>
> The notorious weapon is thus a striking force in which Germany, in Hitler's own opinion, excels in size and/or efficiency and/or strategic position. The nature of the striking force is more difficult to decide; it might be some branch of, or the whole of, the German Air Force; it might be the submarine arm. The latter is improbable if the veracity of Hitler's words may be taken rigorously because his submarines had been extensively used at the time of the speech. It is therefore almost certain that the 'Waffe' is the Luftwaffe.

Jones gave a list of the possible superweapons that the Germans were working on. Apart from the more fantastic rumours, such as those concerned with machines for generating earthquakes and gases which caused everyone within two miles to burst, there were a number of weapons; some of which had to be considered seriously:

1. Bacterial Warfare
2. New Gases
3. Flame Weapons
4. Gliding bombs, aerial torpedoes and pilotless aircraft
5. Long-range guns and rockets
6. New torpedoes, mines and submarines
7. Death rays, engine-stopping rays and magnetic guns.

The scare of a Nazi superweapon was over ... for the time being. But Jones was not finished. His search through the MI6 files had convinced him that MI6 lacked the specialist skills to gather intelligence on enemy scientific research. Although he had only been in MI6 for a few weeks, he submitted a report calling for a new Scientific Intelligence Service that would take responsibility for enemy atomic research. It led to a power struggle for control over British atomic intelligence with another senior MI6 figure, Lt Commander Eric Welsh.

Jones also castigated the British for their lax attitude towards security, although his findings read like an academic paper for a learned seminar in which he compared the German-British conflict to the Peloponnesian War:

A serious disparity in Scientific Intelligence between England and Germany almost certainly exists at the present time. This is due in part to the extra secrecy precautions observed in Germany, and in part to the lack of coordinated effort in our acquisition of information.

Parallels have frequently been drawn between the Peloponnesian War and that between England and Germany but rarely more accurately than in the present connection. A similar disregard for Scientific Intelligence exists now in England to that which existed in Athens.

He then quoted Pericles on Athenian policy:

Our city is thrown open to the world and we never expel a foreigner or prevent him from seeing or learning anything of which the secret if revealed to an enemy might profit him. We rely not upon management or trickery, but upon our own hearts and hands (Thucydides, II, 39).

Jones was still banging the drum for improvements in Britain's approach to scientific intelligence after the war ended. I discovered a report on 'an improved scientific intelligence service' written by Jones in 1945.[6] It is still secret, and held by the Ministry of Defence as a document closed to public scrutiny.

Hitler's Danzig speech was also important for another reason: although the war was barely two weeks old, the Axis powers were already embarking on a fight over the moral high ground. Hitler declared that he had ordered the Luftwaffe to conduct 'humanitarian warfare' by attacking only fighting troops in Poland.

Hitler went on: 'I hope that they will then not suddenly remember Humanity and the impossibility of waging war against women and children. We Germans don't hold with that at all. This is not our nature ... I have issued orders to spare towns wherever possible. But naturally, if a column marches across the market square and is attacked by aeroplanes, it can happen that someone else is unfortunately sacrificed ...' Hitler's words were a cynical lie, given the death and destruction that had rained down on Poland, but Jones later pointed out in his memoirs that the hypocrisy was not one-sided.

Chamberlain told the House of Commons on 14 September 1939 that His Majesty's Government 'will never resort to the deliberate attack on women, children and other civilians for the purposes of mere terrorism' whatever lengths to which others might go. Jones – who later opposed 'carpet bombing' – acidly commented after the war that this made 'curious reading' in view of the Allied bombing offensive in the later stages of the war, including the fire storm in Dresden, which, he said, 'showed how far high intentions can be gradually eroded'.[7]

The battle for the moral high ground would grow into a global struggle at the end of the war over the first use of nuclear weapons.

There was one glaring omission in Jones's report. There is no reference to the threat of a German atomic weapon. Jones was certainly well aware of the threat: one of his first actions on becoming the chief scientific adviser to the SIS was to alert all MI6 agents to be on the look out for tell-tale signs of a Nazi German atomic programme. He may rightly have assumed that it was far too soon after the discovery of atomic fission to poise any immediate threat to Britain.

In this, he was in accord with Winston Churchill, who had been brought back from the 'wilderness' and appointed by Chamberlain to his War Cabinet as First Lord of the Admiralty for a second time when war was declared. Churchill, advised by his 'Prof', Lindemann, wrote to Sir Kingsley Wood, the Secretary of State for Air, pouring cold water on the German threat of an atomic bomb: the Germans had access to only small reserves of uranium in the mines in Czechoslovakia and, even if they produced enough to make a bomb, 'as soon as the energy develops it will explode with a mild detonation before any really violent effects can be produced'. Lindemann and Churchill were to be proved wrong about that; and neither Churchill nor Jones knew that the German high command had already mobilised a group of top German scientists in Berlin to work on an atomic bomb.

3

Hitler's Uranium Club

Erich Bagge, a twenty-seven-year-old assistant researcher at the Department of Physics at Leipzig University, opened his call-up papers on 6 September 1939 with foreboding. He had been ordered to present himself in two days' time at the *Heereswaffenamt*, the Army Ordnance headquarters in Hardenbergstrasse, Berlin.

Bagge was an assistant of the leading German theoretical physicist, Werner Heisenberg, head of physics at Leipzig University, but feared the worst – that he was going to be posted to join the front line troops on the eastern front. 'I had everything that was normal for a soldier,' he said.[1] In his small suitcase, Bagge carried a few necessities to make life a little more bearable for an ordinary soldier on the front line – some warm underwear, a few family photographs and a toothbrush. When he got to the Ordnance office, Bagge was surprised to recognise two people who had approached him a year earlier after he had delivered a lecture in Breslau. At that time, they had wanted him to work for the German military but he had turned them down, saying he was not interested in developing atomic research for the military.

Now the military could order scientists like Bagge to work for them, and if they valued their lives, they could not refuse.

One of the men he recognised was Professor Erich Schumann, the head of weapons research in the Army Ordnance Office. Schumann, the grandson of the composer, and a professor of physics at the University of Berlin, had joined the Nazi Party when Hitler first came to power in 1933 and was a general officer in the army. He had been a physicist at the Reich Ministry of Defence since 1922.

The other was Professor H. Pose of Halle University. Bagge was relieved when he was approached by Kurt Diebner, aged thirty-four, who had worked under Pose, and was invited by Diebner to help him draw up a list of leading physicists for a symposium to be held into the atomic 'problem'.

The list did not take long to prepare. It included Germany's leading physicists – Walther Bothe, Hans Geiger (a member of the team who invented the radiation counter), and professors Stretter, Mattauch, Hoffmann and von Laue, Siegfried Flugge (who had published an article speculating on the enormous power to be unleashed through atomic power), and Otto Hahn, the chemist who had startled the world earlier that year with the discovery of nuclear fission.

Bagge discovered that the world-renowned research laboratories at the Kaiser Wilhelm Institute at Dahlem in the suburbs of Berlin had been brought directly under the control of Army Ordnance by order of its chief General Carl Heinrich Becker. The first conference was fixed for 16 September at the Ordnance Office to discuss the possibility of creating a uranium bomb, and to lay the ground for its development.

The race to an atomic bomb accelerated as Europe prepared for war, but the starting gun had been fired back in 1913 when the Danish physicist Niels Bohr first proposed a theory for the structure of the atom still in use today. He was twenty-eight, and was using experience in experimental science gained at the Cavendish Laboratory in Cambridge headed by a no-nonsense New Zealand physicist, Ernest Rutherford.

Bohr was awarded the Nobel Prize in Physics in 1922 for his discovery, and tried his best to explain his theories in laymen's terms in his Nobel acceptance speech by comparing an atom built up of a nucleus with a number of electrons, 'to a planetary system, such as we have in our own solar system'. This gave us the image of the atom circled by electrons like the sun circled by planets that endures today.

Bohr spent most of the war in his native Denmark after it had been occupied by the Germans and continued to provide important insights into resolving the problems of atomic energy. Bohr predicted that only atoms in Uranium-235 would readily split when struck by a neutron, but the problem for achieving fission was that the more common isotope U-238 would absorb neutrons. Since over 98 per cent of Uranium was U-238, a chain reaction would be stifled. It would be necessary to isolate pure U-235 in sufficient quantities to make a bomb. The difficulty of creating a sufficient quantity of pure U-235 seemed to Bohr to be insurmountable, and ruled out the possibility of making a nuclear bomb. This became the ultimate challenge for the next generation of physicists.

During the 1930s, as Hitler rose to power, Bohr's theories on nuclear physics were eagerly developed by other younger scientists, including Heisenberg, to whom Bohr was a mentor, Otto Hahn, the director of the Kaiser Wilhelm Institute for Chemistry in Berlin, and Hahn's brilliant assistant Lise Meitner.

Werner Heisenberg, a brilliant theoretical physicist, was born on 5 December 1901 in the German city of Wurzburg and studied mathematics at universities in Munich and Gottingen before developing quantum mechanics. He first met Bohr at a festival in 1922 and studied under him in Copenhagen. Together with Erich Bagge and von Weizsäcker, who worked with Heisenberg, they pursued the theoretical postulate – predicted by Einstein's mass-energy equivalence theory ($e = mc^2$) – that colossal amounts of energy could be released if they could reduce the mass of the atom by bombarding it with neutrons so that it split.

For more than three decades, German scientists pitted their brains against those of other international teams: the Cambridge laboratory of Ernest Rutherford, where James Chadwick won the Nobel Prize for his discovery of the neutron in 1932; the Paris laboratory of Frederic Joliot and his wife Irene Curie, the daughter of the pioneering Marie Curie, the first woman to win the Nobel Prize for her theory of radioactivity; and Enrico Fermi in Rome, who had discovered that, using the water in a fish pond outside his laboratory, the radioactivity of a metal bombarded with neutrons increased because the neutrons were slowed down by water, making it easier to split the atom and cause a chain reaction.

What motivated them? For some, it was the intellectual challenge, and the honour of a Nobel Prize. They rushed forward, either not realising or ignoring the fact they were paving the way to a new superweapon making science fiction into scientific fact.

The frightening power of an atomic bomb that could threaten the destruction of Planet Earth had been envisaged as early as 1914 – the year of Bohr's great discovery – by H. G. Wells in his science fiction novel, *The World Set Free*, which foresees the world being turned to smouldering rubble by the 1950s with an atomic bomb.

In September 1933, the Hungarian physicist Leo Szilard, a pupil of Einstein's, suddenly realised Wells's frightening scenario was not merely science fiction. He was walking through the wet streets of Bloomsbury while he was mulling over a remark by Rutherford, that predictions that the neutron would unlock vast stores of energy were 'moonshine', when the truth hit him with the force of a London bus.

> I stopped for a red light at the intersection of Southampton Row ... I was pondering whether Lord Rutherford might not be proved wrong. It suddenly occurred to me that if we could find an element which is split by neutrons and which would emit two neutrons when it absorbed one neutron, such an element if assembled in sufficiently large mass, could sustain a nuclear chain reaction[2]

In his landmark television series, *The Ascent of Man*, Professor Jacob Bronowski described Szilard as 'just the kind of good-humoured, cranky man, who disliked any statement that contained the word "never", particularly when made by a distinguished colleague ...'[3]

Szilard was horrified at his own insights into the potential development of atomic power into a fearful new generation of weapons. Worried that the secret might get out, he patented the idea of a chain reaction and gave it to the Admiralty in London on the condition that it should remain secret. He wrote to Enrico Fermi, who also had developed the fission theory, urging him not to publish his discoveries. However, in 1939 the atomic genie was let out of the bottle when Bohr announced to a startled scientific conference in New York that nuclear fission – the splitting of the atom – had been achieved by Otto Hahn and Fritz Strassmann in their laboratory in Berlin. It had been predicted in theory. Now, it was a scientific fact – and it was headline news across both sides of the Atlantic. British scientists, including the MI6 intelligence officer, R. V. Jones, were well aware of Hahn and Strassmann's discovery, but they were still a long way from developing the theory into an atomic weapon.

Advances increased as war loomed over Europe. In February 1939, the French team of scientists, led by Frederic Joliot-Curie at the Joliot-Curie laboratory in Paris and assisted by Hans von Halban, Lew Kowarski and Francis Perrin, produced some startling results from experiments that suggested they had split the atom. It was to take the insight of a Jewish refugee from Germany – Lise Meitner – to explain how this had happened.

Lise Meitner had been born into a family of Jews in Vienna in 1878, but had been given her own physics department at the Kaiser Wilhelm Institute for Chemistry in Dahlem, Berlin, under Otto Hahn. They were very close, and she became acting head while Hahn was away on a trip to America, but after Hitler was elected to power as German Chancellor in 1933, she became increasingly alarmed and intimidated at the Nazification of the campus. Brown Shirts of Hitler's Nazi Party appeared in the corridors, and Nazi swastikas were put up around the institute.

The Nazi Party set about the systematic persecution of Jews in German society, banning them from professional positions in industry, universities and politics. Meitner, though Jewish, was protected from persecution for a while by her Austrian citizenship but other Jewish scientists, including Meitner's nephew Otto Frisch and Leo Szilard, were dismissed or forced to resign from their posts. Hitler's fanatical anti-Semitism stripped Germany and its war effort of some of the best brains. Frisch went to Copenhagen to work near Bohr's institute before settling at Birmingham University in Britain. Szilard went to Britain and then to America, where he was to play an historic role in helping to persuade President Franklin D. Roosevelt to launch the nuclear programme that would become the Manhattan Project. Enrico Fermi fled from Italy to America because his wife was a Jew. Perhaps their biggest loss was Meitner, an outstanding and intuitive physicist, who was forced to leave Hahn's laboratory and flee, firstly to Holland then on to Sweden.

In March 1938, Meitner's position became perilous when Hitler announced the Anschluss – the annexation of Austria, her homeland, and its incorporation into Germany – and she became subject to German race laws against Jews holding professional posts. She belatedly decided she had to escape, but her Austrian passport was useless because Austria had ceased to exist as an independent country, and she was refused a permit to travel abroad because she was a Jew. Her travel was rejected with a sinister threatening message to Carl Bosch, president of the Kaiser Wilhelm Society, who had applied for it, saying there were 'political objections' to issuing a passport to Professor Meitner: 'It is considered undesirable that renowned Jews should leave Germany for abroad to act against the interests of Germany according to their inner persuasion as representatives of German sciences or even with their reputation and experience.'[4]

She decided to make a run for it, and did so taking only two small cases, the clothes she stood up in, ten Marks, and a diamond ring given to her by Otto Hahn, who inherited it from his mother. He gave it to her to bribe her way past German border guards, if necessary. On 13 July 1938, after spending a nervous night at Hahn's house, she travelled undercover to the Dutch border with an ally, a Dutch physicist, also travelling incognito on the same train. He had smoothed the way days before by urging the Dutch officials to persuade the German border guards it was important to allow her to travel to the Netherlands. She got across the border, but it was a narrow escape.

Four months later, on the night of 9/10 November, the *Schutzstaffel* (SS), the 'protective force' for the Nazi Party, unleashed a crackdown on Jews with a wave of anti-Semitic acts of violence; the windows of Jewish-owned shops, offices and synagogues were smashed; streets were littered with broken glass; with a Nazi sense of humour, it was called *Kristallnacht*, crystal night. There was far worse to come – an estimated 30,000 Jews like Meitner were rounded up and sent off to concentration camps. By then, Meitner was safe in the Netherlands, but when a promised job failed to materialise, she moved on to Stockholm and established a close working relationship with Niels Bohr at his laboratory in Copenhagen.

Five months after Meitner had fled Germany her old boss, Otto Hahn, and Fritz Strassmann made the breakthrough.

They were excited by some findings reported by Irene Curie in Paris that uranium atoms split when they had been irradiated with neutrons. Attempting to replicate Curie's research findings, Hahn and Strassmann studied the reaction of nuclei of different elements by bombarding them with neutrons. When a nucleus absorbs a neutron it becomes radioactive and moves one or two places along a scale used by physicists known as the periodic table. Uranium appeared to jump four places to become radium. In December 1938, Hahn and Strassmann decided to check radium was being formed. They added barium to extract the radium at the bottom of a test tube but after the experiment, they found it contained only barium – thirty-six places away on the periodic table, and the nucleus was halving in size.[5]

Hahn was shocked by the results and, before informing his own institute, wrote to Lise Meitner in Stockholm informing her about their puzzling discovery. 'Actually there is something about the "radium isotopes" that is so remarkable that for now we are telling only you.' Meitner read the letter while she was staying with friends and her nephew Otto Frisch for a Christmas break among the forests by the river at Kungalv, north of Gothenburg. She showed Frisch the letter and they discussed it as they went for some exercise through the snowbound woods; Frisch was on cross-country skis and his aunt followed him at a brisk walk, still talking about the letter. She wondered aloud whether it was a mistake. No, she said, Hahn was too good a chemist for that. Frisch later recalled how she sat down on a log and began making calculations. She reasoned that a nucleus was not like a brittle solid that could be cut or broken; it was more like a liquid drop, as suggested by Bohr. Perhaps a drop could divide itself into two small drops gradually, first becoming elongated, then constricted, before being torn in two. Science historian John Cornwell, author of *Hitler's Scientists*, described Meitner's intuitive solution as 'one of the great insightful moments in science in the twentieth century'.[6]

The calculations she had hurriedly made on scraps of paper while she sat on the log also proved uncannily accurate. Meitner realised her solution chimed perfectly with Einstein's famous equation, $e = mc^2$. She worked out that the two nuclei formed by the division of a uranium nucleus would be one-fifth of the mass of a proton. Using Einstein's equation, she estimated that the loss of this mass would generate 200 million electron volts; splitting one gram of uranium would release energy equivalent to 2.5 tonnes of coal. She was staggered by her conclusion, and wondered why it had gone unnoticed by Hahn and Strassmann in Berlin, Fermi now in the United States and Joliot in Paris. She assumed the energy release was not observed because they had used such small amounts of uranium in their experiments. Thus, Meitner was responsible for articulating the theory behind Hahn and Strassmann's discovery, but it was Niels Bohr who broke the news to the scientific world.

In January 1939, Bohr, after nine days of a very rough crossing, sailed into New York harbour on a passenger liner at the start of a five-month lecture tour with the news of the startling discovery that atomic fission had occurred. He was accompanied by Leon Rosenfeld, aged thirty-three, a professor of physics at the University of Liège, who irritated Bohr by revealing details of the Hahn–Strassmann–Meitner discovery to the physics club at Princeton University. As the news was being openly discussed, Bohr and

Enrico Fermi decided to set out the details to the fifth Washington conference on Theoretical Physics.

Bohr's announcement was such a landmark moment that a memorial plaque was put up outside Room 209 in Government Hall at the George Washington University. It reads: 'In this room, January 26, 1939, Niels Bohr made the first public announcement of the successful disintegration of uranium into barium with the attendant release of approximately two hundred million electron volts of energy per disintegration.'

Scientists were so excited on hearing the news, some left before the conference was over to carry out their own tests in their laboratories. News of the fission breakthrough was independently announced by Columbia University, the John Hopkins University in Baltimore and the Carnegie Institution shortly after the close of the Washington conference.

The American press, however, was more interested in the application of the sensational new discovery for a huge bomb. *The New York Times* reported on 30 April 1939 that Bohr had declared the bombardment of a small amount of pure isotope U-235 of uranium with slow neutron particles of atoms would start a chain reaction or atomic explosion 'sufficiently great to blow up a laboratory and the surrounding country for many miles'.

In neutral America, scientists were already secretly mobilising against a German nuclear bomb. Leo Szilard had switched from moral opposition to the atomic bomb to a conviction a nuclear bomb was inevitable, and that Hitler must not be allowed to win the race to construct it.

He approached his mentor, Albert Einstein, to enlist his help to alert the American President Franklin D. Roosevelt to the danger. Together, they drafted an historic letter to Roosevelt. It was signed solely by Einstein to maximise its impact:

> In the course of the last four months it has been made probable – through the work of Joliot in France as well as Fermi and Szilard in America – that it may become possible to set up a nuclear chain reaction in a large mass of uranium, by which vast amounts of power and large quantities of new radium-like elements would be generated. Now it appears almost certain that this could be achieved in the immediate future.
>
> This new phenomenon would also lead to the construction of bombs and it is conceivable – though much less certain – that

extremely powerful bombs of a new type may thus be constructed. A single bomb of this type, carried by boat and exploded in a port, might very well destroy the whole port together with some of the surrounding territory.

The letter cast doubt on whether it was feasible to construct a nuclear bomb that could be dropped from the air. Such bombs, said Einstein, 'might very well prove to be too heavy for transportation by air.'[7]

Urging the President to be on the alert and take urgent action if required, Einstein's letter added that the US had only very poor ores of uranium in moderate quantities; there was some good ore in Canada and Czechoslovakia, while the most important source of uranium was the Belgian Congo. In view of this situation, Einstein continued: 'You may think it desirable to have some permanent contact maintained between the Administration and the group of physicists working on chain reactions in America.'

One way of doing that, said Einstein, was to appoint a coordinator to keep government departments informed and speed up the experimental work that was being carried out within the budgetary restraints of university departments.

The letter concluded with a specific warning of the threat posed to the United States by Germany:

I understand that Germany has actually stopped the sale of uranium from Czechoslovakian mines, which she has taken over. That she should have taken such early action might perhaps be understood on the ground that the son of the German Under-Secretary of State, von Weizsäcker, is attached to the Kaiser-Wilhelm Institut in Berlin where some of the American work on uranium is now being repeated.

The letter was dated 2 August 1939, but the President was preoccupied with the international crisis and lobbying Congress to lift the arms embargo on Britain, and it was not until 11 October that the White House could find the time for it to be presented to FDR by Alexander Sachs, a Wall Street economist and long-time unofficial adviser to the president. Sachs delivered it as part of a dossier which included a technical memorandum by Szilard and a simplified explanatory memorandum by Sachs.

Szilard's memorandum tried to explain fission in laymen's terms: 'Fast neutrons lose their energy in colliding with atoms of a light element in much the same way as a billiard ball loses velocity in a collision with another ball ...'

Szilard said at present it was an open question whether such a chain reaction could be made to work with fast neutrons that were not slowed down but there was reason to believe they could be used, and, if so, it would be easy to construct 'extremely dangerous bombs ... The destructive power of these bombs can only be roughly estimated but there is no doubt that it could far beyond all military conceptions.'[8] Roosevelt decided something should be done, but America was not yet at war. He put it on hold.

Germany had an undoubted lead in atomic science. German scientists had achieved the key breakthroughs and now Hitler's Third Reich was the first to mobilise its physicists for the war effort. 'In the early days of World War Two there was no country better poised in the world to build an atomic bomb than Hitler's Germany,' said Alan B. Carr, historian at the Los Alamos National Laboratory in the United States.

By calling up gifted scientists such as Heisenberg, von Weizsäcker and Bagge, they also showed they had the will. Paul Rosbaud, an Austrian and publisher of scientific works in Germany, revealed that the first meeting took place in May 1939, at least four months before war was declared.

Rosbaud was to become perhaps the most important agent on nuclear research in Hitler's Third Reich for Lieutenant Commander Eric Welsh, the MI6 officer for the Scandinavian section who was to take the lead in London on atomic intelligence. Rosbaud's code name was GRIFFIN, a mythical beast with the body of a lion and wings and head of an eagle; he knew Welsh as 'Theodor'. Griffin wrote a summary about his activities during the war for American intelligence officers on 5 August 1945 – the day before the atomic bomb was detonated on Hiroshima. In this fascinating report, a copy of which I found in the Pash archives at the Hoover Institution Library in Stanford, Rosbaud said the first meeting of the *Uranverein* was called in the first week of May 1939, after the idea for an atomic bomb was put forward by the German experimental physicist Wilhelm Hanle at Gottingen University to Wilhelm Dames at the Department of Education in late April 1939, five months before war was declared.

Rosbaud said Hanle was 'always busy and in great haste and probably convinced of his own historic mission, was glad to have an opportunity to report to this mighty man [Dames] and laid before him this idea of a bomb which should be able to destroy a town, a province, even the whole of an island ...'[9]

Dames immediately called some handpicked atomic scientists to Berlin to a highly secret gathering. A plan to build a nuclear bomb was discussed and a research association was founded, which was dubbed by the scientists themselves the *Uranverein*, the Uranium Club. Those attending included Josef Mattauch, who had taken Lise Meitner's place in Hahn's laboratory, but Hahn, the discoverer of atomic fission, was not invited. Dames had assumed, as Hahn was the director of the *Kaiser-Wilhelm Institut für Chemie* (chemistry), he would not be interested in a meeting about physics.

Rosbaud, who was the first to publish Hahn's discovery of atomic fission, said this meeting took place in extreme secrecy. 'I don't think that there were many physicists taking Dames too seriously, especially when he offered experiments with the bomb which he probably hoped to be ready before the outbreak of a war for the shooting-grounds of the *Wehrmacht* at Kummersdorft.'

Rosbaud admitted: 'I do not deny that I was somehow alarmed when Mattauch, who was present at this meeting, told me the next day everything about it, though it was obvious that the time required for the perfection either of a machine [reactor] or a bomb would be between five and fifty years.'

He was irritated by the secrecy imposed on the new research. 'I remember the visit of one of the team workers who came to see me at my Berlin office,' said Rosbaud. 'I asked him, "How is the work on the U-bomb going on?" The effect of this question was striking. He clasped both hands over his head and exclaimed in his best Baden dialect: "For Heaven's sake! That will cost us all our lives." He was so excited that he nearly lost control.'

Rosbaud told him: 'Oh, come on! The sparrows are singing it from the rooftops.' Soon, Rosbaud found his publications were gagged by a decree imposing secrecy on atomic research in Germany.

The German development of nuclear energy was channelled through three separate organisations – the Army Ordnance Office, the German Department of Education and, bizarrely, the German Post Office, which had its own research budget at the outbreak of war.

The German Post Office became engaged in atomic research after a German businessman, Baron Manfred von Ardenne, who had made a fortune out of private research and enterprise, found there was a large, unused pot of money for research at the Postal

Department. In order to tap into it, he suggested to the Postal Minister, Ohnesorge, that research could deliver an atomic bomb.

The Department of Education had a separate programme of research into atomic energy through university laboratories. The head of physics at the Ministry of Education, Abraham Esau, was regarded as third rate by some leading German physicists; he was one of the senior figures in Hitler's Third Reich who gained promotion because they were Nazis, rather than for their academic ability. Esau was elbowed aside by the Army Ordnance Office group, who gained the authority of the Reich Economic Ministry to get first call on German stocks of uranium and radium, and was not at the meeting on 16 September.

During the meeting, they heard German intelligence had learned that Britain was engaged in uranium research, discussed the difficulties in extracting enough fissionable U-235 to make a bomb. Bagge later claimed Bothe and Geiger said: 'If there is the slightest chance that it is possible – it must be done.' They agreed, despite some objections from rivals, to bring in Heisenberg, though he was a theoretician rather than an experimental scientist. General Becker set up a new Nuclear Physics Research group with Diebner in charge.

Schumann and Diebner called a second meeting on 26 September at the Office of Army Ordnance in Berlin for their first full conference under Diebner. They included Bagge, Heisenberg, his protégé Carl Friedrich von Weizsäcker, Otto Hahn, and Paul Harteck.

Harteck, thirty-six and a physical chemist at Hamburg University, had worked under Ernest Rutherford at the Cavendish Laboratory, Cambridge in 1932. He was not as well known as the rest, but he was partly responsible for their call-up. Five months earlier, Harteck and an assistant at Hamburg University had written to Schumann at the Ordnance Office calling his attention to the newest developments in nuclear physics, which they said 'will probably make it possible to produce an explosive of many orders of magnitude more powerful than conventional ones ...' The country that first made use of a nuclear explosive would have 'an unsurpassable advantage over the others', they added.[10]

Having grabbed Schumann's attention, Harteck was drafted into the elite group of scientists who made up the Uranium Club.

They had yet to capture the imagination of the Nazi high command, which took little interest in pure science, and regarded much of atomic theory as 'Jewish' science. Many scientists with Jewish blood, however diluted by the generations, chose to flee like Lise Meitner, and this depleted the Germans of vitally needed scientific brains. Inevitably, many joined the American atomic bomb programme, code-named the Manhattan Project, with a heightened fear that unless they won the race to produce the bomb, Hitler would win, and his Nazi Third Reich would rule the world.

In December 1939, Heisenberg made a breakthrough at his laboratory in Leipzig. Bagge recalled how Heisenberg met him on his bicycle outside his laboratory and excitedly told him: 'Bagge, come to me in my room!' Heisenberg explained his breakthrough to Bagge: if you used alternating layers of graphite or heavy water as a moderator, it would slow down the neutrons of U-238 without capturing them; that would make it easier for uranium neutrons of U-238 to collide with neutrons of the rarer U-235, causing a further split. A controlled chain reaction would be possible.

Heisenberg submitted a secret two-part paper to the department of Army Ordnance in early 1940 called the *Possibility of Technical Energy Production from Uranium Fission* in which Heisenberg explicitly referred to the possibility that nuclear energy could lead to a new superbomb:

> As far as we know, you can use the Uranium fission (found by Hahn and Strassmann) for the production of energy. The safest way for constructing a suitable machine is the enrichment of the isotope U-235. The more you intensify the enrichment, the smaller you can construct the machine. The enrichment of U-235 is the only way to keep the volume of the machine as small as possible ...and it's the only way to produce powerful explosions – explosives that outmatch all the up-to-now known explosives at several 10x powers ...

In July 1940, von Weizsäcker published a theoretical report for the Army Ordnance Office called *A Possibility of Energy Production from U-238* in which he speculated that neptunium – element 93, the next element after uranium – could be produced as a by-product of atomic fission and might be more explosive. In August 1941, Fritz Houtermans went further and predicted that plutonium – element 94 – could be created by a reactor.

Houtermans had a remarkably unlucky life; he had worked for EMI in England before going to Soviet Russia where he was denounced by the secret service and imprisoned as a German spy; when Stalin entered the pact with Hitler in 1939, Houtermans was handed over to the Gestapo and then imprisoned in Berlin as a Soviet agent; he was only released after the intervention of Max von Laue. He joined the private laboratory of the colourful Baron von Ardenne in Berlin. He was no Nazi and tried to get a warning out to American intelligence through a refugee acting as a courier. It is thought he realised the potential of plutonium to fuel a bomb, and his message to the Americans was simple: hurry.

The Battle of Britain was over, and the two sides were settling down to all-out war with a bombing blitz of cities. In early October 1940, a team under the direction of Professor Karl Wirtz was given a wooden barrack hut in the grounds of the Institute for Biology and Virus Research next to the Institute of Physics in Berlin-Dahlem, where they could build their first nuclear reactor. In order to deter curious students from prying further, they put up a sign outside their barrack block saying: 'Virus House'. Inside, they excavated a circular pit six feet deep and lined it with bricks for the experimental reactor core. If they blew up the laboratory, it was hoped the radioactive 'virus' would not contaminate the institute. Their fears were not so far-fetched. Heisenberg's laboratory in Leipzig was burned out when an experimental pile exploded in a fireball.

By December 1940, Von Weizsäcker and Heisenberg embarked on their first experiments. It was a frustrating business. They lowered a large aluminium canister containing uranium oxide and paraffin packed in layers in a pit of water to act as a radiation shield. They were unable to measure any increase in neutrons and concluded, rightly, that ordinary water would not work as a moderator with natural uranium to sustain a chain reaction. That left two options to act as a moderator: graphite or heavy water, a mixture of oxygen and the heavy isotope of hydrogen, called deuterium oxide, which was about 10 per cent heavier than ordinary water. It had first been isolated by Professor Harold Urey, who was awarded the Nobel Prize for the discovery.

They were partly led astray by the findings of Walther Bothe in Heidelberg who produced a fatally flawed analysis showing that graphite would not work. Bothe was a gifted experimentalist but his false finding was to disable the German research for years to come. Enrico Fermi, the Italian refugee, was later to make the breakthrough in Chicago using pure graphite as a moderator, not heavy water. This enabled fission with 'fast' neutrons which, in highly refined U-235 or plutonium, would lead to the development of the world's first atomic bomb.

Allied bombing was deliberately targeted at the laboratories in Dahlem, a suburb of Berlin, to disable the German atomic research.

It made life almost intolerable for the scientists. In response, the primitive 'Virus House' was replaced by Diebner with a much larger and more sophisticated laboratory, concealed inside a huge underground bunker with reinforced concrete. It was the largest reactor pile so far, capable of holding 1.5 tons of heavy water and 3 tons of uranium metal in the form of plates in a deep pit. When it was found by American intelligence officers they mistook the deep pit for a swimming pool.

There are still heated debates about the motives of the scientists who answered the call to work for Hitler's Third Reich. All vehemently denied they were seeking to build the atomic bomb for Hitler and some, including Heisenberg, have claimed they deliberately pursued the building of a 'boiler' to avoid handing Hitler an atomic bomb. But by mobilising its nuclear scientists, Germany's military chiefs were clearly intending to steal a march on their enemies, and it was not for the peaceful use of atomic energy.

Heisenberg had to wrestle with a personal dilemma as the world slipped towards war. In the summer of 1939, he was on a lucrative tour of American universities giving lectures on his atomic theories. He had offers to stay in America, which was at that time neutral. However, he refused them all, and returned to Germany as it geared up for war.

Heisenberg was no Nazi. Indeed, Heisenberg had been viciously attacked in a Nazi newspaper, *Das Schwarze Korps*, in 1937 as one of the 'white Jews in science' who were traitors and deserved the concentration camp: 'Heisenberg is only one example of many others ... They are all representatives of Judaism in German spiritual life who must all be eliminated just as the Jews themselves.'[11]

Heisenberg's 'crime' was engaging in the 'Jewish science' by suggesting that Einstein's theory of relativity should be taught in schools. He was subjected to a year-long SS investigation and was exonerated only after a personal appeal to the family of Heinrich Himmler, head of the SS, through Heisenberg's mother's family.

On 21 July 1938, Himmler wrote to SS Gruppenführer Heydrich in Berlin saying: 'I believe that Heisenberg is a decent person and that we cannot afford to lose or to silence this man, who is still young and can still produce a rising generation in science.'

Himmler wrote on the same day to Heisenberg saying: 'Because you were recommended by my family I have had your case investigated with special care and precision. I am glad that I can now inform you that I do not approve of the attack in *Das Schwarze Korps* and that I have taken measures against any further attack against you.'

Himmler added a friendly personal postscript warning him it would be best in future if he made a distinction between the results of scientific research and 'the personal and political attitude of the scientists involved'.

However, Heisenberg's choice of returning to Hitler's Third Reich as it mobilised for war was to raise far-reaching questions about his nationalism.

Heisenberg, the son of a professor of medieval Greek studies, certainly had a deep-seated love of his country, its culture – he loved playing Beethoven sonatas on the piano – and its traditions, including wearing lederhosen and mountain hiking in Bavaria, where he had an alpine chalet, just as Hitler had his 'Eagle's Nest' at Berchtesgaden. Before the war broke out, Heisenberg had joined the Alpenjäger, the German mountain reserve force, which, he said, he enjoyed because it was like 'mountaineering, complicated by the presence of sergeants'.[12]

Asked by US intelligence agents why he returned to Germany in 1939, Heisenberg gave a deceptively simplistic answer: he felt 'Germany needs me'. He later gave a range of reasons, including not wanting to leave his young team of scientists. He also had strong family ties in the Fatherland: he had married Elisabeth Schumacher, the daughter of a Berlin economics professor, in 1937 and within a year 'Li' gave birth to twins, the first of their seven children over the next twelve years.

Several German scientists were torn like Heisenberg and von Weizsäcker between the intellectual challenge of working on nuclear fission and the moral implications of developing a nuclear weapon of untold power for the Nazi war machine.

They could collaborate and survive, in the hope that the war would be over before the uranium bomb was ready, or refuse and face the consequences. Some scientists, such as Paul Müller, ended up in German uniforms fighting on the eastern front against the Russians, where they met their deaths. There was a 'Führer list' of protected citizens who were excused the call-up, but they were mostly artists, singers, and movie stars admired by the Nazis.

Heisenberg explained his reasoning in a letter to Robert Jungk, author of *Brighter than a Thousand Suns*, written after the war:

With the beginning of the war there arose of course for every German physicist the dreadful dilemma that each of his actions meant either a victory for Hitler or a defeat of Germany, and of course both alternatives presented themselves to us as appalling.

Heisenberg claimed Germany mobilised for atomic weapon research because the Americans were doing so. He said news reached Germany almost simultaneously with the outbreak of war that funds were being allocated by the American military authorities for research on atomic energy. Heisenberg claimed that the *Heereswaffenamt* created the special research group under Schumann and Diebner 'in view of the possibility that England and the United States might undertake the development of atomic weapons'. In fact, American funds were allocated as 1939 turned into 1940 – three months after the German Ordnance Office began work, and America remained out of the war until the attack on Pearl Harbour in December 1941.[13]

The German scientists discussed their motivation at the Kaiser Wilhelm Institute at the time. Von Weizsäcker told Otto Hahn that working for the *Wehrmacht*, the German army, was the best way to preserve their laboratories. Hahn, whose discovery had accelerated the drive for the atomic bomb, replied, 'I think you are right.' But Hahn had then become very excited and said, 'If by my work Hitler gets a bomb I shall commit suicide.' Von Weizsäcker added: 'We both agreed this was not very probable.'

Otto Hahn was a complex character. He had been awarded the Iron Cross for his bravery when he commanded a machine gun unit on the western front in the First World War, but he was one of the German troops who famously fraternised with the English in the trenches at Christmas 1914:

I shall never forget the afternoon of that Christmas Eve. At first there were only a few among us and the English who looked over the parapet of the trenches, which were about 50 metres apart. Then there were more and more, and before long all of the soldiers came out of the trenches. We fraternised. The English gave us their good cigarettes, and those among us who had candied fruit gave them some. We sang songs together, and for the night of 24/25 December the war stopped. All was quiet on the 25th too. No shot was fired.[14]

Despite this display of humanity, Hahn was transferred to chemical warfare in 1917 to lead gas attacks on the Eastern Front. He later described how the results on the Russian soldiers left him 'ashamed and deeply agitated' by the 'total insanity of war'.[15]

Hahn was equally troubled by his involvement in the German nuclear programme but said he felt like a soldier acting under military orders. It is not a convincing argument. The excuse of 'acting under orders' proved no defence for Hitler's former henchmen at the Nuremberg tribunal into Nazi war crimes.

Heisenberg said after the war that his friend von Weizsäcker loathed Hitler's personality and the crimes committed by his movement just as much as any other decent human being. But he added: 'To this revulsion undiminished later on as well, there may have, over time, been added a mix of horrified admiration, when he saw from up close (through his family) how Hitler managed to twist power out of the hands of all those highly qualified people whose efforts were directed towards positive ends in German politics.'

On the night before he was due to join the Ordnance Office team, von Weizsäcker, who came from a long line of politicians in the family, debated what he should do with a friend, who was a philosopher.

> When I understood that nuclear weapons were possible in 1939 we debated all night: if this is possible somebody will use it – this means mankind comes into a position where we either overcome the institution of war or we will destroy ourselves. I felt this was the most important political thing that has happened in my life. My feeling was that Hitler will begin a war but Hitler will not persist – but the bomb will be there forever ... I felt that as I am a physicist and I am politically interested, I must in any case enter this field. I cannot keep outside.

Having cleared his conscience, von Weizsäcker volunteered to work for Hitler's Third Reich. 'I approached them. I actually told them I should be glad to work in this.'[16]

Von Weizsäcker admitted after the war that people would question why he had volunteered to work on the nuclear programme for Hitler. Paul Rosbaud wrote:

> I am sorry to say there were – apart from wild Nazis – quite a number of good and even very distinguished physicists, who for some reason – personal ambition, fear that another might be more successful, hope for a chair of physics or a war decoration ... or for

other human weaknesses were only too willing to do their best ... for these or any other war machines.[17]

The fact that he worked on atomic research for Hitler's Nazis was also the source of some embarrassment for von Weizsäcker's brother Richard, who became president of the Federal Republic of Germany in 1984 and presided over the reunification of the democratic West Germany with the communist East Germany following the collapse of the Berlin Wall in 1989. Their father had been German Foreign Minister Ernst von Weizsäcker. He was a member of a leading aristocratic German family, who produced a long line of respected statesmen and diplomats; he died in January 2015 at the age of ninety-four.

Heisenberg and von Weizsäcker became convinced that the way forward was through the use of heavy water as a moderator. Heisenberg predicted a chain reaction would occur if he could obtain at least 600 litres of heavy water, alternating in a layer with 1 metric ton of graphite and 2 to 3 metric tons of pure uranium oxide. Germany had nothing like these quantities of materials. The world's leading source of heavy water was a plant in the south of Norway called the Norsk Hydro where it was produced through electrolysis as a by-product of ammonia for fertiliser. The process required huge amounts of electricity and water, both in abundance at the Norsk Hydro plant. On 9 April 1940, Hitler ordered his forces to invade Norway, which threatened to put the largest stocks of heavy water on earth into the hands of Hitler's Third Reich.

Unknown to Berlin, London or Washington, however, a French team was determined to stop that from happening ... with the help of a British intelligence officer in Paris and an eccentric British peer of the realm.

4

Heavy Water and the French Connection

Raoul Dautry, the French minister for armaments, was several steps ahead of MI6 and the Abwehr, the Germans' intelligence service under the resourceful Wilhelm Canaris, when Hitler ordered the invasion of Norway on 9 April 1940. Dautry had already authorised a daring secret operation by French intelligence a month earlier in March to evacuate the 185 kg of heavy water that made up the biggest stockpile in the world from the Norsk Hydro in Rjukan, south-central Norway, to Paris.

Dautry did the Allies a great service in keeping the heavy water out of the hands of the Germans, but the French were acting out of self-interest. They wanted the stocks of heavy water for their own military nuclear programme. Lew Kowarski, a scientist at the Joliot-Curie laboratory in Paris, convinced Joliot by January 1940 that using heavy water as a moderator was the only practical way to achieve sustained nuclear fission. Joliot sent a secret report to Dautry stating that they needed heavy water. Kowarski wrote a report stating the bulk of the world's stock of heavy water was at the Norwegian factory. Kowarski added: 'And then I wrote this magnificent sentence: "We would need the whole of this stock." It was quite thrilling to write a sentence like that.'[1]

Kowarski was in no doubt when he was interviewed in 1969 that the French programme had a military dimension: 'There is in France a certain tradition of high military thinking allied to the advanced sciences ... It was quite comprehensible to the high military minds that there will be some day an atomic explosive ...

and therefore anything which produces a chain reaction someday will contribute to going toward the explosive.'[2]

Kowarski, aged thirty-three, had been born in St Petersburg, Russia, before gaining French citizenship shortly prior to the outbreak of war. He gained a chemical engineering degree at Lyon University. He was thickset, with heavy jowls, and had been part of the Joliot team since 1934. He was so committed to the role of heavy water in atomic fission that he regarded himself as the 'heavy water man' in the Joliot team. The French minister for armaments, too, was convinced about its importance. Around 20 February 1940, Dautry told Joliot, 'I've decided to get the heavy water for you.'

Lieutenant Jacques Allier of the French Deuxieme Bureau, the French equivalent of the SIS, had discovered that the Germans, who had previously been disinterested in heavy water, had suddenly changed their view. Axel Aubert, General Manager of the Norsk Hydro, had been approached by a representative of the IG Farben company in Germany, who had wanted to buy the entire stock. The need for action was pressing. Dautry decided that Allier should secretly go to Oslo to begin negotiations for the heavy water with Aubert. Allier was accompanied by Captain Muller, Lieutenant Mosse, professor at the Sorbonne, and a Monsieur Knall-Demars as back up.

It was still the period of the so-called 'Phoney War' before a bomb had been dropped by the Germans in Britain or France, and it could have caused a huge diplomatic row because Norway was officially a neutral country. For the French, who were officially at war with the Germans, Allier and his team were putting their lives at risk. As spies, they were likely to be shot if they were caught. There were suspicions the Germans had been tipped off about the French interest in heavy water. Dautry and Allier were so worried that there would be a security leak to the Germans that, for their own good, Kowarski and his German-born colleague, Hans von Halban, were sent out of Paris while the operation took place.

Kowarski was told to take a 'holiday' on an island off Brittany while von Halban was sent to the Cote d'Azur. 'I was less conspicuous in spite of my bulk. I was supposed to do some geological researches. I hired a bicycle and I rode in all directions, having ideas about the slowing down of neutrons and a few other things. I also read the whole of *Gone with the Wind*.'[3]

Allier had been a banker with the Banque de Paris et Des Pays-Bas (BNP Parisbas) for seventeen years before being mobilised and his Paris bank had made a heavy investment in the 'Norsk hydro-elektrisk Kvælstofaktieselskab' (Norwegian Hydro-Electric Nitrogen Company – the Norsk Hydro), which the bank had helped to found in 1905.[4] Dautry assumed that this would give Allier extra leverage over Axel Aubert. Allier found no extra pressure was needed. At their meeting in Oslo, Allier found Dr Aubert was as keen as the French to keep the stocks of heavy water out of the hands of the Germans, even if it cost him his life.

Aubert explained he had been dissatisfied by the answers he got from the Germans when he asked why they wanted such a big order for heavy water, and he had put them off. Now, fearing a German invasion, Aubert readily agreed to give the French their entire stock of heavy water on free loan until the end of the war. 'If later, by bad luck, France loses the war, I shall be shot for what I have done today. I am proud to take that chance,' said Aubert.

An elderly craftsman constructed jerry cans in a small welding yard in Oslo (avoiding the use of boron or cadmium, which would have contaminated the water) to avoid arousing German suspicions. Aubert arranged for the cans to be taken to Rjukan by night and filled with 185 kg of heavy water. The factory manager drove the precious containers himself along icy mountain roads to Oslo, where Allier and his men were waiting.[5]

Allier was travelling under his mother's maiden name, but he was alerted by French intelligence that they had intercepted German orders to detain him. The Gestapo had searched an earlier plane when it landed at Hamburg on its way to Amsterdam. As a result, he set out to confuse the Germans by appearing to board a plane with his colleagues and the jerry cans heading for Amsterdam, but switched to a flight to Britain under assumed names.

They had to seek cloud cover to evade possible interception by Luftwaffe fighters after takeoff, but there was so much cloud over the east coast of Britain they were diverted to Montrose. They spent the night at Edinburgh before catching a train to London. Travel by train was difficult enough in wartime Britain, but Allier and his men managed to transport the world's entire stock of heavy water almost the entire length of Britain by train in a compartment occupied by the four French intelligence agents, with one mounting an armed guard, without telling the British authorities.

The SIS had no idea that one of the most important coups against Hitler acquiring the atom bomb was going on under their noses. The heavy water was taken to the French Military Mission in London, where it was stored pending the next move.[6] The French intelligence team then transported the jerry cans to the coast and across the English Channel into France, where they were delivered safely to an air raid shelter under the College de France in Paris.

It is inconceivable that the British would have allowed a shipment of such vital importance to the war effort to leave their shores if they had known. Dautry only informed British intelligence when the heavy water was safely stored at the College's Joliot-Curie laboratory.

Jacques Allier went to London in April 1940 on the orders of Raoul Dautry to liaise with the British on the atomic bomb, including Dr Herbert John Gough, Assistant Director of Science Research at the Ministry of Supply, and his deputy, the nuclear physicist Professor John Cockcroft. Allier was embraced by British intelligence for his audacious coup and, on 10 August, was invited to the first meeting of an expert committee of scientists to discuss the threat of a Nazi atomic bomb along with the prospects for a bomb being built by Britain. It was held at the headquarters of the Royal Society, then housed in the Palladian-style mansion of Burlington House in Piccadilly, underlining the fact that atomic research was still firmly in the hands of scientists rather than the military in London. Being surrounded by such distinguished scientists may have been daunting, but the former banker sat down at the conference table with the satisfaction that he had already achieved more than anyone in that room to stop Hitler acquiring a bomb. The day before, Hitler's forces had invaded Norway. Allier knew he had beaten them to the heavy water.

The committee had been set up by Sir Henry Tizard, a chief adviser to the Government on science, to investigate the claims by two refugee scientists who had come to Birmingham University, Otto Frisch and Rudolf Peierls, that an atomic bomb could be built with as little as 1 kg of enriched uranium.

It was chaired by George Thomson, Professor of Physics at Imperial College London, who had transferred to full-time research work at the Royal Aircraft Establishment at Farnborough near to his home on the Hog's Back. Its members included Cockcroft, who had been doing pioneering research at the Cavendish Laboratory in Cambridge on splitting the atom in the early 1930s while Professor James Chadwick was working in another part of the laboratory on the discovery of the neutron. Their work would lead to a landmark document that presaged the development of the world's first atomic bomb. It was called the MAUD report.

The Frisch and Peierls Memorandum

Two brilliant young scientists, Otto Frisch and Rudolf Peierls, fled to Britain to escape the Nazis but they were barred from taking part in research into the development of radar because it was too secret to trust to enemy aliens. That left them with plenty of spare time to work on a theoretical problem that had fascinated them: would it be possible to create enough fission to cause an atomic explosion?

Frisch was thirty-five, Jewish, born in Austria; his aunt was Lise Meitner. Rudolf Peierls, a German-born Jew aged thirty-three, was a gifted mathematician and had been studying in Cambridge under Professor Chadwick when Hitler came to power but obtained leave to remain in Britain. They were at Birmingham when they collaborated in March 1940 on the theoretical paper that became known as the Frisch and Peierls Memorandum.

They concluded Einstein was wrong – an atomic bomb could be made small enough to drop from an aircraft.

Frisch and Peierls' findings were blood-chilling: 'The energy liberated by a 5 kg bomb would be equivalent to that of several thousand tons of dynamite, while that of a 1 kg bomb, though about 500 times less, would still be formidable.'

The explosion unleashed would be on scale and of nature never witnessed by Man before. It would be as hot as the sun, they said.

The energy liberated in the explosion of such a super-bomb is about the same as that produced by the explosion of 1,000 tons of dynamite. This energy is liberated in a small volume, in which it will, for an instant, produce a temperature comparable to that in the interior of the Sun. The blast from such an explosion would destroy life in a wide area. The size of this area is difficult to estimate, but it will probably cover the centre of a big city. In addition, some part of the energy set free by the bomb goes to produce radioactive substances, and these will emit very powerful and dangerous radiations. The effects of these radiations is greatest immediately after the explosion, but it decays only gradually and even for days after the explosion any person entering the affected area will be killed.

They also addressed some of the moral questions that still confront the world over atomic weapons. As a superweapon, it would be 'irresistible' and no fortress would be able to withstand its power; but it would also make it impossible to seize land where it had been exploded because of the radioactive fallout poisoning the battle ground. Owing to the spread of radioactivity in the wind, it would be impossible to use it without killing large numbers of civilians.

Most physicists such as Einstein, Szilard and Heisenberg were working on the assumption that, in order to achieve a sustained chain reaction, they would have to slow the neutrons down in a medium such as heavy water. Frisch and Peierls made their calculations based on 'fast neutrons' – using only highly enriched uranium-235, which would fission more freely. It was the difference between creating a uranium-powered 'boiler' – a reactor creating energy – and a bomb.

If one works on the assumption that Germany is, or will be, in the possession of this weapon, it must be realised that no shelters are available that would be effective and that could be used on a large scale.

The most effective reply would be a counter-threat with a similar bomb. Therefore it seems to us important to start production as soon and as rapidly as possible, even if it is not intended to use the bomb as a means of attack. Since the separation of the necessary amount of uranium is, in the most favourable circumstances, a matter of several months, it would obviously be too late to start production when such a bomb is known to be in the hands of Germany, and the matter seems, therefore, very urgent.

They also suggested how it could be constructed: 'It is necessary that such a sphere should be made in two (or more) parts which are brought together first when the explosion is wanted. Once assembled, the bomb would explode within a second or less, since one neutron is sufficient to start the reaction and there are several neutrons passing through the bomb every second, from the cosmic radiation.

A sphere with a radius of less than about 3 cm could be made up in two hemispheres, which are pulled together by springs and kept separated by a suitable structure which is removed at the desired moment. A larger sphere would have to be composed of more than two parts, if the parts, taken separately, are to be stable.

Neutrons would enter the nucleus of other atoms, splitting them, releasing more neutrons, splitting more atoms, repeating the process exponentially in a mega-explosion of energy.

So far, it was only theoretical, a mass of calculations on a blackboard; nobody had found a way of separating enough U-235 to make a bomb. They conceded it was 'quite possible' that nobody in Germany had yet realised that the separation of the uranium isotopes would make the construction of a super-bomb possible.

> Hence it is of extreme importance to keep this report secret since any rumour about the connection between uranium separation and a super-bomb may set a German scientist thinking along the right lines.

They were so alarmed by their own calculations, they wanted to alert the authorities, but had no idea how to warn the British government. They approached Marcus Oliphant, Professor of Physics at Birmingham University, who was involved in secret research work for the Admiralty. He told them to 'write to Tizard', the chairman of the Committee for the Scientific Survey of Air Defence at the Air Ministry in Whitehall.

Their memorandum was to trigger a political chain-reaction that was to change the course of history. But for a time it seemed as though it had produced a damp squib.

Peierls heard nothing, and became so concerned by the apparent lack of action that he wrote to George Thomson, chair of the committee on the atomic bomb, to seek his help in alerting the government to the threat. Thomson was already well aware of Peierls' memorandum when the letter arrived at his home in Puttenham, near Farnborough, where he worked at the Royal Aircraft Establishment. Though Tizard was sceptical whether an atomic bomb would ever work, he had already asked Thomson to study a range of options, including work on isotope separation, with the claims raised by Frisch and Peierls in their memorandum.

Thomson pulled in a network of associates: James Chadwick, who pioneered the study of fast neutrons using Britain's first cyclotron at Liverpool University; Professor Oliphant from Birmingham; physicist Philip Moon, a student of Oliphant and Rutherford; Patrick Blackett, a member of Tizard's committee at the Air Ministry working on radar; and John Cockcroft, who shared the Nobel Prize for splitting the atom and was Herbert Gough's deputy assistant director of scientific research at the Ministry of Supply.

Apart from science they had one other thing in common: they were all members of the Athenaeum Club. It was reassuring when they were discussing the biggest secrets in the world that they were all members of the same gentleman's club.

Thomson's uranium subcommittee commissioned a series of theoretical and experimental research programmes at Liverpool, Birmingham, Cambridge, and Oxford universities and at Imperial Chemical Industries (ICI) to test the Frisch and Peierls findings. They confirmed the essentials; suddenly, the threat of an atomic bomb being dropped on London became a shattering possibility ... unless Britain and American scientists built the atomic bomb first.

Crucially, they predicted an atomic bomb could be achieved by 1943, early enough to influence the outcome of the war. It would be a game changer.

As yet, the Americans had not entered the war and were less focused on the need to build the bomb. That was not the case in London. Fear that the Nazis would win the race to the atomic bomb proved a powerful driver for progress on the uranium problem in London.

Thomson realised it would be better for security to adopt a code name for his committee. It adopted the obscure title of the MAUD Committee. Some suggest it was an acronym for Military Applications of Uranium Detonation, but if so, it would have been a huge hint about its purpose. The more compelling reason is that it came from a mysterious telegram sent to Frisch by Bohr when the Germans invaded Copenhagen. It ended with an apparently coded message: 'Tell Chadwick and Maud Ray Kent.' The best brains in Britain tried to unravel the mystery of the 'Maud Ray' code without success. It was so enigmatic, they adopted 'Maud' as the code name for Thomson's committee. They only later discovered from Bohr himself that he was trying to get his message to Maud Ray, who was his children's' former governess from Kent.

*

Allier also met his British opposite numbers in intelligence and supplied them with a list of German scientists capable of engaging in uranium research. He suggested they should discover whether the scientists on his list were still working in their own universities or had been called up by the Third Reich. MI6 had already asked Frisch and Peierls for reports on all they knew about the Nazi bomb programme. Peierls said:

> One of the first things that we did was to provide Intelligence with a list of names and the request that we were kept informed of where they were working ...
>
> We decided that quite a lot could probably be picked up from German scientific literature. For instance, one German journal, which was published twice a year, included a lecture list showing who was lecturing where, and when. We realised that this could hardly be false, because that would have been obvious in so many places.
>
> This showed that most of Germany's nuclear physicists were working at their normal universities, doing normal work, and publishing normal papers. Therefore we could assume that nothing particularly important was going on ...
>
> It seemed that Heisenberg was up to something. There was for instance a Ph. D. thesis, which was published by a student at his laboratory. At the end of the paper the student acknowledged the help of a number of people – but not of Heisenberg, although the thesis dealt with his subject. One wondered at the omission ...[7]

Frisch and Peierls suggested to MI6 where they might start their inquiries:

> Information that could be helpful in this respect would be data about the exploitation of the uranium mines under German control (mainly in Czechoslovakia) and about any recent German purchases of uranium abroad.
>
> It is likely that the plant would be controlled by Dr K. Clusius (Professor of Physical Chemistry in Munich University), the

inventor of the best method for separating isotopes, and therefore information as to his whereabouts and status might also give an important clue.

Their advice was remarkably prescient; Heisenberg and Clusius were among the key figures in the Nazi atomic energy programme, but it would be another four years before action was taken to seize them.

The Germans launched their blitzkrieg against France on 10 May 1940. On 15 May the Germans crossed the river Meuse at three points between Namur and Mezieres, where the bridges had been left intact. The next day, Allier's team decided at a hurried meeting with Joliot that the heavy water should be taken out of Paris to Clermont-Ferrand with heavy equipment from the Joliot-Curie laboratory. The plan was for von Halban, together with Joliot's deputy director of the lab, the chemist Henri Moureu, to leave Paris and relocate the laboratory to the south of the Loire. 'The Loire for some reason was given a mystical significance,' said Kowarski. 'It was considered that the Germans might occupy France as far as the Loire but certainly not below the Loire. So they had to go below the Loire and put the heavy water in safety, perhaps the gram of radium that we had, and a few other things and then we would see.'[8]

The last days of May were essentially spent by the Joliot-Curie laboratory in preparation for the evacuation, since the Germans were getting closer and closer to Paris. From his windows in Paris, Joliot could see the ominous black clouds of smoke billowing up from the burning oil refineries seventy miles away. In the meantime, von Halban rented a villa in Clermont-Ferrand. The idea was that they would continue on experiments in the villa, which had to be fitted out as an emergency laboratory. On 5 June, Kowarski found himself commanding half-a-dozen soldiers considerably younger than him in a convoy carrying the laboratory equipment to von Halban's villa. The journey took two days and Kowarski's family travelled south separately by train. Kowarski's daughter, aged four, had accidentally suffered serious burns to her leg with a pan of boiling water a few days before, and her leg was heavily bandaged. Kowarski was worried, but everybody seeing the little girl with the bandaged leg assumed that they had been in some way bombed out and were full of sympathy for her.

The French government also fled Paris and arrived among the shaded, tree-lined streets of Le Mont-Dore, the spa town in Central

France, by the hills of the Massif Central, about the same time as Kowarski. It seemed a world away from the fighting, but Kowarski was arrested by the local mayor who suspected from his foreign accent and his suspicious behaviour that he was a German spy.

Fortunately, a safe place had been found for the heavy water: the jerry cans were stashed in the local women's prison for safekeeping. The following morning, Kowarski was released from custody, and Allier moved the heavy water to another prison at Riom that later became infamous for the trial of French political leaders responsible for declaring war on Germany.

When he reached Clermont-Ferrand, Kowarski was surprised to find that von Halban appeared to be settling in to the little villa, *Clair Logis*, for the duration of the war, going down to Vichy to buy furniture for the villa at an auction sale, as though he expected to be able to stay there. Contrary to von Halban's domesticity, Kowarski was convinced that they would have to leave Clermont-Ferrand very soon.

A few days later Joliot arrived with his wife, Irene Curie, the daughter of the Nobel Prize winner, who was suffering from tuberculosis of the lungs. 'They were completely exhausted, and I remember, characteristic of Irene, as soon as they arrived, Irene immediately lay down on the floor and went to sleep. She had this simplicity of behaviour.'

Meanwhile, a huge drama was being played out on the sandy beaches of Dunkirk. By 4 June, most of the British forces had been expelled from France in the evacuation from Dunkirk – code-named Operation Dynamo – and on Monday 10 June the French government declared Paris a 'free city' to avoid the Germans destroying their historic capital and its people, and decamped to Bordeaux. The Germans rolled into the beautiful boulevards of Paris at 3 a.m. on 14 June.

The victorious Führer and his architect, Albert Speer, with a couple of artists donning grey German uniforms, carried out a private tour of Paris in open top Mercedes sedans so that Hitler could inspect its finest buildings, including the opera house, over which Hitler became animated with excitement. Hitler told Speer it had been his dream to visit Paris, which he readily conceded was the most beautiful city in Europe. He confided to Speer he had thought it would be necessary to destroy Paris, but he had changed his mind. Why destroy Paris? Paris would be a mere shadow of the new Berlin he planned to build with Speer.[9] Speer claimed that, from that moment, he realised that the Führer was not only a megalomaniac, but also a nihilist and a misanthrope. What so shocked Speer was Hitler's casual threat to destroy the most beautiful city in the world. It did not stop Speer working for him, though. Speer helped Hitler rebuild the centre of Berlin to eclipse Paris, including Hitler's Chancellery, with vast, cavernous public buildings. In his memoirs, written in Spandau prison, Speer relates with amusement the way Hitler's ministers vied with each other to have the widest doors and the highest ceilings in their vast echoing halls that were supposed to invoke the grandeur of the Roman era. None of it survived the war, but a remnant of Speer's designs can be seen in the interior of the former German embassy in London (now the Royal Society) at 7–9 Carlton House Terrace, where his work, stripped of its Nazi fixtures and partially covered by carpets, remains.

Sunday 16 June 1940 was a tumultuous day for France. That day, two days after the Germans entered Paris, the embattled French Prime Minister in Bordeaux Paul Reynaud, resigned and fled to the south of France with the intention of reaching North Africa to lead the resistance in exile from one of the French African colonies, such as Algeria. He crashed his car and spent the rest of the war as a prisoner until the liberation. Reynaud's veteran deputy, Marshal Philippe Pétain, a hero of the First World War with the famous white soup-strainer moustache, took over the French government, saying they must share the trials of the French people by staying to act as the civil power under Nazi control from Vichy; the Vichy government won the undying hatred of de Gaulle's Free French for collaborating with the Nazis.

As his government collapsed, Jacques Allier decided to act. A Simca screeched to a halt outside *Clair Logis*, the scientists' villa in Clermont-Ferrand. Allier, still in the uniform of Dautry's cabinet, jumped out, and ran inside to tell Joliot, von Halban and Kowarski that they would have to leave with the heavy water for England. Their only hope of escape was through the port of Bordeaux, which would not remain open for long.

5

The Crown Jewels

Charles 'Wild Jack' Howard, 20th Earl of Suffolk and 13th Earl of Berkshire, stumped around the deck of the tramp steamer SS *Broompark,* with a walking stick in one hand and a bottle of 1928 *Pommery Grenot* in the other, dispensing vintage champagne to female passengers who were feeling queasy. Champagne, he said, was the best cure for seasickness.[1]

The earl had good reason to feel like celebrating. He had just pulled off a coup that could sabotage the German efforts to produce an atomic bomb.

As France capitulated in June 1940 under the shock of the Nazi blitzkrieg, the Earl of Suffolk had commandeered the Scottish collier in Bordeaux harbour and had smuggled onboard a cargo far more precious than gold: twenty-six jerry cans containing the world's stockpile of deuterium oxide D2O, known as heavy water.

SS *Broompark* slipped its mooring at Bordeaux harbour at 6 a.m. on 19 June 1940, and headed down the river Garonne for the open sea, with its weather-beaten master Olaf Paulsen on the bridge, quietly smoking his pipe and wondering if they were going to make it to England. Two days before, the Cunard liner *Lancastria* had been sunk by Ju 88 bombers leaving the port of Saint Nazaire, on the west coast of France, with the loss of around 3,000 lives – the biggest death toll on any British ship in history.

Paulsen was a seasoned skipper. Born in Oslo, he had lived most of his life in Scotland, and had been forced into retirement in his sixties, allegedly for grounding a ship. He had been recalled in 1939 to skipper the 5,136-ton cargo vessel SS *Broompark,* recently built by Lithgows in Glasgow for J. and J. Denholm of Greenock. The steamer was registered in Glasgow, manned by a mixed Glaswegian and Arab crew and flew the Red Ensign of the British Merchant fleet. She was every dusty inch a classic tramp steamer, carrying freight across the world's oceans to wherever it was needed most. Her log shows she had sailed from Singapore, Saigon and Suez, and had criss-crossed the Atlantic, risking sinking by U-boats, to deliver vital materials such as timber and metal to Britain for the war effort; but she had never carried a cargo like this.

Over three anxious days, while she was moored like a sitting duck at the Bordeaux quayside, the earl and an army intelligence officer, Major Ardale Vaultier Golding, arranged for an extraordinary consignment to be loaded on board: two crates of industrial diamonds, worth millions of pounds, from the famous diamond houses of Antwerp and Amsterdam; over 600 tons of heavy American machine tools they had discovered by chance in railway wagons on the docks; the British embassy cars which had been lifted into the coaly hold; twenty-seven French scientists and their families; and the world's largest stockpile of heavy water. Twenty-six jerry cans containing the heavy water were now sitting in the small cabin next to Paulson's cabin, along with the diamonds and an armed guard on the door.

The bearded earl had welcomed them on board stripped to the waist and showing off the tattoos of his youth like a pirate, shouting orders and cracking jokes in fluent French with a raw English accent. He dispensed the champagne – part of the spoils of war – as the ship headed out to the open sea and started to pitch and roll.

'There were seasick people; he was limping around the ship to treat them with champagne, which he proclaimed to be the best remedy against seasickness,' Kowarski recalled. 'All this was completely in keeping with the ideas of British aristocracy I had gathered from the works of P. G. Wodehouse.'[2]

The Earl of Suffolk was more Lord Peter Wimsey, Dorothy L. Sayers' wily sleuth, than clueless Bertie Wooster. He had been a soldier, but was unable to serve in the regular army when war broke out because of a 'gammy' leg, caused by rheumatoid arthritis, which required him to use a walking stick. Instead, he was hired as a special agent for the scientific arm of the Ministry of Supply, although he remained a civilian. It seems extraordinary that British intelligence could find space for a buccaneering amateur like Charles Henry

George Howard, but the old boys' network was strong inside the intelligence services – as the recruitment of the Cambridge traitors including Burgess, Blunt and Maclean later showed – and it was always ready to make exceptions for colourful characters like the 20th Earl of Suffolk. To say he was an eccentric is an understatement. He inherited the title at the age of ten in 1917, when his father had been killed in the First World War at the Battle of Istabulat in Iraq. He went to the Royal Naval College at Queen Victoria's Osborne House estate on the Isle of Wight, and then Radley College, but in 1923, when he was seventeen, he joined a merchant sailing ship, a wool clipper called the *Mount Stewart*, bound for Sydney as a naval cadet.

He soon returned to Britain and joined the Scots Guards, but resigned his commission in 1927 – there are rumours he was forced to do so because of his 'wild ways' – and sailed back to Australia, where he jointly bought a share in a sheep farm in Queensland with the master of the *Mount Stewart*. After a few years, he returned to London and fell in love with an actress and singer from Chicago, who was then a hit on the London stage. Mimi Forde-Pigott, whose stage name was Mimi Crawford, became the Countess of Suffolk in 1934 upon their marriage. There are four stage photographs of the Countess of Suffolk in the National Portrait Gallery, one showing her in ballet dress, with blonde hair in shingles, the style of the time. The marriage of the earl and the showgirl may have confirmed his reputation as 'Wild Jack' but their marriage lasted until his death, and they had three children together.

The earl was hospitalised with rheumatoid arthritis, a recurrence of an old illness that left him with a permanent limp. At a loose end on his discharge from hospital, he took his wife's advice and signed on for a graduate course at Edinburgh University. He emerged with a first-class honours degree in chemistry and pharmacology and was made a fellow of the Royal Society in Edinburgh. When the Second World War broke out, he offered himself as an unpaid scientific expert to the government through a family friend who was a government whip in the House of Lords. He arranged for the earl to have an interview at the Ministry of Supply at its headquarters in the Shell-Mex building in the Strand. The ministry had taken over all army scientific research establishments, including explosives, in 1939, which interested the earl. He was sent to see Herbert John Gough, the ministry's Assistant Director of Scientific Research, who was based at the nearby Adelphi House in the Strand, with a request to find him some unpaid post in the research department.

Gough admitted later he was alarmed at being landed with a titled member of society about whom he knew next to nothing, but he was won over by his infectious enthusiasm and his gay, buccaneering spirit. Gough discovered Suffolk was fluent in French and had a solid grounding in science and engineering, and Gough felt he had just the job for his titled recruit: he could go on a secret mission to Paris to liaise with Raoul Dautry, the French minister for armaments. Acting as an undercover agent in a city rife with intrigue, spies and Nazi sympathisers appealed to Suffolk's love of the dramatic and his devil-may-care attitude to danger. But he was an unpaid amateur and acted like it. It was a role for a low-profile man, but that was not Wild Jack's style ... especially not in Paris. He had orders to work with an experienced British army intelligence officer, Major Golding, thirty-seven, who was three years older than Suffolk and had been a professional soldier for thirteen years. He was officially in the Royal Tank Regiment but had joined the War Office as an officer in Military Intelligence, specialising in the development of tanks and artillery.

The earl ignored the rules of tradecraft for spies along with the advice of the more experienced Major Golding by installing himself at the Ritz, where he quickly made an impact with his lavish lifestyle, his love of parties and his inquiring mind. Golding implored his new partner to take a lower profile for his own security after being denounced as a spy by a Nazi propaganda sheet. Suffolk responded by hiring a bodyguard, but refused to drop his champagne lifestyle. After his death, a 'friend' described in his obituary a typical scene of the earl in top form, holding court at a late-night café soirée in Paris:

A Sorbonne professor was treated, in rapid, fluent French, which Suffolk spoke like a native – to a dissertation on pharmacology, lapsing into some Parisian gossip which the professor certainly appeared thoroughly to enjoy. Then arising from a remark of an Army officer, a feat of conjuring produced from hidden shoulder holsters a pair of automatics, lovingly referred to as 'Oscar' and 'Genevieve', whose merits were expounded with boyish delight. At a later stage the company were entertained with a masterly and dramatic rendering of a dialogue between a Cockney using 'rhyming slang' and a Chicago gangster conversing in his local idiom: a very extensive knowledge of these 'argots' was another unexpected possession of this most versatile man ...'

His obituary in *The Times* was signed J. H. G. – John Herbert Gough.[3]

It enhanced the enduring myths that still surround 'Wild Jack'. His private correspondence to Gough, which I found in the National Archives, shows that he was a diligent scientific agent, passing on technical intelligence gathered in Paris about a variety of inventions, from a metal detector to smoke bombs and antihistamine substances. In one letter to Gough, he reveals Dautry invited him to move into an office at the Majestic Hotel so that it was nearer to his ministry, but Suffolk says he prefers to stay close to the scientists at the Armaments Ministry in the Rue de l'Universite. The earl's 'party' in Paris was suddenly over when the Germans threatened the city. Wild Jack was all for staying in the city until the last possible moment, but the more experienced Golding realised they would soon have to evacuate their Paris office, at least for the sake of their two civilian secretaries, Eileen Beryl Morden, whom Suffolk had brought with him from the Ministry of Supply in London, and Marguerite Nicolle, who worked for the Major. They set about hurriedly packing up all the files that might be useful to the Germans in a large packing case. They made plans to drive with their secretaries in their office cars for Bordeaux, where they boarded a ship back to Britain. The historic port city on the Garonne on the west coast of France, world-famous for its wine, became the last bastion of unoccupied France, but they had to accelerate their escape as the Germans approached.

Suitcases were in short supply as Parisians rushed to escape south with what little of value they could carry. Major Golding and Marguerite Nicolle drove out of Paris in the early hours of 10 June in an official car, with Golding at the wheel, and Bloch, the official chauffeur, in the back with the luggage. Miss Nicolle, Golding's super-efficient secretary, recorded their dramatic flight to Bordeaux in her diary:

> Major Golding calls me at 11.30 p.m. instead of 4 a.m. as originally planned. This means things are hot ... Finally leave Paris by the Porte de Versailles about an hour or so before the arrival of the Germans. Our progress on the road is necessarily very slow as we are continually held up by military convoys, lorries and war material that seem to go both ways. We are caught in an air raid just on the outskirts of Paris. We drive without lights and in a thick mist. We drive non-stop until dawn.[4]

Hitler's troops marched into Paris four days later on 14 June. The roads to the south of France became blocked with refugees fleeing the Nazis. Major Golding, in his British army uniform, had to clear a path through them, shouting 'mission militaire'. Suffolk and his loyal secretary, Miss Morden, followed in their own car, but they hit trouble after staying overnight at Le Mont-Dore, the town where the fleeing French government had stopped. French officials seized their car, but Marguerite Nicolle noted: 'Maj. Golding gets him fixed up with a lorry in which he piles all his luggage and travels to Bordeaux with Miss Morden in this conveyance.'

Marguerite noted that the weather was glorious, and the Massif Central was lovely. They might have been touring on holiday but for the urgent need to get to Bordeaux. It was not until 2 a.m. on Sunday 16 June – after six days on the road – that they reached Bordeaux. Marguerite recorded it was 'absolutely blacked-out and none of us know why.'

The Earl of Suffolk and Beryl Morden had safely made it to Bordeaux in the lorry, but found that the British consulate was besieged by hundreds of refugees waving British passports. One newspaper reported that Bordeaux was a 'city in agony – ladies bent on saving themselves and their lap dogs, poor artisans with large families, Frenchmen and foreigners, civilians and soldiers, had swollen the population of the port threefold. Food and water were scarce and millionaires who had left their villas in Paris a week before were camping, hungry and unwashed in the public squares. The single thought in everyone's mind was escape. Civic authority had given way to martial law.'

Major Golding and the Earl of Suffolk fought their way through the crowds to find the Commercial Attaché at the British embassy, Mr Irving. He told them that they could have a merchant vessel called the SS *Broompark*, skippered by Captain Paulsen, which had steamed into Bordeaux harbour on 13 June to unload coal from the Tyne, with French authority collapsing around the port.

Golding and the earl had yet to gain access to the ship. The obstacle appeared to be General Maxime Weygand, the French defence minister, who was described by Suffolk as a 'ferret-faced little soldier who listed Englishmen among his principal allergies'. The earl forced his way past protesting sentries into Weygand's office to demand Weygand's authority for loading the cargo that he needed to get back to Britain, along with 'certain French nationals' who were vital for the war effort.

Weygand was secretly pressing Reynaud for an armistice. Suffolk and Golding knew the French capitulation would wreck their hopes of an orderly evacuation. Pétain had already put out feelers to the German high command indicating that he wanted to sue for peace with Hitler. Weygand infuriated Suffolk with his defeatist attitude, saying he preferred 'Hitlerism to French Socialism'. Suffolk showed his disgust and walked out.

While Bordeaux sank into chaos, Churchill, who had fought off appeasers in his own Cabinet in May after taking over from Chamberlain, embarked on a frantic mission to shore up the French resistance to the Nazi onslaught. Churchill flew to France on Wednesday 12 June to appeal to Reynaud to hold out; it proved hopeless – Weygand said to Reynaud that Britain would have 'her neck wrung like a chicken'. Two years later at Ottawa, Churchill defiantly roared: 'Some neck, some chicken!'

Churchill returned to Britain, but, despite the risk of being shot down, flew back to France the next day, on Thursday 13 June – the same day Paulsen and *Broompark* steamed into port at Bordeaux. He went to a final crisis meeting with Reynaud at Tours, where Churchill tried to persuade the French to establish a fighting redoubt with their backs to the the sea in Brittany as favoured by de Gaulle. Reynaud was prepared to fight on, but Reynaud's Cabinet – led by Pétain and the defeatist Weygand – met later that day and decided to retreat to Bordeaux, utterly demoralised. According to the British officer, Brigadier-General Sir Edward Spears, who was Churchill's personal representative with the French, Weygand and Reynaud saw the Nazi hordes coming for them 'like a Martian invasion under a swarm of Stukas'.[6]

On Sunday 16 June, Churchill was woken up early at Chequers to receive a telegram from Bordeaux telling him the French were seeking American help to secure an armistice with the Germans. Churchill issued a defiant message of solidarity with France, promising the French to keep on fighting to free it from the Nazis, but it was no good. Reynaud had resigned the night before, and Pétain had replaced him.

Meanwhile in Bordeaux, Major Golding and the Earl of Suffolk were loading the SS *Broompark*. After getting nowhere with Weygand, 'Wild Jack' decided to see if he could get Pétain to overrule him. The official report of the Suffolk–Golding mission did not try to conceal Suffolk's contempt for Weygand:

> Until representations were made by one of us, i.e. Lord Suffolk, to the highest quarter and in the most uncompromising and bald terms, we met with nothing but the most obstructive and defeatist attitude from the higher members of the Bordeaux government. However, the demands to Marshal Pétain having been made,

we succeeded in extracting from him permission to embark the technicians and scientists which we had brought with us.[7]

Two members of the Joliot team – von Halban and Kowarski – had left the villa in Clermont-Farrand with the cans of heavy water for Bordeaux after Jacques Allier's dash to alert them to the danger of arrest by the Germans.

Von Halban and his family escaped from Clermont-Ferrand in one car, with the burly Kowarski on top of the jerry cans in the back of a second car. It was an uncomfortable, high-speed journey. 'On the back were piled up some 20 cans of heavy water, with a few blankets and so on, and I was lying on the blankets and reacting in an obvious way to a rather fast drive through very curved roads and the deep hills of French central Massif.'[8]

It took them all day to race across France and they entered Bordeaux after nightfall on Monday 17 June. They immediately went in search of the Ministry of Armaments, which was then occupying a school, to get help and fresh orders. They found Captain Jean Bichelonne, Dautry's aide, who had orders to look after them. He tore a sheet out of a schoolboy notebook and wrote out their orders. They were to board the ship that had been commandeered by the Earl of Suffolk and go to England.

'The order was very short, and we had to put ourselves at the disposal of the British authorities and observe absolute secrecy. Also we had to put at their disposal our materials and our records,' said Kowarski.

The order was to cause serious trouble with Colonel de Gaulle and his Free French followers when they reached London. Von Halban and Kowarski decided that their orders specifically ruled out informing de Gaulle and the Free French in London about the heavy water. They steered clear of de Gaulle's group in London and de Gaulle was furious when he found out.

The next day, Tuesday 18 June, Churchill delivered his famous 'finest hour' speech in the House of Commons with a promise that Britain would always remain a friend of France:

What General Weygand has called the Battle of France is over … the Battle of Britain is about to begin. Upon this battle depends the survival of Christian civilisation. Upon it depends our own British life, and the long continuity of our institutions and our Empire. The whole fury and might of the enemy must very soon be turned on us.

Hitler knows that he will have to break us in this island or lose the war. If we can stand up to him, all Europe may be freed and the life of the world may move forward into broad, sunlit uplands.

But if we fail, then the whole world, including the United States, including all that we have known and cared for, will sink into the abyss of a new dark age made more sinister, and perhaps more protracted, by the lights of perverted science ...

Churchill concluded with the ringing promise that if the British Empire lasted for a thousand years, people would still say 'this was their finest hour'. This was stirring stuff for the audience at home, but in Bordeaux, the Earl of Suffolk and Major Golding were still anxiously loading their precious cargo. Suffolk and Golding spent three frustrating, nerve-jangling days loading up the ship, while the chaos at the port got worse.

The British Commercial Attaché, Mr Irving, introduced them to four diamond dealers: Paul Timbal, managing director of the Antwerp Diamond Bank, Hubert Jacques, Nicholas Sansiaux and Andre Van Campenhout. They came with two crates containing over £3 million worth of diamonds – in effect the European diamond market. Timbal had transported the diamonds across Belgium and France to the safety of the vaults in a bank in Bordeaux before flying secretly by military plane to London for talks. With the approval of the British Ministry of Economic Warfare, he agreed with Sir Ernest Oppenheimer, the chairman of De Beers in London, to relocate the European diamond market in London, providing he could carry the diamonds safely to England.

Suffolk was also approached by von Halban and Kowarski with the news that they wanted to get on board with their families and some jerry cans carrying heavy water. Kowarski said in the last gasp of the belligerence, France had quite naively and touchingly put its faith into these two departing magicians (himself and von Halban). 'We were not just refugees leaving the country. We were carriers of a mission, we had been entrusted with something important ... You know the story of these two scientists fleeing for their life from an implacable enemy and carrying the world's supply of rare material which will enable them to master a new force of nature, it was preposterous, it was dime-novel stuff.'

There were a few cabins left for women and children. Von Halban and Kowarski were left to fend for themselves, as well as they could. 'I found in the hold a heap of coal, collapsed on it and fell asleep,' said Kowarski.[9] He was awoken during the night by bombing of the port by German warplanes, but he was too tired to stir.

A British embassy official, Mr Harvey, secured an omnibus passport and clearance through customs at the quayside for the scientists and technicians and their families. The extraordinary group passport is one of many precious mementoes of the Suffolk–Golding mission still held by Ian Golding, one of Major Golding's sons. which he kindly allowed me to use. The roughly typed sheet of names bears an official stamp and a signature, with a hurriedly scribbled declaration: 'All above, and their wives – where applicable, will proceed to the United Kingdom, by authority of His Majesty's Ambassador to France.' Those named included Charles Berthiez, who they met in Le Mont-Dore, and twenty-two others who were listed as technicians with firms such as Citroën, Panhard, arms maker Hispano Suiza, Renault and tank builders Société d'Outillage Mécanique et d'Usinage d'Artillerie (SOMUA).

Suffolk and Golding succeeded in persuading the naval authorities in Bordeaux to let them have two anti-aircraft 75 mm guns, a pair of 'under and over' 9 mm Hotchkiss machine guns and one single-barrelled Hotchkiss anti-aircraft machine gun of the same calibre. They also secured a gun crew of picked members of the French navy, especially skilled in anti-aircraft defence.

Kowarski said that they had all sorts of officials of the Ministry of Armament, some with fairly high military rank, including colonels, to help them load their belongings on board at midnight before the Reynaud government completely handed over power to Pétain. They had bowed to the 'force of nature' called the Earl of Suffolk.

Suffolk feared Fifth Columnists – Nazi sympathisers – had tipped off the Germans that something valuable was being loaded at the docks. An attempt was made on Tuesday morning, 18 June to bomb the *Broompark* while it was at the quayside, but the bomb missed. He had the ship moved to another part of the docks on the fringes of the city. As a result, when Joliot arrived, he could not find the SS *Broompark*. He would have been trapped on board, if he had found her.

Joliot had travelled with his wife, Irene, but had left her in a sanatorium because she was weak and sick. Kowarski said: 'He told me later on that he debated within himself whether to look for it [the *Broompark*] and took his decision: "Oh, well. Anyhow I have to stay. They will carry on and I will stay here." It is still interesting to speculate on what would have happened if he had found the boat. He would certainly have gone on board without knowing that he would not be allowed to leave.'

They carried on loading the heavy machine tools they had found in railway wagons in the docks area until 5 a.m. on Wednesday morning, 19 June, when they decided to head for home.

The sun was rising as Paulsen edged the *Broompark* out of the harbour and headed towards Le Verdon-sur-Mer, fifty miles down river at the mouth of the mighty Gironde, which they reached shortly before noon. It was on the south bank, and therefore safer from attack by any German forces spreading across northern France. Kowarski later recalled:

> There was a captain of the ship, but Lord Suffolk was obviously in charge – a very picturesque personality looking like an unkempt pirate. I read a lot of stories about the eccentricities of the British aristocracy, and here was Lord Suffolk, something like the 19th or 20th Earl in a line, which was considerably older than the house of Windsor. It went together ... He was dressed in rags, with a very picturesque beard. He walked with a noticeable limp, which had nothing military about it; its origin was purely civilian. He was limping around the ship with two secretaries, one blonde and one brunette.[10]

They moored and loaded up with ammunition, but as the current changed with the tide a neighbouring passenger ship, the *Mexique*, blew up. It had hit a magnetic mine – a secret German device that needed only proximity to a vessel to trigger it – as the tide turned the *Mexique*. The passenger ship sank within a couple of hours. The passengers were rescued, but it caused an enormous shock among the passengers on board SS *Broompark*. It was a stark reminder, if any were needed, that their ordeal was not over; they still faced the danger of being blown up by mines or torpedoes on their voyage back to Britain. The sinking, however, enabled Joliot to convince the Germans when they questioned him that the heavy water had gone down with that ship.

Suffolk thought the danger of sinking was so great that he lashed up a wooden raft, which he and the ship's carpenter hammered together using heavy nails. But it was not for people. It was for his precious cargo of diamonds and heavy water, which he was determined would float if the ship went down. He drew up a memorandum in French for von Halban and Kowarski to sign, giving him authority to take over 'les biens', the goods, if they did not survive. Kowarski still had his copy thirty years later.

The raft was rigged up by the bridge with the cans of heavy water and a large bag of diamonds lashed on it.

Officially, the records describe their voyage as 'uneventful', but it was nerve-racking for the passengers, who saw Captain Paulsen as a calm hero who would get them through. The English Channel was busy with shipping taking part in the final evacuation of France, and they followed a convoy about thirty miles ahead. They were horrified to see the convoy come under attack by German bombers.

Paulsen cleared the decks for action, and ordered the passengers to go below. The gun crews manned their anti-aircraft guns. There was absolute silence on board, apart from the throbbing of the engines.

Paul Timbal, who was in charge of the diamonds, described how Paulsen stood on his bridge, bronze-faced, unflinching, lit by the setting sun, as he steered his ship full steam ahead with the Red Ensign flying, quietly smoking his pipe, towards England, and freedom.

Three days after leaving Bordeaux, the Earl of Suffolk and Major Golding arrived safely with their precious cargo in Falmouth harbour, Cornwall. The log of the *Broompark* carries no hint of drama or its role in transporting the stocks of heavy water to Britain. It simply stated 'Current Voyage and Cargo – Tyne 5/6, Bordeaux 13/6, Bordeaux – Verdon 19/6 – Falmouth 21/6.'[11]

Marguerite Nicolle noted in her diary their safe arrival at Falmouth at about 6 a.m. on Friday 21 June. 'The authorities come on board.' It was not until 5.30 p.m. that Suffolk managed to get a telephone call through to Gough's office at the Ministry of Supply. The official report called 'Matters Arising from the Telephone Call received from the Earl of Suffolk' concealed the excitement – and consternation – it must have caused. Suffolk told them that, with Major Golding, he had brought a 7,000-ton ship across from Bordeaux to Falmouth, carrying:

1. 600 tons of machine tools
2. £3 million-worth of diamonds
3. All the heavy water in France taken from the Joliot-Curie labs
4. The entire secret archives of the Ministry of National Education
5. Two pieces of apparatus of considerable scientific importance
6. All the secret documents belonging to himself and Golding from Paris
7. A new secret machine for the manufacture of a 20 mm Hispano-Suiza gun

8. Another machine tool of similar nature
9. Some anti-aircraft guns.
10. Twenty-four French scientists and technicians of very high rank.

The report added: 'Suffolk proposed, after depositing the diamonds, to get the personnel on board a train from Falmouth to London … it was necessary to bring them to London as Falmouth is full of refugees. It was agreed that Suffolk should himself come to London on that train.'

Major Golding organised a special train to take their party of VIP refugees, including the French atomic scientists, to Paddington, London, with their special cargo. The jerry cans containing the heavy water were put in the guards' van under armed protection. The special service was laid on by Great Western Railways, whose chairman, Charles Jocelyn Hambro, was soon to be recruited for his own cloak-and-dagger role in the war, as head of the Scandinavian section of the Special Operations Executive.

The earl fired off a telegram to Gough: 'OHMS (On His Majesty's Service) Priority – Trainload leaving special train Falmouth 2300 Approx Stop Will telephone Department on Arrival – Suffolk and Berkshire.' He was being optimistic about the departure time. After helping with the passports, Miss Nicolle was 'carried off to some Club and provided with sandwiches and a whisky' by Major Golding. Once on board, they found a compartment to themselves and managed to catch some sleep.

The Suffolk–Golding special train arrived at Paddington at 9 a.m. on 22 June, the same day that Hitler, in a carefully choreographed show of revenge, arranged for the defeated French Pétain government to sign the armistice at the Forest of Compiègne in the same railway carriage and on the same spot where the Imperial German command signed the armistice in 1918 with the French Marshal Foch to end the First World War. It shut the door to foreign travel from France without the Nazis' approval, making any further rescues from Bordeaux impossible. A few days later, Hitler ordered the Compiégne site to be razed, leaving just a forlorn statute of Marshal Foch.

At Paddington, the doors of the carriages were locked to prevent the other passengers stepping onto the platform. Paul Timbal complained about not being allowed onto the platform but Suffolk told them to be patient, while he waited for the armed guards to arrive with Gough. They turned up after about half an hour, cleared the platform, threw a cordon around the train, and ensured the priceless cargo could be taken off safely into waiting trucks.

Suffolk and Major Golding met up with Gough and they were told that breakfast was waiting for all the passengers at Paddington's Great Western Railway Hotel, where some rooms had been allocated for the arrivals. An army truck, followed by another truck full of armed soldiers, transported the diamonds to the Diamond Corporation at 8 Charterhouse Street. Paul Timbal first took his party in a taxi to the Mayfair Hotel in Berkeley Square where, despite his dishevelled appearance, he was immediately recognised as a regular guest and given a room, a hot bath and a cooked breakfast. But he had one more duty to perform, when he was cleaned up. He went to the Diamond Corporation and witnessed the diamonds being delivered by Major Golding's squad of armed guards. Golding was given a signed receipt for the consignment: 'I confirm that I have today received two sealed boxes put under guard of Major A. V. Golding, R. T. R., at Bordeaux for transmission to the above address.'

Von Halban and his family was also given a room at the Mayfair Hotel, where on hotel-headed notepaper he provided details to the British authorities about his identity. Von Halban wrote in blue ink that he had been 'engaged in nuclear fission and nuclear reaction chains since February 1939 in collaboration with Professor Joliot and Mr Kowarski'.

Kowarski scribbled his details on a scruffy sheet of notepaper. Under military data, he wrote: 'Fit for auxiliary service only (decision of the French recruiting board, January 1940).'

Captain Paulsen and the SS *Broompark* had no time to relax. Six days later, on 27 June, they sailed for Panama, arriving on 18 July, before sailing on for Vancouver, where the log says they were due by 31 July. They were carrying 5,130 tons of timber and metal en route from Vancouver to Glasgow in Convoy HX-72 when, at 23:38 hours on 21 September, they were hit by a torpedo fired by the U-boat U-48 captained by Heinrich Bleichrodt. But the ship refused to go down.[12] Paulsen filled in the log with red ink. It says: 'Torpedoed +23/9'. Then, in pencil, he later added a line below: 'still afloat'. Most of the forty crew abandoned ship but returned when Paulsen and eight crew members managed to bring her on an even keel by shifting ballast and restarting the engines. Paulsen and his crew managed to sail *Broompark* across the Atlantic, despite the damage. The logbook says: 'Arr Rothesay Bay 25/9 for Clyde. Repairs Clyde 10/10.' Paulsen was awarded the OBE and the Lloyds War Medal for Bravery at Sea for his courage in bringing the ship home, but he was eventually retired.

His ship continued to steam across the world's oceans under a new master, John Leask Sinclair, until it was sunk on the home leg of a journey from Buenos Aires via Hampton Roads, Virginia, in Convoy ON-113 when, at 04:09 on 21 September, it was torpedoed by Erich Tropp, skipper of the U-552. She still refused to go down and was taken in tow by the US tug, *Cherokee*. A note in her logbook in red ink says: 'Vessel in tow of *Cherokee* ... Sunk in tow at 18.13 1/8 in 90 fathoms.' Sinclair and three crewmembers went down with the ship, which sank about fifty miles south-west of St Johns.

Gough told Suffolk that the Labour minister Herbert Morrison, the Minister for Supply, wanted an urgent briefing. In the event, Morrison was not available and Suffolk saw Morrison's Tory deputy, Harold Macmillan, a lofty aristocrat, who thought the socialist Morrison would have found the Earl of Suffolk very remote, and could not make him out at all.[13] Morrison, however, fully understood the importance of the Suffolk–Golding mission.

In the Commons secret session – with the public and press barred from hearing his statement – Morrison told MPs that two officers of the Ministry in Paris had brought back 'large quantities of valuable and secret stores, some of them of almost incalculable scientific importance'. He added, 'A considerable service has been rendered to the Allied cause by the safe arrival of this shipload.'[14]

Von Halban and Kowarski were also carrying information of vital importance about the remaining stocks of uranium oxide in France. They told British officials including Gough that Union Minière, the Belgian company in charge of the uranium mines in Katanga in the Belgian Congo, had 500 tons of uranium oxide; some had been shipped to the USA but the rest had been transported to France. It would be four years before the hunt for this ore could begin on the ground.

Nothing could be said in public about their Top Secret exploits. For his part in the liberation of the heavy water, Major Golding was awarded a military MBE in the 1941 New Year's Honours List. He was later promoted to the rank of Colonel and was posted to Washington as a wartime military attaché, which almost certainly involved the exchange of secrets about atomic weapon development; after the war Colonel Golding returned to his former life as an expert in research and development of weapons at Fort Halstead, in the North Downs of Kent. He took early retirement to take part in the integration of a re-armed Germany into a united Europe, and then worked in Paris as a diplomat in arms control before retiring to the United States in 1967. He died of heart failure in Nantucket in the United States in 1992, at the age of eighty-nine.

The irrepressible Earl of Suffolk, true to his daredevil reputation, volunteered as a civilian bomb disposal officer. Beryl Morden continued loyally to act as his secretary, taking notes as he dismantled the bombs. She would take cover only in the last moments when he finally defused the explosives. He also recruited a Cockney Pickford's Removals van driver, Fred Hards, along with his removals van, which the earl converted into a custom-made bomb disposal workshop. The earl called the threesome the Holy Trinity, and cheerfully smoked cigarettes while he set about defusing bombs. He took the fatalist view that 'if my name is on a bomb, that's it.'

His name was on a 500 lb bomb that exploded at 2.45 p.m. on 12 May 1941 as he attempted to defuse it. The bomb had been taken from London, where it was found, to the bomb disposal area on the soggy ground at Erith Marshes, Kent to be rendered safe. He had safely defused thirty-four bombs, including many with booby traps. He told Beryl, his secretary, he was removing a Type 17 delayed-action fuse with a clockwork mechanism, and a Type 50 anti-handling fuse with a motion sensor for training purposes. Unknown to the earl, a third fuse, a Zus 40, had been fitted as a booby trap by the German bombmakers underneath the Type 17. It was not immediately visible, and was designed to explode as soon as an attempt was made to remove the Type 17. The Type 17 fuse was ticking and the earl had followed normal procedure by attaching a clock stopper to the bomb to neutralise it. He was listening through a stethoscope to make sure the ticking had stopped, before using steam to neutralise the second fuse. Two sappers were fetching water for the steamer when the bomb blew up.[15]

The blast was so great that little was left of 'Wild Jack', the buccaneering earl. He was thirty-five. Beryl Morden, aged twenty-eight, was caught in the blast and died of her injuries while being rushed to hospital in an ambulance. The earl's driver, Fred Hards, thirty-six, also died with a number of the sappers who were nearby. His famous bomb-disposal van was set on fire by the bomb, and the earl's finely made shotgun and his Parabellum Luger pistol No. 1741 were so badly burned that they were disposed of with the rest of the wreckage.

The earl's bravery as a bomb disposal officer made headline news after he was killed but his evacuation of the heavy water was kept secret until long after the war. The *Daily Sketch* on 19 July 1941 ran the headline: 'Earl and Girl die for bomb secret.' The

London Gazette announced that Charles Henry George Howard, 20th Earl of Suffolk and 13th Earl of Berkshire, had been awarded posthumously the George Cross, the highest civilian award for 'supreme gallantry'. There were also commendations for 'brave conduct in Civil Defence' for 'Frederick William Hards (deceased), Van Driver, and Miss Eileen Beryl Morden (deceased), Shorthand-Typist both from the Experimental Unit, Ministry of Supply'. *The Times* obituary by Gough said Britain 'has lost the services of a very gallant gentleman … with a fearless and forceful personality, tempered with great charm of manner and infinite courtesy and tact.'

Gough was one of the few who knew about the heavy water. It was estimated that the 185 kg of heavy water brought to England had a commercial value of £100,000 – worth £5 million today – but in truth, it was priceless.

Six cans were deposited at Wormwood Scrubs prison, where MI5 had established a wartime headquarters. The remaining twenty cans were taken to the safest hiding place in England – Windsor Castle.

Every tourist knew that the Crown Jewels were stored in the Tower of London, but they had been secretly removed to Windsor to avoid the Blitz. Now they were to be joined by the twenty jerry cans of heavy water.

General Sir Maurice Taylor, senior military adviser to the Ministry of Supply, wrote to Lord Wigram, the king's private secretary, at the Norman Tower, Windsor Castle, on 4 July 1940:

> We have rescued from France a small stock of what is probably the most valuable and rare material in the world and one which is most urgently needed, in very small quantities, for what we hope may prove to be without exaggeration the most important scientific contribution to our war effort … I have been racking my brains to think of the safest place in this country to save part of this stock. Since I am told it is the only stock in the world you will understand my anxiety on the score of its safety. The conclusion to which I have come is that some small chamber in the depths below Windsor Castle would most nearly meet the case.

Lord Wigram, deputy constable of Windsor Castle, gave his assent. Five days later, the Earl of Suffolk personally delivered the remaining twenty jerry cans – twelve square cans of more concentrated material and eight round tins of less concentrated water – into the hands of Sir Owen Morshead, the Royal Librarian at Windsor Castle.

It was a formidable fortress, built 1,000 years before for William the Conqueror near a strategic crossing of the Thames, and still in use as a home for the House of Windsor. There had been speculation that the royal family, including the two princesses, Margaret and Elizabeth, would be evacuated to Canada if an invasion looked imminent. There were also contingency plans for the royal family to use Madresfield Court, a 120-room mansion in the Malvern Hills, and Pitchford Hall in Shropshire, but the princesses remained at Windsor for the duration of the war, despite being disturbed by the nightly German bomber raids over the capital. During 1940, the two princesses made their first radio broadcast from Windsor Castle; ostensibly, it was a message to the 'children of the Empire', but it was aimed at the American audience to bolster support for Britain in its hour of need.

There are stories that the two princesses were taken to see some hat boxes by Mr Morshead in a dungeon of his library, and he showed them the Imperial State Crown set with its glittering array of 3,000 gems, including the Black Prince's Ruby, the Stuart Sapphire and the huge diamond known as the Second Star of Africa.

Morshead could be counted on to be the soul of discretion. He was a distinguished soldier, and had been awarded the Military Cross in the First World War. It is said he was trusted with recovering secret letters written by Edward VIII to Hitler. On 11 July, Morshead wrote to Gough at the Ministry of Supply confirming the consignment was safe and that 'the King knows that it is here'. He said Suffolk's precious consignment of heavy water was held in the same wartime hiding place as the Crown Jewels:

> The King knows that it is here and Lord Wigram knows. But it is I who hold the keys and exercise executive control. No-one else at this end is, or will be, in the secret.
>
> But in case of extreme necessity, should I not be accessible (for Lord Wigram would not actually know how to get at it) I will give you another way round.
>
> There are two people here who would know how to get it if you told them that it is in the same spot as the Crown Jewels. They know nothing of this stuff; but they do know how to get at the Crown Jewels. They are (in order of preference) Commander Dudley Colles (Secretary of the Privy Purse) and Mr McIntosh (the Superintendent of the Office of Works here, who made the dugout). Either of these could manage somehow to obtain access to it; they haven't got the keys but would know how to get keys.[16]

I asked the research staff at Windsor Castle if they knew about a 'dugout', and was met by bafflement. But then I saw an old 'behind-the-scenes' documentary on Windsor Castle repeated on BBC Four in January 2016 and was convinced I had the answer. The cameras follow a senior castle officer, Major Alan Denman, into the bowels of Windsor to a basement room where the Castle 'tender smiths' – the men who tend the fireplaces – have made their office. The carpet was rolled back, a wooden trap door was opened, and a second, metal manhole cover was taken off, revealing a tunnel. The passageway was narrow, about six feet high, and rough-hewn. It was clearly dug by hand; the palace thinks it was constructed in the medieval period when the occupants might have needed a secret escape route. 'We are not quite sure what this tunnel was used for,' said Major Denman. 'We believe it might have been used for an air raid shelter during the Second World War.'[17]

The tunnel, unknown to even most of those who live in the Castle, would have been the perfect place to hide something as precious as the Crown Jewels, and the world's largest stock of heavy water. Was this Owen Morshead's secret 'dug out'? I was proved right in January 2017 by a BBC documentary, *Coronation*, which uncovered a further letter by Morshead which confirmed the most precious Crown Jewels had been gouged out of the regalia, wrapped in paper, placed in a sealed jam jar and hidden in a Bath Oliver biscuit tin. The jewels included fragments of the Cullinan diamond, the Koh-i-Noor diamond, St Edward's Sapphire and the Black Prince's ruby 'the size of a frog'. Morshead said he had placed the tin in the dug out in a tunnel under the castle. The Queen said: 'We were told nothing. We were only children but we didn't know anything. It was a secret I suppose … Did he remember where he put them because he might have died in the middle?' Oliver Urquhart Irvine, the current Royal Librarian, said: 'I think the king was told, ma'am.'

Most of the fabulous jewels in the Crown regalia, including the Imperial State Crown with which King George VI was crowned in 1937 after Edward VIII's abdication, date from the Restoration in 1660. The capture of the ancient crown and the sovereign's orb used for coronations for four centuries would have been a terrible blow for the morale of the British people and a huge coup for Hitler and the Third Reich. The loss of the heavy water would have been worse. It could have given Hitler's scientists the material they needed to develop the atomic bomb.

6

Catastrophe

Lieutentant Commander Eric Welsh, the head of the MI6 Norwegian section, received a telegram from an agent in Trondheim that made R. V. Jones jump when he read it. It came from one of Welsh's top agents in Norway and warned that the Germans had ordered production of heavy water at the Norsk Hydro in Rjukan to be stepped up.[1]

One of the first things that Jones had done when he was transferred to MI6 was to put all agents on the alert for any signs of atomic research by the Germans, including any signs of an increase in the production of heavy water. 'I therefore jumped one afternoon of 1941 when I received a telegram from Norway saying the Germans were stepping up the production of heavy water.'[2]

The spectacular coup pulled off a year earlier by Jacques Allier, the French intelligence chief, to stop the Norwegian stockpile of heavy water falling into the hands of the Germans had bought time, but may have lulled British intelligence into a false sense of security. Jones, the assistant director of scientific intelligence at MI6, had been concentrating on inventing counter-measures to the 'Knickebein' system that had been used by German bomber crews to find their targets for their blitz on British cities.

The telegram in the autumn of 1941 brought Jones back to the atomic bomb threat with a jolt. Jones saw it as a clear signal that the Germans were serious about building a bomb. They needed the heavy water for an atomic pile, but the intelligence that the SIS had about the progress made by the Nazis towards an atomic bomb, despite the help of Paul Rosbaud, Agent *Griffin*, was sketchy to say the least.

The anonymous source of the signal in Norway said he would be ready to supply further information if the British intelligence services would say what was required. He also demanded an assurance before supplying any more information that Jones was not merely looking after the interests of Imperial Chemical Industries (ICI), a competitor of the Norsk Hydro. 'Remember, blood is thicker than heavy water!'

According to Jones, Welsh said, 'Bloody silly telegram. Whoever heard of heavy water?' If so, Welsh was being disingenuous. He was familiar with Rjukan, a remote town in the mountains of southern Norway that took its name from the nearby *Rjukanfossen*, the 'Smoking Waterfall', and Welsh knew all about the production of heavy water at the Norsk Hydro there.

Welsh had worked for two decades as an analytical chemist in Bergen for International Paint Limited, which specialised in marine and industrial paints. He had settled down in Bergen, married Johanne Brun Svendsen, a relative of the composer Grieg, and raised two daughters; but he was living a double life as a British naval intelligence officer spying on the build-up of the German navy, which came to his firm for special anti-fouling paint for its warships' hulls.

Welsh was an officer in the Royal Navy and a spy, but he was no James Bond figure: he was forty-four years old, hard-smoking, hard-drinking, and portly. Eric Welsh was born in August 1897 in windswept Newbiggin-by-the-Sea, the fifth child, with a twin brother called Leslie, in a family of eleven; they were crammed into a terraced house at 215 Rawling Road, Gateshead, a red-brick end-of-terrace house on the corner of Kelvin Grove. An adopted baby boy brought the total number of children in the Welsh household to nine. Over the road was a chapel, the Church of Christ Meeting Place; it was non-conformist, like most of the people around there.

His father, John, put his occupation down in the 1911 census as an insurance agent, which, in those days probably meant collecting insurance payments door-to-door around the terraced streets of Gateshead. The area was working class and poor, but Eric was clearly bright; he spent most of the First World War at Durham University where he gained a degree in chemistry. He had been in the Royal Naval Volunteer Force in his youth, serving for a short time on a minesweeper. His military record describes him as five feet eight inches tall, with brown hair, brown eyes and fresh complexion, with a chest measurement of thirty-four-and-a-half inches. He is put on the general reserve list in 1919 and then goes under the radar for more than two decades.

With the onset of war, Welsh became a full-time MI6 officer with the rank of Lt Commander in the RNVR, organising the resistance in Norway. He was to become one of the most powerful figures in British intelligence involved in the race to the atomic bomb.

His deep cover as MI6 Agent 'Theodor' in Norway was to pay dividends. He had been to the Norsk Hydro plant to supply special caustic-resistant floor tiles in the building where the heavy water was processed. That gave him a unique insight into the layout of the plant, its production processes and its employees, who he recruited as agents for MI6.

Twelve days after the Germans invaded Norway on 9 April 1940, Welsh escaped to England. He left behind his wife Johanne, who refused to go, and his two children, but the official history of SIS remarks that Johanne was 'an asset to SIS', indicating that she continued to work for them.

The humiliating defeat of the British forces in Norway had given the Germans the access to the heavy water production they needed. It also destroyed British spy networks in Norway. When Welsh reported back for duty at MI6 on 1 May 1940, he was immediately tasked with rebuilding the spy networks that had been rolled up by the Germans. Welsh used fishing boats to send agents to and from the Norwegian coast, a system known as the 'Shetland Bus'. One of the fishing boats was sent from the Shetland Islands to Norway in September 1940 to infiltrate two large teams, Skylark A with twelve agents in Oslo, and Skylark B with twenty-one agents in Trondheim.

The Skylark B team was based around the Norwegian Institute of Technology and its head of chemistry, Professor Leif Tronstad, aged forty-seven, who had helped to create the Norsk Hydro heavy water plant with Jomar Brun, its chief engineer.

Lt Commander Welsh knew that the Trondheim professor was the author of the telegram. Trondstad was unusual. He was an academic, who was prized for his organisational skills, but he was also a fighter. He insisted on getting his hands dirty in the resistance against Hitler's hated occupying force, and he was to pay for it with his life.

Tronstad had learned that Kurt Diebner, the head of the German atomic research, had demanded a sharp increase in production at the Norsk plant of an extra 1,500 kg of heavy water in 1941 – more than eight times the volume shipped back to Britain by the French on board SS *Broompark*. It was this new contract that sparked Tronstad's telegram to the MI6 headquarters in Broadway Buildings.

The professor was asked to come to London, where R. V. Jones and Professor Frederick Lindemann, later Lord Cherwell, Churchill's scientific adviser, questioned him about the production at the heavy water plant at Vemork. Tronstad confirmed that Diebner was demanding a big increase in production. Tronstad's information helped sway Roosevelt's decision to launch a full-scale industrial programme to build the bomb even before America had entered the war. Roosevelt's team believed the German anxiety about raising heavy water production showed that the Germans were 'taking it seriously'.[3]

Anxiety about Hitler acquiring the atomic bomb had been increased by the results of the review by the MAUD Committee of the startling Frisch and Peierls findings. The MAUD Committee's final report was delivered in March 1941 in two parts, on the bomb and atomic power. They admitted at the opening of their report that they entered the project 'with more scepticism than belief'. As they proceeded, however, they became more and more convinced that the release of atomic energy on a large scale:

is possible and that conditions can be chosen which would make it a very powerful weapon of war. We have now reached the conclusion that it will be possible to make an effective uranium bomb which, containing some 25 lbs. of active material, would be equivalent as regards destructive effect to 1,800 tons of T.N.T. and would also release large quantities of radioactive substance, which would make places near to where the bomb exploded dangerous to human life for a long period.

They estimated it would cost £95 million (£3.3 billion at today's prices) to produce enough enriched uranium to build three atomic bombs per month. Despite such a large expenditure, they concluded:

We consider that the destructive effect, both material and moral, is so great that every effort should be made to produce bombs of this kind. As regards the time required, Imperial Chemical Industries after consultation with Dr Guy of Metropolitan-Vickers, estimate that the material for the first bomb could be ready by the end of 1943 ... We know that Germany has taken a great deal of trouble to secure supplies of the substance known as heavy water. In the earlier stages we thought that this substance might be of great importance for our work. It appears in fact that its usefulness in the release of atomic energy is limited to processes which are not likely to be of immediate war value, but the Germans may by now have realized this, and it may be mentioned that the lines on which we are now working are such as would be likely to suggest themselves to any capable physicist.

The MAUD report showed that an atomic bomb was not only feasible but could be delivered in time to change the outcome of the war. However, the committee failed to realise that highly fissile plutonium could be created as a by-product of the heavy water reactor, and that would in turn provide another route to a bomb.

At Cambridge, Kowarski and von Halban had made substantial progress in this direction, working on the heavy water they had brought back from France. With two other scientists at the Cavendish Laboratory, Bretscher and Feather, they said that a reactor using heavy water to create fission might lead to a new element – nuclear number 94 – capable of undergoing fission with slow neutrons. Without entirely realising it at the time, they had pointed the way forward to the production of an atomic super-bomb using plutonium at its core.[4]

On 18 December 1941, Professor James Chadwick sent von Halban and Kowarski's research findings in a sealed envelope for safekeeping to the Royal Society in London with a covering letter saying, 'The paper is such that it would be inadvisable to publish it at the present time.' The paper and Chadwick's covering note lay in the Royal Society Archive until 2007 when they were opened to mark the seventy-fifth anniversary of Chadwick's discovery of the neutron. It revealed just how far ahead Kowarski and von Halban were. They described how to control nuclear chain reaction, gave an outline plan for building a nuclear reactor and explained how to produce plutonium. Professor Brian Cox, then a particle physicist at the CERN (European Organisation for Nuclear Research) project in Geneva, said:

I can see why these papers were locked away during the war – they contain details that could be used to build a nuclear reactor ... The sheer amount of knowledge that these papers contain amazes me – only eight years after Chadwick discovered that a neutron even existed, these scientists are already looking at how to use neutrons to bring about nuclear fission and energy.[5]

The breakthrough was made in America by the Berkeley team under the chemist Glen Seaborg, using cyclotron separation pioneered there by Professor Ernest Lawrence. The new element 94 was called plutonium after the planet Pluto because in the solar system it comes after Uranus, which was taken for uranium, nuclear number 92, and Neptune, used for neptunium, nuclear number 93.

Seaborg's team was to prove plutonium underwent slow neutron fission even larger than that of U-235. Plutonium would form the core of the 'Fatman' bomb dropped on Nagasaki and the basis for Britain's development of the bomb after 1945. At the same time, other American teams were pursuing other routes to the bomb by separating U-235 by centrifuge, thermal diffusion and gaseous diffusion.

In November 1941, on the recommendation of the MAUD Committee, a new body was set up to oversee the development of the British weapon. It was given the cover name of the Directorate of Tube Alloys with an office at 16 Old Queen Street, a short stroll to the SIS headquarters at 54 Broadway Buildings. Churchill appointed the former Whitehall mandarin Sir John Anderson, then Lord President of the Council, to take ministerial responsibility for the Tube Alloys project.

Unlike most ministers, Anderson understood the rudiments of nuclear theory; as a chemistry student at Leipzig he had written a paper on uranium. But Churchill valued Anderson because he possessed a greater political asset: a 'safe pair of hands'. Anderson had been the top civil servant at the Home Office during the General Strike of 1926 and had established a reputation for sound judgment. In 1938, at the height of the turmoil over Appeasement, he decided to run for Parliament and was elected to the House of Commons as the National Independent MP for the Scottish Universities. He was brought into the wartime coalition cabinet by Chamberlain as Home Secretary in 1939, and became famous for introducing 'Anderson shelters', fabricated from tin sheeting and dug into back gardens to protect the public against the Blitz.

The MAUD Committee was wound up, and Tizard, who had been 'Chamberlain's man', was eclipsed by Churchill's 'Prof.' – Frederick Lindemann, who was made a peer by Churchill in the King's Birthday Honours List on 4 June 1941 as Baron Cherwell. The strong message from the MAUD Committee, however, was that if they could make such strides in England and America, so too could Hitler's scientists in Berlin.

In Germany, Hitler's atomic scientists were following the path which von Halban and Kowarski had pursued, a nuclear pile using heavy water as a moderator. But Diebner was growing impatient. Production of heavy water had dropped from 140 kg a month to 91 kg in the first two months of 1942. Diebner summoned the Norsk Hydro's chief engineer, Jomar Brun, to his office at 10 Hardenberg Strasse in Berlin to explain why. When he got there, he was confronted by a panel of experts including Harteck and Karl Wirz, who was a pre-war friend of the British physicist Charles Frank. Wirz arranged to inspect the Vemork plant to see how far production could be increased and Brun visited German firms to place orders for the equipment. As a supporter of the Norwegian resistance, Brun was keen to discover more about the reason why the heavy water was so important to the Germans so that he could inform Tronstad.

The race to the bomb was gaining pace in Germany. In February 1942, Hitler had appointed Albert Speer, his favourite architect, as the Third Reich minister for armaments to replace Friz Todt within hours of Todt's death in a air crash. Speer had become one of Hitler's closest confidantes – the Führer said they were 'kindred spirits' – but it was a daunting prospect. Speer had been given the task of improving the delivery of weapons for the German war machine at a time of crisis – the Allied bombing coupled with global embargoes on materials was squeezing the German economy, and the Führer's Russian offensive, Operation Barbarossa, had stalled. The mood about the war among the German high command was also becoming increasingly bleak after the setbacks in Russia. Like Napoleon 130 years earlier, Hitler was facing his first defeat by the sheer vastness of Russia ... and the Russian winter.

The war of attrition in Russia had spread to the German economy. Defence contracts were being cut, production pared back wherever possible. Goering issued a decree that state funding should only go to projects for the war. Funding for esoteric subjects or longer-term projects where the results would not be known for more than six months was banned. Schumann at the Army Ordnance Office had already ordered a thorough review of the cost effectiveness of its weapons projects. He informed the Uranium Club that it could only carry on funding its research into atomic power 'if a certainty exists of attaining an application in the foreseeable future.'

Speer was aware of the scientists engaged on atomic research but so far it had seemed highly theoretical, and not so promising as some had hoped. On 26 February 1942, a few weeks after Speer's appointment, the Reich Research Council and the Army Weapons Bureau held a conference at the Council's offices in Berlin to discuss the military applications of atomic energy. It was intended to explain the possibilities of the new science to Hitler's military chiefs, but most of Hitler's military high command had other, more pressing engagements and regretfully turned down the invitations. Field Marshal Keitel, Admiral Raeder, and Heinrich Himmler, head of the SS, sent apologies. They were too busy fighting a war with conventional weapons to take time off to hear a bunch of scientists pontificating about science fiction. Not even the promise of 'an experimental repast' for lunch could tempt them. The conference menu boasted traditional German favourites – sausage, broth, roast pork and mixed vegetables – cooked in an experimental way, using synthetic fats.

The invitation declared 'a series of important questions in the field of nuclear physics will be discussed that so far have been worked on in secret because of their importance to the defence of the country'. The conference was opened by Schumann who spoke on the subject of 'Nuclear Physics as a Weapon', followed by Professors Hahn and Heisenberg on uranium energy, Bothe, Geiger, Clusius on uranium isotope separation, Harteck on heavy water, and concluded with Esau on 'Expansion of Nuclear Physics Projects'.

Heisenberg began by explaining nuclear fission for his lay audience. He said neutrons acted like a population: with normal uranium, the death toll of neutrons far outweighed the births, leading to the gradual death of the neutrons; but with highly fissionable refined uranium, U-235, the 'population' of neutrons would increase at an enormous rate.

In a key passage, Heisenberg envisaged the use of the new element 94, plutonium, to make a bomb. He told his audience:

If one collects a quantity of U-235 so large that the loss of neutrons through the surface is small compared to the increase inside, the number of neutrons will increase enormously in a very short time and the total fission energy of 15 trillion calories per ton will be released in a fraction of a second. The pure isotope U-235 represents thus an explosive of unimaginable effectiveness. However, it is very difficult to produce this explosive.

A large part of the Army Ordnance research group is assigned to the problem of enrichment, total separation of the isotope U-235. It appears that American research also stresses especially this work programme.'

Heisenberg foresaw nuclear-powered submarines:

One can think of the practical use of such an engine in vehicles or ships, which will gain an enormous action radius because of the large energy storage in a relatively small amount of Uranium. Such an engine does not burn oxygen which would be especially advantageous for use in U-boats.

As soon as such an engine is in operation, the question of producing an explosive gets a new twist, according to an idea of Von Weizsäcker. The transformation of uranium in the machine produces a new substance (element 94) which very probably is an explosive of the same unimaginable effectiveness as pure U-235. This new substance is much more easily obtained from uranium since it can be separated chemically.[6]

He added:

Admittedly, heavy water is not easy to obtain in large quantities. The task force has initiated thorough investigations into the production of heavy water and other substances that are possibilities such as beryllium and carbon.

Following an idea of Harteck, it has proved advisable to separate the uranium and the moderator so that the kind of arrangements result in a layered ball, which was built as a small-scale experiment at the Kaiser Wilhelm Institute. Whether this kind of layering of natural uranium and moderator can lead to a chain reaction ... has to be regarded as a completely open question ...

Heisenberg's speech was characteristically laced with caveats but it intimated that the production of more heavy water from the Norsk Hydro was vital.

Little of the secret Berlin conference filtered back to London, but the messages coming from Tronstad convinced Welsh and Jones the Germans were on the way to making an atomic pile in which plutonium might be produced. They decided an attack had to be made on the Norsk Hydro. The question was: how?

Welsh proposed the destruction of the Norsk Hydro plant by bombing or sabotage. 'The removal of this source of supply would completely cripple any designs the Germans may have with regard to this type of weapon,' Welsh wrote. 'And on the other hand, the allies are not in a position to use this potential weapon themselves for at least 18 months, as they are only now considering building a suitable plant in America.'[7]

Tronstad was totally opposed to a bombing mission by RAF Bomber Command, arguing that too many civilian casualties would be caused if they blew up the liquid-ammonia storage tanks used in the process for transforming plain water into heavy water. The plant was in a very deep valley with thickly forested sides rising almost vertically to 3,000 feet from a narrow riverbed. It was perched on a plateau halfway down the ravine with massive water abstraction pipes leading to it from the reservoir above. The plant harnessed power from the Rjukanfoss waterfall in a ravine at Vemork, a village three kilometers to the west of Rjukan. The ravine was so deep that the sun never reached Rjukan's streets in the winter. When they came to study surveillance pictures of the plant, the intelligence and air ministry chiefs agreed the task of bombing it looked too difficult. It was a job for the commandos.

The commandos had been borne out of Winston Churchill's demand for a 'reign of terror' along the enemy coastline of Continental Europe after the fall of France. Churchill said he wanted a new style of war: aggressive, 'butcher and bolt', hit-and-run; highly mobile units operating in enemy territory, mobilising local resistance fighters who were to risk their lives to kill the enemy, led by the likes of Brigadier Ben Ritchie-Hook, the one-eyed fictional commando leader who loved 'biffing Jerry' in the Evelyn Waugh *Sword of Honour* trilogy.

The defence chiefs did not share Churchill's eagerness for unconventional Special Forces. Despite the modern infatuation with Special Forces such as the Special Air Service, the Special Boat Squadron and the US Navy Seals, the War Office and the Army chiefs regarded commandos with suspicion. Churchill, however, was typically dogged in his determination.

On 6 June 1940 Churchill minuted General 'Pug' Ismay, his chief of staff and main channel of communication to the Joint Chiefs of Staff of the three armed forces, that:

We have got to get out of our minds the idea that the Channel ports and all the country between them are enemy territory. What arrangements are being made for good agents in Denmark,

Holland, Belgium and along the French coast? Enterprises must be prepared with specially-trained troops of the hunter class, who can develop a reign of terror down these coasts, first of all on the 'butcher and bolt' policy; but later on, or perhaps as soon as we are organised, we could surprise Calais or Boulogne, kill and capture the Hun garrison, and hold the place until all preparations to reduce it by siege or heavy storm have been made, then away. The passive resistance to war, in which we have acquitted ourselves so well, must come to an end. I look forward to the Joint Chiefs of Staff to propose me measures for a vigorous, enterprising and ceaseless offensive against the whole German-occupied coastline.

Churchill reinforced the message later in a memorandum to the Secretary of State for War, Sir Anthony Eden:

The defeat of France was accomplished by an incredibly small number of highly-equipped elite, while the dull mass of the German Army came on behind, made good the conquest and occupied it ... We must develop the storm troop or Commando idea. I have asked for five thousand parachutists and we must also have at least ten thousand of these small 'bands of brothers' who will be capable of lightning action.

Churchill said the memo was intended to help Eden in his struggle with the War Office against official Army opposition to having commandos or 'storm troops' in the regular British Army.[8] But even Churchill was thwarted – he later bemoaned the fact that instead of 10,000 commandos, as he envisaged, he had to settle for 500.

The commando raid on the Norsk Hydro was to be a first big test for Churchill's 'bands of brothers'. It was mounted by Combined Operations Headquarters at the War Office, which combined assets of the three services under the direction of Lord Louis Mountbatten, uncle of Prince Philip, (who was later to marry Princess Elizabeth).

The raid was code-named Operation Freshman and it began with a stroke of luck. In March 1942, Einar Skinnarland, the construction manager of the Norsk Hydro, hijacked the 520-ton coastal steamer *Galtesund* at gunpoint from Egersund in Norway with five friends intent on joining the Norwegian forces in Britain, and sailed the boat to the port of Aberdeen on the north-east coast of Scotland. Two of his compatriots were already members of the Ligne company of the Norwegian resistance fighters with contacts to special forces in

England through Lieutentant Colonel John 'Jack' Skinner Wilson, head of the Special Operations Executive, Norway section. When Wilson interrogated Skinnarland, he was astonished to learn that Skinnarland worked at the Vemork plant near Rjukan and happened to be on one month's annual holiday. Professor Tronstad had given British intelligence details of the layout of the plant but Skinnarland was able to provide the most recent intelligence on German security around the plant. He had observed around 100 German soldiers around the site, and hawsers had been strung across the Rjukan ravine to stop a low-level bombing raid. Skinnarland agreed to return to Vemork to act as guide for the future sabotage operation.

After a comprehensive debriefing on the current situation at Vemork and an SOE crash course, including parachute training, Skinnarland, a champion skier, was dropped over the Hardangervidda plateau by an RAF aircraft – just eleven days after he had reached Aberdeen. It was only the second RAF parachute drop on Norway, but he returned to work as if nothing had happened, without being missed. Skinnarland made contact with Jomar Brun, who furnished him with the most detailed plans of the plant's layout.

A team of over thirty Commandos from two engineer field units skilled in explosives were to carry out the attack. They were to be guided by four Norwegians with expert local knowledge of the region – Lieutenant Jens Anton Poulsson, Knut Haugland, Claus Helberg, and Arne Kjelstrup. They would be sent in first by the SOE to direct the Freshman teams to their target from the Hardangervidda, the barren mountain plateau above the plant where roads are snowbound for eight months of the year. The advance party was given the code name Grouse by Sir Charles Hambro, the head of the Scandinavian section of SOE and a merchant banker who loved grouse shooting on the North York Moors by the small village of Gunnerside.

No attack could be launched until the autumn of 1942 because the summer nights were too short to give adequate cover of darkness. That gave plenty of time for the Grouse advance party to be trained in the use of radios, sabotage and irregular warfare, at the Special Training School 026 at Glenmore Lodge, Aviemore, run by Hambro's Scandinavian section.

They would fly out from RAF Tempsford, by the A1 on the Huntingdonshire/Bedfordshire border. It was Britain's most important clandestine airfield, and had been used for drops in enemy-occupied Europe by countless SOE and MI6 agents – known as 'Joes'. They would go when the moon was full.

RAF Tempsford

RAF Tempsford, now part of the farmland owned by the Errol estate, won the reputation of being Churchill's most secret airfield in Britain.[9] But it was difficult to disguise the airfield with a main runway 2,000 yards long, running north-east to south-west; a second runway 1,500 yards long, running north to south; and a third runway 1,300 yards long, running west-north-west to east-south-east. Together, they formed an extended 'A' pattern on the ground that made it possible to take off and land whichever way the wind was blowing.

There were six hangars, five clustered around the main buildings complex in the south-east area; the other was approximately in the centre of the west boundary station headquarters. The operations block, stores, workshops, Motor Transport and other services were all bunched in the south-east area; messes, RAF and WAAF quarters were widely dispersed. There were thirty concrete aircraft dispersal points laid out at irregular distances from the perimeter track. The bomb dump and shooting range were to the north of the airfield.

The main aircraft used for special ops were four-engine Halifax bombers, Stirlings, twin-engine Hudsons and light single-engine Lysanders, which were slow but prized for being able to land and take-off from farm fields in occupied territory. When Halifaxes were needed for bombing raids, the redundant Stirlings were used for airdrops. Although old, the Stirling had more room than the Halifax and was able to go much slower, making the exit more comfortable for the parachutists, and more time for kit bags to be dropped on the target zone. The Halifax and Stirling had a round drop hole in the underside of the fuselage behind the bomb bay in which the containers were carried.

The Halifax, a heavy bomber with four powerful engines, was unable to go much below 140 mph, which meant that a body had a pretty hefty bump when it dropped into the slipstream. Oluf Reed Olsen describes in his memoirs, *Two Eggs on My Plate*, how he was nearly killed at the start of a mission to Norway when he hit his head on leaving the aircraft on the rear wheel of a Halifax and was knocked out; he regained consciousness to find himself attached to the parachute and a load weighing 80 lb, with a badly dislocated knee heading for the ground at break neck speed; he crashed with his parachute into a dense forest of fir trees, but by a miracle he survived.[10]

Hudsons suffered from lack of room and weight-carrying capacity but were liked by the 'Joes'. The Hudson had a rectangular hole cut in the floor and the bomb bay was taken up with a long-range petrol tank, seriously limiting the amount of baggage that could be taken. There was a chute set-up, which sloped down to the forward edge of the hole, which meant Joes slid out in a semi-reclining position and were cushioned by the slipstream. Reports of this type of exit were very favourable because it was comfortable and reduced the chance of spinning or somersaulting, which could result from a faulty push-off or a clumsy vertical drop from the Halifaxes and Stirlings. However, the chute took up valuable space and limited the load to two Joes and two or three parcels.

The SIS had to share RAF Tempsford and its aircraft with the Special Operations Executive, which was a source of constant friction for most of the war. The Air Ministry did its best to apportion the flights according to priority but both the SIS and SOE were constantly demanding more flights for their agents and operations. Squadron Leader Cautley Nasmyth-Shaw, who showed R. V. Jones around Bletchley, had been promoted to Wing Commander and put in charge of the top-secret MI6 training establishment at Farm Hall. He had arranged for an old friend, Bruce Bonsey, a flying officer at nearby Pathfinder headquarters in Huntingdon, to join him as an air-liaison officer at Farm Hall. Their job was to organise the clandestine flights abroad for MI6 agents. They were jealous of the extra room that the SOE had commandeered on the airfield. They had to put up with a shed as their ops room at RAF Tempsford. SOE had taken over the roomy Gibraltar Farm north-east of the control tower and its very large barn, where 'Joes' made their final arrangements before walking out of the barn doors to a waiting plane to take them on their mission.

Kit

The standard kit issued to the 'Joes' was made up of:

Helmet – made of rubberised sorbo, which covered the entire head and nape of the neck with tapes, tied under the chin.

The Striptease – a one-piece parachutists' suit, made of strong camouflage cloth with large pockets, and of generous proportions to be worn over all civilian clothes, it had a central zip up the middle and zips at the wrists for fast entry and exit. There was a large pocket on the behind, which could hold clothing that could also protect the base of the spine from injury in the drop. There were two pockets, one on either thigh, and a small slot for the special knife that was held by a piece of silk chord stitched on the inside of the slot.

Overboots – these were designed to be worn over shoes and trousers in order that an agent could get across ploughed fields to a road with clean shoes and trousers to avoid suspicion after being dropped. They were made of strong course material with three pairs of strings for tying on. The soles and heels were sorbo, which assisted in breaking the shock of landing.

Gloves – leather gauntlets, silk flying gloves, soft wash-leather or brown leather.

Spine pad – made of sorbo rubber tucked into position in the 'Striptease' when the kit was arranged.

Bandages – crepe, used to bandage the ankles for support on the drop.

Knife – a dagger with a two-edged blade, it was a jackknife, with a locking device to prevent folding back when used as a weapon.

Spade – in two parts, head and handle. The head was enclosed in a small khaki webbing bag and the handle round in shape with a wooden knob packed in a slot at the back of the case. Straps were attached to the case so that it could be fixed to the thigh of the agent. It was an invaluable tool for burying and disposing of equipment on landing.

Flask – capacity: about one fifth of a bottle of whisky or rum. It was useful for lifting the morale of tired cold agents or reception committees of Resistance fighters.

Rations – held in a small but extremely well-packed tin, the rations had a highly concentrated vitamin content for about 48 hours: fruit gums, Horlicks tablets, chocolate, toffee, Benzedrine tablets, and water-purifying tablets.

L (for lethal) Tablets – 'suicide pills' to prevent torture being used to extract information from an agent.

*

Close to midnight on 18 October 1942, the Grouse scouting party, led by Poulsson, dropped by parachute on the snowbound plateau called the Hardangervidda. The Telemark region has leant its name to a form of skiing using ski bindings that allow the heel to swing free. On long wooden skis, it takes an expert to turn at speed, but Telemark skiing is ideal in the deep snow that covers the mountain plateau for eight months of the year, and the quartet of young Norwegian resistance fighters who dropped that night were expert skiers. They spent fifteen days trekking on skis from their drop zone across the snowy wastes of the Hardangervidda to the Mosvatn dam fifteen miles from the target where they met up with Torsten Skinnarland, Einar's brother. They were out of contact for a considerable time, raising suspicions in London that they had been captured. In order to check the SOE radio set was not in enemy hands, they were sent a prepared question:

'Who did you see in the Strand in the early hours of 1 January 1942?'

Haugland, the radio operator, provided the prepared answer: 'Three pink elephants.'

Hambro and the SOE chiefs in London were immensely relieved to get Haugland's reply about the pink elephants. Freshman could proceed.

The plan was to land about three miles from the target on the Hardangervidda, and attack the plant in two teams of Commandos from above to evade the patrols below. The Grouse team was to guide them safely down the mountains.

The Commandos were sappers, drawn from the 9th Airborne and 261st Airborne squadrons Royal Engineers. They had undergone rigorous training in mountain survival in Wales to bring them into peak fitness before being transferred to the area of Fort William in Scotland to familiarise themselves with the workings of an operational hydroelectric plant located there.

Nothing could have prepared them for what lay ahead: it was a catastrophe.

Norway was not suited to clandestine air operations. Possible dropping grounds were few in number and in a very small area. Sir Colin Gubbins, later Commanding Director (CD) of SOE, said the mountains were thickly clustered, precipitous and 'angry' like the Norse Gods – the broken countryside threw up air-pockets and atmospheric currents. Weather conditions on both sides of the North Sea are seldom the same but that autumn there was no let-up by the 'Gods'. Weather conditions on 19 November 1942, when two Halifax bombers towing Horsa gliders took off from Wick on the east coast of Scotland, were described as 'vile'. The foul weather turned into a snow blizzard over Norway. The conditions were so bad that their onboard location finder, code-named Rebecca, failed to hook up with a portable ground beacon called Eureka set up by the advance Grouse party.

The pilot of the first Halifax tried to fly low under the cloud cover, but when they reached the coast, it was hit by a snow squall and heavy turbulence; the tow rope iced up and broke and the glider crashed into the mountains at Fylgjesdalen, near Lysefjord on the south-west coast. The other Halifax had flown higher, but circled twice in heavy blizzard conditions, buffeted by the wind, unable to see and unable to find the landing zone. The pilot turned for home, but the ice-bound bomber had been dragged low by the glider, lost height, and crashed into a mountain, killing the crew of seven. The glider pilot managed to cast off the tow rope, but could not avoid it crashing into the ground, inflicting serious injuries on the commandos it was carrying.

Both pilots in the gliders, and fourteen of the thirty-four commandos were killed; the rest were rounded up by the Germans. Some had gone for help and returned to the crash site, believing they would be treated as prisoners of war under the Geneva Conventions and their friends would be given medical help. The Gestapo treated them brutally, gave them no medical treatment, and treated them all as spies. Their justification was Hitler's infamous decree for all commandos to be executed. Of the surviving twenty soldiers, some badly injured, eleven from one glider were taken to a German army camp at Slettbo and were executed by firing squad. Five from the other glider which crashed at Fylgjesdalen, including the seriously injured, were taken to a German concentration camp at Grini and held there until 18 January 1943, when they were marched into Trandem Forest and shot, their bodies dumped into a mass grave. The remaining four were taken to Stavanager and murdered, despite wearing their army uniforms, in breach of the Geneva Conventions of war. In all, forty men were killed. Only the crew of the first tug plane got back alive.

An agent code-named George sent a radio signal to London at 2.24 p.m. on 11 December 1942, after the extent of the tragedy became known, to alert Lieutenant Commander Welsh at MI6 to the disaster: 'Glider plane fell down at Helleland Church Stop Five men Stop Two killed certainly some wounded Stop All taken prisoner interrogated for two hours Stop All gave Norsk Power Station as target Stop They were all subsequently shot Stop George.' George's message removed any doubt that the Germans knew the Allies' target and would be ready for another attempt.

The grisly details of their deaths emerged after the war, when some of the German officers were tried by a war crimes tribunal for the murder of four captives: Corporal James Dobson Cairncross, twenty-two, who was about five feet six inches tall, with fair hair and green eyes, from Hawick, Scotland; Lance-Corporal Trevor Louis Masters, twenty-five, five feet seven inches tall, with fair hair and blue eyes, from Cobh, Eire; and two Londoners, Driver Peter Paul Farrell, twenty-six, five feet eight inches tall, with dark brown hair and hazel eyes, from Marylebone, and Sapper Eric John Smith, twenty-four, five feet seven inches tall, blue eyes and brown hair, from Paddington.

The military court in Oslo heard evidence by a Luftwaffe doctor, Werner Fritz Seeling, of appalling savagery meted out to the four commandos by *Hauptscharführer* Erich Hoffman, one of three accused Germans. Hoffman stamped on the throat of one of the prisoners, destroying his Adam's apple. He shot another in the head, just behind his right ear. The other two were throttled with a rope and a leather strap, one by being tied to a radiator by the neck and then lifted until he choked to death.[11]

The Germans weighted the four bodies and dumped them in the fjord. Hoffman was sentenced to death and hanged at Hemelin Jailhouse at 3.30 p.m. on 15 May 1946. Seeling was executed by firing squad for his part in the atrocity at 9.05 a.m. on 10 January 1946 at Askerhus Prison, Oslo. A third was handed over to the Russians for atrocities on Russian prisoners of war. His fate was unknown, but could be guessed.

Lieutenant Colonel Wilson, head of the SOE Norwegian section, telephoned the Combined Operations Executive to express his regret at the deaths, but offered to take over the mission. Major General Sir Colin Gubbins, the operational head of SOE, was at first reluctant to agree.

At MI6 headquarters, Lieutenant Commander Eric Welsh broke the news of the Freshman disaster to R. V. Jones and told him that the decision whether or not a second attack would be made on the plant would depend on his expert opinion as a scientist. Was the threat of Hitler acquiring a nuclear bomb so great that another sabotage operation should be mounted on the Norsk Hydro?

After the failure of Freshman, Jones said he felt that Welsh was using him like a puppet – 'as he ultimately used others in a more eminent position' – to drive the case forward for another attack on the plant. Jones spent a sleepless night tossing the issue over in his mind, considering whether it was worth losing more lives in the event of another failure. In the morning, Jones told Welsh it was so important they had to have another crack at it.

On 20 November, Tronstad briefed the SOE on the available intelligence and Gubbins agreed to mount a second attack. Churchill approved. Churchill insisted that this time his 'baby', the Special Operations Executive, should run the show.

7

The Real Heroes of Telemark

The instructor was blunt. Holding up a pistol in his right hand, he told his young Norwegian pupils 'this is your only friend ... the only friend you can rely on. Treat him properly and he'll take care of you.' The message was instilled in them: 'Never give a man a chance – if you've got him down, kick him to death.'[1]

The handpicked team from the Ligne Company, the Norwegian army in exile, were led by First Lieutenant Joachim Rønneberg, aged twenty-two. He had been summoned to an office of the SOE above the Baker Street Underground station in London by Charles Jocelyn Hambro, the head of the SOE's Scandinavian section, and asked to undertake a special mission with five volunteers. Hambro, a rich banker before joining the SOE at the outbreak of war, had chosen the code name for the operation; he named it Gunnerside after the grouse moor in North Yorkshire where he loved to go shooting.[2]

Knut Haukelid was appointed Rønneberg's deputy. The four other members of the Gunnerside team were: Fredrik Kayser, Kasper Idland, Hans Storhaug and Birger Strømsheim. Haukelid was American – he was born in Brooklyn, New York, the son of Norwegian parents. He had been the director of a company importing equipment from the US into Norway when the war broke out. He had joined the resistance to fight the Germans in Norway and, after throwing a supporter of Quisling, the Nazi collaborator, off a ferry, he escaped to Britain to join Norwegian forces in exile.

On the bare wastes of the Hardangervidda, the Grouse team endured one of the most savage winters on record. Temperatures plummeted to minus 30 degrees Celsius most nights, and the team spent up to fifteen hours a day keeping warm in their sleeping bags. Only the radio operator, Haugland, had to get up at night to keep in touch with Baker Street by sending and receiving messages in Morse code. He had to take off his gloves in order to tap out the messages, because each operator had a 'signature' rhythm and anything that interrupted it would raise suspicions the operation had been blown.

While Grouse waited, the Gunnerside team was sent to a series of training schools to teach the six volunteers how to be saboteurs. Stodham Park, Liss, near Southampton in Hampshire – code-named Special Training School 3 – was known as 'gangster school' because that is where they were given exercises by their SOE instructors in the ungentlemanly art of killing with explosives, their bare hands, small arms and even poison.

Churchill approved the creation of SOE at a Cabinet meeting on 22 July 1940. He wanted to hit back at Hitler after the fall of France and had few other ways of doing so. Its twin aims were subversion and sabotage in occupied Europe. It was given the cover of the Ministry of Economic Warfare, presided over by a left-wing Labour minister Hugh Dalton, a well-known critic of SIS. He brought in Colin McVean Gubbins, a specialist in irregular warfare, as 'M', Director of SOE Military Operations, to knock it into shape. SOE moved from 2 Caxton Street to 64 Baker Street on 31 October 1940, where it remained under the guise of the Inter-Services Research Bureau. Gubbins, a wiry Scot who had won the Military Cross in the First World War, and his loyal secretary, Margaret Jackson, moved into an office on the upper floors of 82 Michael House, the headquarters of Marks and Spencer, while SOE expanded rapidly into mansion flats along the street. SOE became known generically as 'Baker Street'.

Army chiefs would have preferred SOE to be strangled at birth. The commandos were at least regular soldiers. SOE, armed with a seemingly unlimited budget, was hiring all and sundry with no military training at all; they included many attractive women, from well-heeled debutantes to office girls, earning Gubbins, who believed girls made good couriers because they had a better chance of evading intimate body searches by the Gestapo, a reputation as a bit of a 'letch'.[3] The defence chiefs regarded SOE as a bunch of dangerous amateurs. If the Gunnerside team screwed up now, the whole future of SOE could be put in jeopardy.

The Gunnerside boys were given intensive training at another SOE safehouse called Brickendonbury Manor in Hertford – SOE Special Training School 17. Here they learned all about the layout of the target and were taught skills in industrial sabotage. The manor was cleared of other 'students' to preserve the secrecy of the mission. They had a detailed full-scale mock-up of the plant in a shed in the grounds that they studied until it was fixed in their memories. Tronstad rehearsed the operation in the minutest detail, like a professor with a star class; he required them to memorise photographs and drawings and then run through the mock-up laying dummy charges with the lights out, all while being timed, so they could do it in the dark.

Occasionally, a question of detail about the plant would come up, and the professor would come back the next day with an answer, suggesting he had a source inside the plant. Einar Skinnarland, who was now back in the plant, undoubtedly helped but another source was clearly involved. The information was so detailed, Tronstad was able to tell them where they kept the keys to the lavatory near the heavy water battery cell hall, should they need to lock up any workers in the plant.[4]

Haukelid recalled: 'Tronstad had been the technical adviser when the works were being planned and knew the factory inside out. But sometimes we raised some special question which [Tronstad] could not answer and then he took it away and gave us the answer next day. So we guessed that he was in contact with someone who knew the factory even better than he did.'[5]

He was unaware that Jomar Brun, the chief engineer of the Vemork plant, had escaped to England with his wife and a pile of documents and blueprints, microfilmed by the Norwegian underground in Oslo. They stayed for a time at the De Vere hotel in South Kensington, enabling Tronstad to check on details with Brun when they were raised by his 'students'.

One day, Haukelid saw some papers from the Supreme Command of the Armed Forces marked 'strictly secret' on Tronstad's desk. 'It's the heavy water,' Tronstad told him, 'It's manufactured at Vemork and can be used for some of the dirtiest work that can possibly be imagined. If the Germans can solve the problem, they'll win the war.' That was all the detail they got about the purpose of the mission. 'They just said it was important and had to be blown up,' said Rønneberg.[6]

They were sent to Glenmore Lodge in Aviemore, Scotland – Special Training School 026 – among some of the wildest mountains in the country, where they lived the outdoor life, sharpening their survival skills, including poaching stags with their rifles. It was perfect training for establishing a base on the 3,500-square-mile Hardangervidda. They were taught how to parachute at Dunham House near RAF Ringway, now Manchester Airport, then known by SOE as Special Training School 51.

Tronstad warned the volunteers that, although they would be wearing British uniforms, if they were captured they must be prepared to be treated the same as the commandos who were shot. The Germans had strengthened security around the plant, with a minefield around the pipelines, and time was pressing.

SOE had planned to carry out the raid on Christmas Eve 1942, to catch the Germans off-guard. There was a full moon but the unlikely Christmas present from SOE had to be postponed because of more bad weather. Even Knut Haukelid complained about the rain that winter, and in Norway, it was falling as deep snow.

The atrocious weather continued and the Grouse team had no option but to hunker down in a mountain hut and hold out until the operation could take place. The barren mountain plateau, at over 3,000 feet high, is one of the harshest places in Europe, where the wind whips snow into deep drifts. They survived on their wits and mountain survival skills through Christmas and into the New Year of 1943. They killed reindeer for the meat, but when they could not make a kill, they resorted to making soup from reindeer moss.

On 23 January 1943, the Gunnerside team was at last told the mission was on. They were taken by lorry to RAF Tempsford where their SOE handlers gave them their final kit check, and issued them with suicide pills – cyanide enclosed in a rubber cover and hidden in emergency bandages. It could be kept in the mouth but once bitten through it would ensure death within three seconds.[7] It was a standard piece of kit issued to 'Joes'.

When they flew over Hardangervidda, they failed to locate their reception squad, which had been optimistically renamed Swallow by Hambro, and had to turn back for RAF Tempsford. At their own request, rather than going back to Brickendonbury Manor, the Norwegians were transported to a remote stone house in Scotland to await the next full moon. The cottage was on an island in the north of Scotland where they shot seals and stags, and went for long walks as they waited another month. It was lonely, healthy and tedious, said Haukelid. The winter in Scotland was even wetter than it was in Vestlandet on the Atlantic coast of southern Norway. Haugland, in the Swallow team, radioed London to warn Tronstad that the Germans had stepped up security around the plant. They were obviously expecting another attack, making it vital that the planes carrying out the parachute drop stayed well clear of Rjukan valley to avoid alerting the guards. It meant a new dropping point had to be fixed at Lake Skyrken, but that was thirty miles away from the Swallow team base at Sandvain on the snowy mountain plateau.

As the date for the next full moon approached, the Gunnerside six were flown south to England in driving rain from their rest-camp on the east coast of Scotland for their flight to Norway. It is claimed they stayed at Farm Hall, but one of the officers there was adamant that no SOE operations were run out of Farm Hall.

The Gunnerside team actually stayed at another SOE stately safehouse (they had so many mansions under their wing that wags suggested SOE stood for Stately 'Omes of England). This mansion was code-named Special Training School 61. It was near the hamlet of Perry, among the flat fields of Cambridgeshire, and handy for RAF Tempsford. Its real name is Gaynes Hall.

Gaynes Hall

There is no sign that the stately home on the flat plains of Cambridgeshire played a role in one of the most important clandestine missions in the Second World War. Today, Gaynes Hall is owned by a London property company and rented out as offices to a national fleet management company.

The house is largely forgotten, off a service road through the hamlet of Perry, near the great reservoir, Grafham Water. Where Haukelid and his five saboteurs were briefed for secret operations, fleet managers answer phones and organise fleets of vehicles.

The SOE 'Joes' hotel' at Gaynes Hall was spread over three floors, with a ballroom and great bow windows, twenty-three acres of parkland and sweeping lawns, all protected from prying eyes by an encircling high garden wall. Dating from the Civil War era, the hall was once the home of Sir Oliver Cromwell, uncle of the Lord Protector of the Commonwealth. It was owned by a Mrs Jubilee when it was requisitioned by the war office for use as SOE Special Training School 61.[8]

The bedroom dormitories where dozens of SOE agents slept before dangerous missions behind enemy lines, many never to return, are now palatial offices overlooking the grounds.

'There's no sign at all of its wartime use,' Mike Smith, director of Fleet Assist, told me. 'The commanding officer's room is on the ground floor overlooking the gardens and the ballroom is still there. It was a big room and must have been a hive of activity.' Mr Smith has found no trace of the hall's wartime use, and sadly no blueprints of the Norsk Hydro hidden in cupboards. If there are ghosts, he has not encountered them. A reminder of Gaynes Hall's past was unearthed in 1973 when unexploded hand grenades and live mortar shells were dug up in the dry moat.

There is no blue plaque to the Gunnerside team and the others who risked their lives to beat Hitler in the race to build the atomic bomb.

Oluf Reed Olsen, a Norwegian SOE recruit who went to Gaynes Hall on a separate mission, said the house behind high walls contained an extremely cosmopolitan collection of agents from various European countries. They tried to guess from which country they came by their accents when speaking English, but all were silent about their missions. They were looked after by 'FANYs', the young SOE women who had been recruited into the First Aid Nursing Yeomanry and acted as house matrons, and entertainers singing hits of the time such as 'Wish Me Luck As You Wave Me Goodbye' around the piano. They also occasionally acted as nurses with a shoulder to cry on for the times when the young men in their care became overstressed.

Knut Haukelid said: 'It was a station for people who were going to Europe on secret errands and who had to wait for planes. The place was very closely guarded. A number of service women kept the house in order, cooked the meals and gave the men some social life. These girls did an uncommonly good job, seeing that everything went as it should and doing their best to prevent the delays from getting on our nerves.'[9]

Eggs were considered a luxury, but for the Joes two eggs on the plate was an ominous sign – it meant they were going on Ops that night. Olsen recalled:

Fresh eggs were at that time largely unobtainable by the English public. Only dried eggs from Canada and America were used. At suppertime, it might happen that two fine fresh eggs were carefully laid on a plate before a particular person. The person in question, even if he liked eggs better than anything, seemed suddenly to have lost taste for this previously so tempting delicacy which now actually lay before him. His turn had appeared on the programme for the night's operations ...[10]

Gaynes Hall was abandoned in 1945 when SOE was wound up and absorbed in SIS. Gaynes Hall became the governor's house for the Gaynes Hall Borstal that was built nearby. From 1945 to 1983 the elegant rooms of the old hall were used by the governor, and the private flowerbeds and lawns were tended by some of the young offenders who were locked up nearby.

The borstal has gone too, replaced by the Category Three low-security Littlehey Prison where inmates have included the public relations man for countless celebrities, the late Max Clifford, who was jailed in 2014 for eight years for indecent assault.

The Gunnerside team enjoyed the conviviality of the 'FANYs' on nights out in Cambridge, but they had one overriding thing in mind – the daunting mission ahead. 'We might be drinking champagne in Cambridge one evening and landing in the snow on the cold and lonely Hardangervidda the next,' said Haukelid. Occasionally, Tronstad's elite class of saboteurs broke out of their close confinement at Gaynes Hall by crawling through the barbed wire fence to shoot pheasant with pistols in the fields and copses. Sometimes, the farmers would complain about bandits poaching their birds, but the Commandant denied all knowledge of any visitors to the hall. They enjoyed the roast pheasant, but not the kitchens. 'It is a curious thing about English cooking that the best food is often cooked in the dirtiest kitchen,' said Haukelid.

The Gunnerside team offered to clean the kitchens for the 'FANYs' in return for their favours. The 'FANYs' remained amiable but unyielding. Tronstad was remembered by one of the Gaynes Hall girls, a Cockney who joined the 'FANYs' at eighteen years of age without realising she was joining its secret warfare section:

We used to go out with some of the Bods [agents] but we had to go right away from where we were stationed so that we did not draw attention to it. I am sure that some people must have known that something was going on.

'We were not supposed to get attached to them but we did and when they went on a mission you never saw them again. I remember a man called Tronstad; he was advising the men on the building that contained the heavy water at Vemork that Hitler intended using in atom bombs. He knew this building that they were going to blow up inside out. Many years later I read that this man had been murdered by Nazi followers. It made me feel very sad.[11]

Tronstad was an invaluable source of intelligence and an outstanding hero of the war for Norway. He was also partly responsible for alerting the allies to the existence of the Baltic German rocket site at Peenemunde where V-1 and later V-2 rockets were launched at London and the South of England. He was killed in March 1945 when he and a small resistance team were dropped into Norway on Operation Sunshine to force the Germans out of Norway. Tronstad's team captured a German collaborator in a mountain hut, but the man's brother tracked them down and killed Leif Tronstad in a shoot-out along with another member of the team.

*

At eleven each morning, a notice was put up in the hall saying whether an operation was expected that night. Each day, they would be told: 'No operation today.' Occasionally, they were told to be ready to go that evening, only to be stood down later. At last however they were told the mission was on. Rain was falling in torrents on the night of 16 February 1943, when the six-man Gunnerside team was driven in a lorry to the airfield at RAF Tempsford. The six bearded men in white winter combat suits headed towards the Halifax bomber waiting on the tarmac a hundred yards away to take them on their secret mission. Professor Tronstad was there to see them off. Their bulky snow suits made it difficult to move around in the aircraft, and they threw themselves down as the door was slammed to.

Flight Lieutenant John Douglas Charrot, who was a navigator but listed as the second pilot on board the bomber that night, recalled:

The first thing to see was these six chaps arriving and you did see them because they were huge. They were all carrying a tremendous amount of equipment which they dumped in the aircraft. They didn't come in a car. They came in a big lorry then the ground crew loaded up their containers. I think they had the maximum, which was twelve [containers]. The Dispatcher was told there would be these six big chaps and was told to watch their heads [on exit]. That is what I was told – 'Watch their heads as they go out.[12]

They took off and headed across the North Sea to Norway; the Halifax came over land near Stavanger, just where the navigator – a station navigation officer who had joined the trip – had planned. By the time they reached the drop zone over the Hardangervidda plateau in the mountains of Telemark, the rain had gone, the moon was out, and they could see miles and miles of snow lit by moonlight. 'It was a lovely night,' Charrot said. But that is when it got difficult.

Their pinpoint was over a frozen lake and everyone, including Charrot, who was in the nose of the plane was straining their eyes to identify the drop zone in the white landscape as they flew low beneath what appeared to be fluffy white clouds. 'I think we got fairly near it, but we weren't sure. Everyone was looking out including the rear gunner. He said, "You are talking about fluffy clouds. I'm not sure they are fluffy clouds. I think these are the tops of mountains." It was as bad as that.'[13]

They could not find the lights for the rendezvous with Swallow. The pilot was Squadron Leader Christopher Gibson, (not Guy Gibson who later led the Dambusters' raid). He spoke to Joachim Rønneberg, the leader of the saboteurs, who thought he could recognise points in the landscape. It was the last night of the full moon in February, and Rønneberg knew the Swallow team would have difficulty surviving on the mountains if another month went by. Rønneberg decided that it was such a vital operation that, rather than ditch it again, they had to risk a 'blind drop' without lights to guide them. They would have to parachute by moonlight.

The hole in the bottom of the aircraft was opened, the warning lamp in the roof went to green, and Joachim Rønneberg jumped out first with a clatter. In quick succession, the other members of the team dropped out. Knut Haukelid was the last out and as he felt the blast of the slipstream tug at his body, he saw the plane bank and turn.

Inside the plane, the rear gunner reported to Gibson that the six parachutes had opened. They went around the drop zone again and on the second circuit, the crew dropped the containers out of the bay doors and they turned for the long haul home. Charrot's logbook shows the mission took eight hours and twenty-five minutes before they touched down again at RAF Tempsford. They were never told the purpose of the Gunnerside mission.

Charrot, who was filling in on special operations at RAF Tempsford while he regained a new crew, was the only member of the crew on board that night to survive the war. A month later, on Sunday 14 March, Squadron Leader Gibson was shot down and killed with the crew of Halifax BB281 near Munich on another clandestine operation to Czechoslovakia. He was thirty-one and was posthumously awarded the Distinguished Flying Cross.

On the snowbound plateau, the Gunnerside team gathered up their kit and disposed of the parachutes under the soft snow. They found a hut nearby and that night, after a brief rest, set out to make their rendezvous with the Swallow team members, but the wind got up and they realised a storm was coming. They took the depressing decision to retreat back to the hut. It saved their lives. The storm was the worst that Haukelid had ever experienced and the blizzard did not let up for another four days. When it finally subsided, they were able to emerge from the hut onto the plateau, but their concealed kit was buried under metres of deep fresh snow, which they had to dig out.

At over 3,000 feet, the Hardangervidda, covering 6,000 square miles of bare snow, ice and rock, is the loneliest mountain area in northern Europe. They found they had been dropped thirty kilometres from the intended pinpoint; it was an energy-sapping journey to their rendezvous point at Svensbu where the Swallow team was hiding. Carrying heavy loads, it was difficult to make progress in four feet of snow, even for expert cross-country skiers like the Gunnerside team. They contacted the Swallow team by radio and they agreed to walk towards them.

After sixteen hours slogging on their skis across the white wasteland, the exhausted Gunnerside team spotted two skiers in the wilderness. Rønneberg asked Haukelid to find out who they were. He sped after them, going as silently as he could for the last few hundred metres, and from a short distance at last recognised Arne and Claus from the Swallow team. He hailed them, and there was plenty of backslapping and joy at the meeting.

The Swallow team members were heavily bearded and emaciated but were quickly restored with the rations that the Gunnerside team brought with them. They returned to the mountain hut occupied by the Swallow team in Svensbu and celebrated with reindeer steaks, chocolate and dried fruits.[14] Jointly they got down to preparing their attack on the heavy water plant. Rønneberg, under orders agreed in London, said the attack was to be carried out by a nine-man team, combining the six-man Gunnerside team and three of the Swallow team, leaving Claus Helberg to scout out the town of Rjukan for the latest intelligence about their target.

They broke into a mountain hut in the Fjosbudal overlooking the plant ravine, and waited for Claus Helberg to return. Rønneberg's plan agreed with Tronstad was that they should go down the mountainside on the north side of the valley near Vaaer, leaving their winter kit and packs up on the top, carrying only arms and explosives. It would avoid the heavily guarded suspension bridge across the gorge but there was unease about the plan because it would mean retracing their steps to pick up their skis when they made their escape, which could be dangerous. Some favoured an alternative route, going down the side of the mountain on their skis. It looked a sheer drop from the top, but aerial photographs showed that the mountainside was clothed in trees, suggesting that there were just enough ledges for them to get down the mountain on their skis.

Knut Haugland knew the area and said it was impossible to ski down this side of the ravine. Rønneberg asked Claus Helberg to recce the area around the edge of the cliffs that plunged down into the valley. He could see the plant on a vast ledge, halfway down the ravine, where it could process the water coming from the falls above. At the back of the plant, the mountain rose up steeply, covered with rough ice. There was a long flight of steps down the side of the pipeline leading to the plant, but they had detailed maps showing the area around the pipeline had been heavily mined since the failed Freshman attack. There were machine guns and searchlights on top of the factory that could light up the whole area.

To get to the plant, all traffic had to cross a narrow suspension bridge seventy-five feet long spanning the deep ravine cut by the River Maan. There was only one weak spot – a railway line which led from the town of Rjukan to Vemork, cut deep into the hillside and used for transporting machinery to the works or shipping heavy water out.

There was a storm on Saturday 27 February but Helberg returned with the news that it was feasible for them to get down. This route would have the advantage of surprise, because the Germans clearly thought that Vemork was so well protected by nature that it needed no guards to cover the direct ravine route. It would also enable them to take a different escape route out of the valley and back up the mountain.

Rønneberg consulted his team, one by one, about which plan they should follow. Some members of the team wanted to stick to the original plan, but the majority preferred to tackle the steep side of the ravine, avoiding the bridge and its guards altogether. The only other obstacle appeared to be a guard hut in the centre of the plant, which they would somehow have to slip past to get into the hall where the lines of heavy water collecting vessels were located. Spies inside the plant had told them that the Germans had a guard of thirty men using a hut as a guardroom in the middle of the yard between the main buildings. They thought it would hold between eight and twelve guards at a time; it would have to be covered, but it seemed possible the explosives party could slip by and enter the plant unseen. They waited in the hut near the gorge until it was dark.

At 8 p.m. on 27 February 1943, the combined Swallow and Gunnerside team set out on their long wooden skis for the most audacious sabotage mission of the war. They dropped silently through the snow, took a look down at the drop before them, and then slipped over the lip of the cliff. They sideslipped on their skis down the mountainside in the deep snow, grabbing bushes to brake their descent. Any noise they made was drowned out by the constant whine of machinery in the seven-storey factory across the ravine, and the incessant sound of running water. At a safe point, they scrambled out of their white winter combat suits. They hid their snow kit, skis and rucksacks among the trees, and wearing the khaki uniforms of the Norwegian army, slithered down on foot to the road to the plant. They ducked out of the lights when two busloads of workers turning up for the night shift drove past. They followed the tight bends of the road between Rjukan and Mosvatn but broke off at the bottom to ford the partly frozen river Maan. Across the icy river, Rønneberg and his men followed a break in the wooded hillside that had been cleared for pylons carrying power cables, and climbed steeply up the mountain through the deep snow; the snow was wet after a thaw, making climbing the mountain more of an effort. With their lungs heaving, and drenched in sweat, they reached the railway line running from Rjukan to the plant without a challenge, and struck right along the tracks towards the plant. They gratefully reached the cover of a snow-covered electricity transformer at 11.30 p.m. It was on a ledge carrying the rail line, 500 yards from the Vemork plant. They halted and ate chocolate while they waited for the sentries to change at midnight.

They had timed their attack for 12.30 a.m., just enough time for the new guard to settle down in their hut for the night; at the appointed time, Rønneberg went forward to cut the heavy chain on the railway gates guarding the entrance to the plant. Rønneberg was glad he brought his own heavy-duty chain cutters, which he had bought in a shop in Cambridge; the hacksaw the British intelligence had supplied would have made too much noise and could have alerted the Nazi guards, wrecking the mission.[15]

He cut through the chain, and the teams followed him into the plant. They split into two – four to lay the charges and five to cover the guard hut with 'Tommy' guns, grenades and two sniper rifles. Their target was a battery of eighteen cells, the last stage in the production of the heavy water, in the cellar of the plant.

Rønneberg inched past the guard hut with his team and tried a door to a cellar, which they had been told would be open. He found it was locked, because the worker who should have left it open had unexpectedly gone on sick leave. They searched for another way in. Two of the team found a cable intake that had been identified by Leif Tronstad, following advice from Jomar Brun, as a possible way in during their training. They squeezed inside the cable canal and crawled along like rats among a quantity of pipes under the floor, pushing their packs ahead of them.

'From the open hole, we could look into the heavy water concentration room and saw there was only one man, a Norwegian caretaker,' said Rønneberg. 'So we climbed down without being spotted, rushed the open door and shouted: "Hands in the air!"'

The startled Norwegian watchman instantly saw the two men in khaki battledress were carrying guns. Rønneberg recalled:

There was a Norwegian workman inside the factory reading the instruments and filling out the logbook. He heard us talking Norwegian, discussing whether we should put on a thirty-second fuse just to be sure that we heard the bang as soon as possible. That was when he asked for his glasses. It was difficult to get glasses in Norway, so he wanted to have them before we lit the charges. I remember I threw away what I was doing and searched for the glasses and found the case and handed it to him ... He was very pleased and I started getting ignition sets ready when he suddenly said that the glasses were not in the case. I said: 'Where the hell are they then?' And he said, 'Well, they were there when you came in.' In the end, I found them being used as a bookmark in his logbook, and gave them to him.

As they pacified the watchman, the window was kicked in, and three other members of the sabotage team, who had failed to gain entry by the cable chute under the floor, burst in. There were four charges of plastic explosives in two strings, each with a two-minute fuse, and they were laid against the battery cells. Rønneberg decided to cut the fuses to thirty seconds. 'I don't know how long we were there, but it was very easy. The charges fitted like a hand in a glove.'[16]

The demolition team ordered the workman to give them the key for the cellar door so that they could go out through the door. 'We opened the door and I remember Major Tronstad saying that in case we needed to lock up the guard, the key for the lavatory was on the left-hand side of the door. I remember just after we had lit these thirty-second fuses, I saw the key but we did not need it.'

Watching nervously, the watchman said: 'Take care not to short-circuit. If you do there may be an explosion.'

'Explosion!' said one of the demolition team. 'That's just what there's going to be!'

Rønneberg told the man: 'You just run around the corner, up the staircase, lie down and keep your mouth open, until you hear the bang. There will be only one bang, so when it is over you can go down and see the result.' Rønneberg said he met the man two years later and he had followed his advice. It was just as well; if he had had his mouth closed, the pressure of the explosives would have blown out his eardrums.[17]

Once they had set the thirty-second fuse, they all ran for cover. Because of the wind and the noise of the power station, none of the German guards heard the explosion.

Outside, the team watching the guardroom wondered when they would hear the bang. Knut Haukelid and the team covering the guard hut watched and waited an agonising twenty minutes for the big bang. When it came, it was an 'astonishingly small, insignificant one'. It broke the windows and there was a flash of light in the dark, but it hardly seemed big enough to destroy the capability of the plant to make heavy water.

The noise disturbed a German guard, but it was not enough to raise the alarm. The guard emerged from the hut to inspect the door leading to the electric-light plant with a torch. Haukelid considered killing him with a burst of automatic fire, but decided to hold fire. The German returned inside the hut, and they slipped away. They were down at the bottom of the valley when the air-raid sirens sounded, raising a general alarm to mobilise all troops in the area. Floodlights carved through the night sky.

They watched as several armoured cars raced along the road to the plant. The German guards discovered their line of retreat and gave chase along the railway line, but instead of turning left, the way they came, the Norwegians turned right on the road to Rjukan, then cut up to the left, following the line of a funicular railway, up a steep zigzag route six or seven hundred metres to the top of the ridge leading to the Hardangervidda. They were exhausted after their climb carrying heavy loads, but they were exhilarated at their own audacity. They put on their skis, their white combat kit and slipped away into the night.

The sun came up at 6 a.m. 'It was a mackerel sky,' said Rønneberg. 'It was a marvellous sunrise. We sat there very tired, very happy. Nobody said anything. That was a very special moment.'

Operation Gunnerside was remarkable because it was carried out without a shot being fired. It was regarded as a textbook exercise in sabotage, and was turned into the highly fictionalised Hollywood epic *The Heroes of Telemark*, with Richard Harris playing Haukelid and Kirk Douglas as Professor Leif Tronstad. Those who took part in the mission were the real heroes of Telemark.

Haukelid said they left behind just one clue as a calling card – a British 'Tommy' gun, to limit the reprisals against the local workforce, which had been accused in the past of sabotaging the heavy water production process.

Michael Foot, a former army officer who was decorated for his operations with the Special Air Service (SAS) in Brittany, said if it had never done anything else, the SOE's Operation Gunnerside would deserve the 'gratitude of humanity'.[18] Former SOE members Peter Wilkinson and Joan Bright Astley, in their biography of the SOE commander, Sir Colin Gubbins, said the Gunnerside operation 'was probably the most important act of sabotage carried out by either side during the Second World War'.[19] Gubbins said the Gunnerside raid had 'put paid to the German efforts to produce the atom bomb before their final defeat'.[20]

It is easy to understand why such hyperbole should be lavished on Operation Gunnerside, but it was an exaggeration. The heroics of the Gunnerside team did not fully stop production of heavy water, and it was decided to risk a daylight bomber raid by B-17s and B-24s of the US 8th Air Force in November 1943, despite the earlier misgivings by the British at the difficulty of hitting the target.

They were to target the plant in two waves at lunch hour to minimise civilian casualties, as the workers would be away from the plant, but they hit bad weather. The first wave of B-17 bombers only managed four direct hits on the plant after dropping 435 bombs; the second wave of B-24s scored direct hits, but it was the wrong target – they destroyed a nitrate plant three miles away. The Norwegian government in exile lodged a formal protest that more than seventy Norwegians were killed in the raid.

The mission report of the 392nd Bomber Group who carried out the second wave said:

> Bombs were dropped from 14,000 feet at 1212 hours. Photo analysis on return showed that 29.5 tons of bombs were dropped on the Norsk Hydro Nitrate Plant three miles east of the secondary target with only 2.5 tons dropped on the hydro-electric plant. This was unfortunate, as the bombing was excellent. Using the centre of the large centrally-located building as an MPI, the 392nd had 37 per cent of its bombs within 1,000 feet and 85 per cent within 2,000 feet.

The US bomber attack, though it failed to stop heavy water production, finally convinced Schumann and Diebner in Berlin that they could no longer rely on supplies of heavy water from the Norsk Hydro. They moved production to Germany.

The bitter struggle to stop the Germans obtaining enough heavy water from Norway to make an atomic bomb was not over. Knut Haukelid bravely remained in Norway under cover and later planted charges that sank a ferry transporting railway wagons carrying the last supplies of the precious heavy water to Berlin.

The success of Gunnerside was used by the SOE to answer criticism from MI6 and the regular army that their efforts were counter-productive to the war effort. Gubbins said:

> It was one of the most important individual actions of the war for which we received the thanks of the Chiefs of Staff and the congratulations of the Prime Minister in a personal note. This undoubtedly was also a turning point for SOE, underlined by a directive from the Chiefs of Staff to SOE on 20 March 1943 and circulated to all the exiled governments in London and Cairo [Allied headquarters in the Middle East].

The Chiefs of Staff directive decreed that SOE was the authority responsible for co ordinating sabotage and other subversive activities, including the organisation of resistance groups in all occupied countries and for providing advice and liaison on all matters in connection with patriot forces.

Gubbins said SOE had been 'working for months to get this directive from the Chiefs of Staff'. In future, the Chiefs of Staff would not be able to consider anything from foreign governments without it passing through the SOE's 'sieve'. It also put a shot across the bows of MI6 and the Foreign Office who had been complaining about SOE interfering in their strategic operations. The success of the Gunnerside raid carried Hambro and Gubbins through a disastrous downturn in the SOE's fortunes over the next six months.

German intelligence penetrated their spy networks in Holland. SOE chiefs ignored security checks designed to show that networks had been turned and continued to send Joes into the arms of the Nazis. The blunders were so great that claims were made after the war that Gubbins' assistant at Baker Street, Vera Atkins, was blackmailed into acting as a double agent for the Nazis. My former colleague at the Independent, Sarah Helm, author of the outstanding biography on Atkins, *A Life in Secrets,* told me she was convinced the blunders at SOE were more cock-up than conspiracy. However, the crisis came when the army chiefs of staff in Cairo sent a delegation to Churchill to complain about SOE interference with their operations in the Balkans. Churchill had no option but to put SOE in the Middle East under the army chiefs. Hambro was furious and, in the resulting fall-out, was forced to resign from SOE.

Hambro had detractors inside SOE who saw him as a dilettante, and grumbled about the excessive amount of time he was devoting to his City interests and running the Great Western Railway while also acting as the head of SOE. He treated Colin Gubbins as a competent general manager. Dalton's top civil servant, Gladwyn Jebb, who had been Hambro's fag at Eton, grumbled to Dalton, another Old Etonian, 'Hambro lives by bluff and charm.'[22]

Hambro had more than 'bluff and charm' to emerge smelling of roses from SOE. He had the personal support of Churchill, who appointed him to Washington as the British liaison officer with General Leslie R. Groves, the head of the US atomic bomb programme code-named the Manhattan Project. Churchill rightly believed Hambro, six foot three with his easy charm and moneyed contacts, would hit it off with 'the Yanks'. He became a key player with the Americans in the race to beat Hitler in the race to the bomb.

Charles Jocelyn Hambro was an extraordinary character, even for the odd assortment of people attracted by the operations of SOE. Like the Earl of Suffolk, he would not take any pay for his services during the war. He did not need to.

A scion of the Scandinavian Hambro banking family, by the age of thirty Hambro was a director of the Bank of England, a director of Hambros Bank, and would shortly take over as chairman of the Great Western Railways. He was also a close personal friend of the Prime Minister, a fellow Old Etonian. Hambro had been a star at Eton, skippering the cricket first eleven and excelling as a batsman and a medium pace bowler. *Wisden*, the cricket 'bible', records in one match he took seven wickets for six runs. In 1916 he joined the Coldstream Guards as an ensign and, after a short stint at Sandhurst officer training college, was sent to the Western Front, where he spent two years in the trenches, and won the Military Cross for conspicuous gallantry. His citation describes how he led a raiding party across a canal, rescued an injured soldier who could not walk, and charged the enemy, using his revolver to kill four of them.[21]

After the First World War, he became managing director of the family bank, Hambros. His first wife, Pamela Cobbold, a member of the Cobbold brewing family, died in April 1932 after a tragic accident. Aged only thirty two, she died from pneumonia after contracting septicaemia in a wound from a kick by one of her hunting horses. He married again in 1936 a Mrs Dorothy Wallenberg, ex-wife of a Danish banker and industrialist.

He was forty-two when he wangled a post in the cloak-and-dagger world of intelligence through Sir Ronald Cross, one of his contemporaries at Eton and Hugh Dalton's predecessor as Minister of Economic Warfare. Hambro's expertise in finance and the City was undoubtedly an asset at the Ministry of Economic Warfare. He was originally viewed as a useful addition for British attempts to stop the Germans shipping iron ore from Sweden for its war effort, but Hambro proved to be very well connected with business and family networks around Europe. He was put in charge of SOE operations in the Scandinavian countries, including Norway, where he used a journalist, Ebbe Munck, to gain intelligence on the German occupation.

He quickly made an impact with sabotage operations, for which he was knighted in 1941, shortly before being put in charge of the French, Belgian, German and Dutch sections of SOE. In

1942, Hugh Dalton, the Labour minister for economic warfare responsible for SOE, was moved by Churchill and replaced by Lord Selborne, a peer with a long family pedigree in the Conservative party, who promptly promoted Hambro to replace Nelson, the worn-out head of SOE.

Tall and with a great domed head, Hambro was an impressive figure. He was despatched by Churchill to Washington under the cover of leading a British mission on 'raw materials' – code for uranium. The suave merchant banker impressed the hard-headed General Groves, who exploited Hambro's expertise in finance to lead the hard-bargaining over the price of uranium. Hambro led talks with Edgar Sengier, the head of Union Minière, the Belgian uranium mining company, to buy up world stocks of the ore to stop it falling into the hands of Hitler's Third Reich or Stalin's Soviet Union. Groves also wanted guaranteed supplies for America for years ahead. That required huge sums of money to be committed beyond the war, but such expenditure for peacetime was not covered by the war emergency powers. To avoid US Congressional scrutiny, Groves set up the Combined Development Trust, with the approval of Roosevelt and Churchill, with Hambro as its deputy director. Although there was no suggestion of fraud, Groves admitted to the highly questionable dodge of siphoning off some of the money and depositing the enormous sum of $37 million into a secret personal bank account held with the Bankers Trust Company of New York. But then, almost everything to do with the Manhattan Project was kept secret from Congress.

Groves had been chosen to organise the logistics of the atomic bomb programme in September 1942 by Lieutenant General Brehon Somervell, chief of the Army Services of Supply, and Major General W. D. Styer, his chief of staff, with the approval of Roosevelt's chief scientific adviser, Dr Vannevar Bush, Henry Stimson, the US Secretary of War, and George Marshall, the Army Chief of Staff. He was appointed because of his vast experience with the US Army Corps of Engineers in delivering army construction projects on time and on budget. They included the construction of the new defence building which would become known as the Pentagon. His office was at the Manhattan Engineer District building in New York, which is how the US atomic bomb programme gained its code name. One of Groves's first acts was to move his office from Manhattan to Washington to be close to the centre of power. Before long, he would be directing all aspects of the Manhattan Project.

The burly Groves – at fifty-five, he had a bulging waistline which he tried to keep in check by playing tennis – was described by one US army officer who knew him as 'the biggest son of a bitch I ever met in my life but also one of the most capable individuals'.[23]

Groves was an engineer, not a nuclear physicist, and he was initially responsible for the logistics – the engineering, construction and operation of the atomic plants – but he quickly became the driving force behind everything to do with building the world's first atomic bomb, from choosing the sites for the industrial complex to selecting the target cities in Japan.

Even so, the American start was faltering. The official history of the Manhattan Project by the US Department of Energy says the Maud report 'served as a sobering reminder that fission had been discovered in Nazi Germany almost three years earlier and that since spring 1940 a large part of the Kaiser Wilhelm Institute in Berlin had been set aside for uranium research'. That is only part of the story. The prod to get going came from the British. Roosevelt had responded to the warning in Einstein's letter by appointing a senior US official, James Briggs, to head up a secret advisory committee for the president on uranium. Briggs was hugely respected by Roosevelt for the work he had done during the Great Depression but progress on an atomic weapon under Briggs ran into the sand. Vannevar Bush, the president's chief scientific adviser, successfully lobbied Roosevelt to set up a new National Defence Research Committee (NDRC). It was headed by Bush, and took the lead on atomic research in America, but Briggs remained chairman of the nuclear advisory committee.

Members of the Maud Committee in London had kept Briggs informed of its findings, crucially its new conclusion that a bomb could be created by 1943. But in August 1941, when Mark Oliphant, a member of the Maud Committee, made a follow-up trip to Washington, he was annoyed to find from American physicists that Briggs had not passed on its findings, and left the landmark report in his safe. Oliphant enlisted the support of Ernest Lawrence, director of the Radiation Laboratory at the University of California in Berkeley, who went to see Arthur Compton, an American physicist working for the NDRC, to intervene over Briggs's inaction. Compton forwarded Lawrence's work to Vannevar Bush, with a warning that Germany was undoubtedly making progress and that Briggs and the Uranium Committee were moving too slowly. Bush briefed Roosevelt at the White House on 9 October 1941 that an atomic bomb was feasible. On 7 November 1941, Compton, chairman of a working party set up by Bush, confirmed the basic Maud findings that it was possible that a critical mass of 100 kg of uranium-235 would produce a powerful fission bomb, although he was more conservative in his estimates. Compton's report was presented to Roosevelt on 27 November 1941.

With America still not at war, the President was tentative. Then the attack on Pearl Harbour happened on 7 December 1941, which plunged America into the conflict it had been avoiding. Naval Marshal General Isoroku Yamamoto says in the Hollywood movie *Tora! Tora! Tora!* that he is afraid all they have done is wake a sleeping giant; the movie scene may have been apocryphal but for US atomic research it was true. Roosevelt sent a scribbled note on White House notepaper to Vannevar Bush on 19 January 1942 which has been preserved in the Roosevelt archives: 'V.B. OK – returned – I think you had best keep this in your own safe. FDR.' That is the only record of a decision having been made to launch the US nuclear bomb programme, but by then, Roosevelt was the commander-in-chief of a country at war.

Progress in America on the atomic bomb then gained momentum. Roosevelt's 'OK' transformed the atomic research project into a programme to make an atomic bomb.

Groves quickly acquired the vast tracts of land where he would create the 'secret cities' for the Manhattan Project, after taking over from the dithering Colonel James Marshall.[24] They were: Oak Ridge, Tennessee, where uranium was refined in two separate plants, Y-12 and K-25, by electromagnetic and gaseous diffusion; Los Alamos, a former Boy Scout camp in the wooded mountains of New Mexico, where the laboratories under J. Robert Oppenheimer assembled the bombs; and Hanford, Washington, where the world's first plutonium-producing reactors were built.

On 2 December 1942, history was made when the Italian Enrico Fermi's experimental pile in a racket court under the west grandstand of the Chicago University stadium achieved a sustained atomic reaction. It used graphite – not heavy water – as a moderator with 350 tons of pure graphite, and 42 tons of uranium. Groves received the news in a coded message from Chicago: 'The Italian navigator has just landed in the New World. The natives are friendly.' That spurred him on, but he was troubled by the nagging worry: if the Americans were making such strides, so must be the Germans.

8

The Bomb and the Carlsberg Brewery

Albert Speer slipped into a private room at his favourite Berlin restaurant, Horcher's, in April 1942 for one of his regular lunches with General Friedrich Fromm, head of the German army reserve.

They would chat in private about how the disastrous Russian campaign was going, the future for Germany, and exchange their private thoughts about Hitler. But there was a pressing issue on Fromm's mind. He had heard that a group of German scientists were working on a weapon that could destroy whole cities like London and perhaps throw England out of the war.

Speer had been unimpressed by reports from the February conference of Diebner, Heisenberg and the Uranium Club, but Fromm gave him fresh hope that something useful for the war effort may come from the new science about splitting the atom. Speer realised that he first needed to sort out the confusion between the competing groups of scientists. German atomic research was spread thinly over too many laboratories and ministries, the Army Ordnance Office under Schumann and Diebner, the Education Department under Berlin-educated scientist Abraham Esau and even the Post Office. Diebner coordinated nine research groups, including two engaged on building reactors – the Kaiser Wilhelm Institute for Physics in Berlin under Diebner's direct control and Heisenberg's laboratory in Leipzig University.

Diebner had replaced Peter Debye, a highly respected Dutch-born scientist, as head of the Kaiser Wilhelm Institute with the Nazification of the institute at the outbreak of war, but Diebner was regarded by Debye's former staff, von Weizsäcker and Wirtz, with professional contempt, although his design for the experimental pile at the Army's explosive research site in Gottow, sixty kilometres south of Berlin using cubes of uranium proved more successful than Heisenberg's attempts.

Albert Vogler, president of the Kaiser Wilhelm Society, complained to Speer in April, around the same time as Speer had lunch with Fromm, that Abraham Esau, a Nazi Party apparatchik, who paraded under the title of *Bevollmachtigter* (plenipotentiary) for nuclear physics, lacked a grip on the research. Esau was regarded as worse than Diebner by Heisenberg and his colleagues. On 6 May 1942, Speer spoke to Hitler and suggested that atomic research should be unified under one powerful individual who had a reputation for knocking heads together to get things done: Hermann Goering, Speer's boss and the head of the Luftwaffe.

While Hitler ruminated, a second secret conference on how atomic energy could be utilised by the Third Reich was held on 4 June 1942 at the *Kaiser Wilhelm Gesellschaft* at Harnack House in Berlin. Speer's office diary noted: 'On June 4, the Minister [Speer] flew back to Berlin ... that evening there was a lecture in Harnack House on atom-smashing and the development of the uranium machine and the cyclotron.'

There was no specific mention in Speer's diary of a bomb, but Heisenberg's lecture was a landmark. It was here that many of the military leaders of Hitler's Third Reich heard for the first time that an atomic bomb was possible. Speer attended with Professor Porche, designer of the VW who was engaged in designing new, more powerful Panzer tanks. The scientists included the cream of German physics with Heisenberg, Hahn, Diebner, Harteck, Wirtz and Thiessen. The military chiefs included Fromm and fifty-year-old Field Marshal Erhard Milch, a veteran of the Norway and French campaigns, now in charge of aircraft production.

Heisenberg's speaking notes were discovered in the files of the KGB but they could not convey the drama of what happened in a question-and-answer session after he had finished his scripted lecture to the military chiefs gathered in the Helmholz lecture room. Standing at the lectern in front of the semi-circle of tiered seats, Heisenberg launched immediately into the application of atomic research for war, going over the ground he covered at the February conference.

Theoretically, he said, there were two routes to a nuclear bomb, U-235 or element 94, plutonium. He went on to explain how a bomb could be made. It was news to many at the lecture who were not there in February, according to Telschow, the secretary of the Kaiser Wilhelm Foundation. Heisenberg said he had American technical journals that showed the Americans had plenty of technical and financial resources for atomic research, which meant that America might have gone ahead of the Germans in the race to a bomb, even though Germany had a head start only a few years before.

In the question-and-answer session at the end of his speech, Field Marshal Milch asked Heisenberg how big would a bomb have to be to reduce a large city like London to ruins? Milch wanted revenge after the British bombing of German cities. Heisenberg encompassed a space with his hands and said it would be about the size of a 'pineapple'.[1] Heisenberg's reference to a bomb the size of pineapple caused a ripple of excitement among generals in the audience.

Milch had another question for Heisenberg: how long would it take the Americans to build an atomic bomb? Heisenberg recalled telling Milch: 'Our careful estimate was – even if the Americans worked on this with full effort – they would not finish their reactor before the end of 1942, and an atom bomb most likely not before the end of 1944.'[2] He added: 'Actually, we believed it would take very much longer ... We physicists knew for certain and could state with a clear conscience: in under three or four years nothing could be done.'

After the meeting, Speer asked Heisenberg how much extra funding he needed. He assumed Heisenberg would want millions of marks. Speer said he offered a budget of two million marks, and Fromm offered to release hundreds of scientists, but Heisenberg made only modest demands, saying that more money could not be utilised at that moment. Milch and Fromm shook their heads in dismay at what they saw as Heisenberg's naivety. Milch later put funding into a weapon that was more likely to see a return on his investment: the vengeance rockets then being tested at Peenemunde.

Heisenberg strolled with Speer to the Institute of Physics, with its giant high-powered particle accelerator that Speer had wanted to see. Heisenberg quietly asked Speer how he thought the war would end for them. Speer left it an open question. Instead, he asked the theoretical physicist bluntly whether he could build an atomic bomb. Heisenberg assured him it was technically possible to build a bomb, but said it would take 'two years at the earliest' to put a programme in place. Speer said he found the answer 'in no way encouraging'.[3] With the Nazi campaign grinding to a halt in Russia, Hitler needed a superweapon in six or nine months, not two years.

Heisenberg said the technical problems were compounded by the fact that Europe possessed only one cyclotron to produce enriched uranium – located at Joliot's laboratory in the College de France in Paris. Because of the need for secrecy, it could not be used to the fullest extent to increase isotope separation in uranium. Speer offered to build cyclotrons to match the American ones, but Heisenberg said it would only be possible to use a relatively small type, because Germany lacked the experience to use them.

Despite this disappointing answer, Speer was not put off by Heisenberg's vagueness about the timescale; he knew scientists were like that. On the other hand, Hitler's armaments minister was cautious of whetting the Führer's appetite for a new weapon before being sure it could be delivered. There was no doubt in Speer's mind that if Hitler had an atomic weapon, he would use it against Churchill's little island. Speer recalled Hitler's excitement at seeing a German propaganda movie that ended with a montage of a plane diving towards the outlines of the British Isles; the islands erupted into a ball of fire. 'That is how we will annihilate them,' Hitler yelled. 'I am sure that Hitler would not have hesitated for a moment to employ atom bombs against England.'[4]

Speer, like most members of Hitler's inner circle, wanted to cover his own back against recriminations and he was acutely conscious of the risks involved. Once the Führer became excited by a project, he placed crazy demands on the armaments industry to produce it. Schumann confided to von Weizsäcker that if the Führer demanded the atom bomb in nine months and they could not deliver, it would be 'bad' for them all. Their fears were well founded. When he was in a rage, Hitler would strike at those closest to him. He operated like a Mafia boss – if you stepped out of line, you could be eliminated. Fromm was later executed for failing to stop the 20 July 1944 plot to assassinate Hitler. Speer cautiously doubted the Führer's mental capacity to understand the technology.

Speer reported to Hitler on the support his office was giving to the atomic scientists. Speer's Office Journal records their brief conversation on the 23 June 1942 *Führerprotokoll* (the minutes of Hitler's meetings): 'Reported briefly to the Führer on the conference on splitting the atom and on the backing we have given the project.' It was item sixteen on the agenda, and the only mention on record of atomic weapons being discussed with Hitler. The Führer made one of his little jokes – he told Speer his scientists might lay bare all the secrets of the universe only to turn Planet Earth into a new glowing star. Speer said Hitler did not relish the thought of ruling the world just when it became a supernova.

Heisenberg almost proved Hitler right when he returned to his laboratory in Leipzig. His assistant, Dopel, noticed that the experimental pile was acting strangely; a sphere containing uranium metal that had been in a tank of water for two weeks suddenly started releasing bubbles. He notified Heisenberg and interrupted him during an evening tutorial when he realised the sphere was becoming hotter and hotter. They were wondering what to do, when they saw the sphere shudder, and then start to swell. Both scientists ran for the exit as an explosion blasted burning uranium into the air. The fire brigade put out the fire, and covered the pit with a blanket of foam. It was a reminder about the dangers of pushing at the boundaries of known science.

Hitler accepted Speer's advice, and drew together the Army Ordnance Office uranium research programme of Schumann's team and uranium research in universities under Esau at the Ministry of Education. He gave Goering overall responsibility for the *Reichsforschungsrat,* the State Research Council. It was reconstituted with military chiefs, not scientists, but, crucially, it was scientists, not the military, who remained in charge of research in the laboratories. Heisenberg was promoted to replace Diebner as the full-time scientific head of atomic research at the Kaiser Wilhelm Institute. He moved from Leipzig to Berlin and sent his wife, Elisabeth, with their six children, his mother and a maid to their Bavarian summer house – a log cabin in the mountains overlooking a vast lake – for the duration of the war. A year later, Heisenberg persuaded Speer and Goering to replace Esau with his ally Gerlach as the plenipotentiary.

Heisenberg's promotion was seen as worrying evidence by Arthur H. Compton, the head of the Metallurgical Laboratory at the University of Chicago, that the Germans were stepping up the race. He wrote on 22 June 1942 to his friend, Dr Vannevar Bush, head of the US Scientific Research and Development Office, to alert the Roosevelt administration to the growing threat of Germany acquiring an atomic weapon. Compton, chair of a special committee set up by the National Academy of Sciences to investigate the prospects for the bomb, said he had heard that Heisenberg had been appointed director of the Kaiser Wilhelm Institute. Compton said his colleagues estimated that a German atomic bomb could be ready by December 1944 and urged Bush to warn the president of the need to move fast because of the fear that the Germans might be gaining a decisive lead in the nuclear race.

Dear Van,

We have recently become aware that the threat of German fission bombs is even more imminent than we supposed when I made my budget report to Mr Conant and Mr Briggs a month ago. This is because we have just recognised how a chain reaction started with a small heavy water plant can quickly supply material for a high power plant for producing 'copper' [American code name for plutonium]. If the Germans know what we know – and we dare not discount their knowledge – they should be dropping fission bombs on us in 1943, a year before our bombs are planned to be ready.[5]

There were three 'chances' for the US to avoid defeat, said Compton: complete domination of Germany before about June 1943, when they got the bomb; destruction of their fission plants by sabotage, air or commando raids; and to 'speed our schedule to beat theirs'. He urged Roosevelt to carry out destructive raids, accelerate the production of a US atomic bomb, and take urgent steps through the secret service to locate and disrupt Nazi bomb-making activities.

Groves was driving ahead with his own timetable for a US bomb. He convened a key meeting of the Military Policy Committee on 12 November and the S-1 committee – a Presidential advisory body on the bomb and successor to the Briggs committee – for two days later to thrash out the best route to the weapon from the competing options. It decided on the use of plutonium as the most promising path and gave the go-ahead to gaseous diffusion, the use of a full-scale reactor to produce plutonium, and electromagnetic separation, but dropped the centrifuge process. The official history of the Manhattan Project by the US Department of Energy says: 'Now that the committees had chosen which horses to back, the only things left to do were to get final presidential approval and to run the race.'

In London, little was known about the struggles going on inside the Third Reich's Uranium Club, or about the progress of the atomic bomb in the laboratories of Berlin. As in America, there was an assumption that if the Allies could make progress on splitting the atom, so could the Germans. Eric Welsh, the leading MI6 officer on the Tube Alloys project, recognised there were huge gaps in Allied intelligence about the Nazi bomb. He began drawing up a list of foreign scientists who could prove useful to the Third Reich. Top of his list was Niels Bohr in occupied Denmark. Welsh sent a message to Bohr at the end of March 1943, via a clandestine under-sea telephone cable to Malmö, southern Sweden. Captain Gyth, a member of a Swedish resistance cell called Prinserne (the Princess), told Bohr that arrangements would be made for him to escape to England. The scientist refused to discuss it without evidence that it was genuine.

Welsh came up with the idea of getting one of Bohr's old friends, Sir James Chadwick, then at Liverpool University, to write a letter to Bohr appealing to him to come to England. Chadwick had to be persuaded to write it by Welsh, who said the future of Britain depended on it. Chadwick's letter was, in the best spy tradition, put on a microdot and hidden inside the handle of a hollow door key by MI6, and delivered to Bohr through the Swedish underground.[6] Bohr carefully opened the key, read the message and replied by a microfilm letter that was carried in a courier's denture. When Welsh read it, he was astonished. Bohr refused.

Six months later, in September 1943, Bohr changed his mind after he had learned from resistance sources that he and his family were to be arrested in a round-up of Danish Jews. Bohr approached the Swedish resistance cell, and on 30 September he was smuggled to Limhamn on the Swedish coast in a fishing boat. On 12 October, Bohr was secretly flown to Britain from Bromma airport in a fast, low-level Mosquito to Scotland. He had to crouch in the bomb bay, with a parachute and instructions to jump if they were hit by enemy fire. He almost perished shortly after take-off because the flyer's helmet with an intercom he was given was too small for his unusually large forehead, raising the headphones above his ears. He was unable to hear the pilot telling him to switch on the oxygen to his mask as the plane climbed, and Bohr passed out. He only regained consciousness when they descended to land.

Having recovered, Bohr was entertained to a convivial dinner at the Savoy Grill on the Strand in London. Underlining his importance to the Allied war effort, Lieutenant Commander Welsh laid on the cream of British scientific intelligence for their Top Secret supper, including 'C', Sir Stewart Menzies, the head of SIS, Churchill's 'Prof' Lord Cherwell, Wallace Akers and Michael Perrin of Tube Alloys, Sir Charles Frank, R. V. Jones and Welsh. That night Bohr told them a curious story: that in the autumn of 1941 – as nuclear research was reaching a crisis in Germany – Heisenberg and von

Weizsäcker had secretly ventured to visit him in Copenhagen. Bohr claimed it was to enlist his help in solving the atomic problem of sustaining a chain reaction to create a bomb.

Bohr, fifty-five, was Heisenberg's mentor and a long-term family friend. Heisenberg had worked at Copenhagen University before the war; they had gone on long mountain walks and had gone skiing together; they had shared each other's family homes for convivial evenings.

Heisenberg and von Weizsäcker were attending a German cultural conference in the Danish city, but Heisenberg had an ulterior motive. He wanted to discuss with Bohr the growing likelihood that uranium could be harnessed to make a bomb of a type that the world had never known before. They never had a formal meeting with notes being taken, but they had plenty of opportunity for private conversations as they strolled the streets late at night to the tram stop where Heisenberg would catch a tram to his hotel. Exactly what was said between the two men has become wreathed in controversy and the mists of time. They came away with divergent views of the same conversations.

Bohr claimed Heisenberg was seeking to recruit him to the German war effort; Heisenberg claimed he was seeking Bohr's help in stopping the race to a nuclear bomb.

Whether Heisenberg was seeking Bohr's help to build the bomb or stop it, as Heisenberg claimed, has been the subject of heated controversy in the academic world ever since. Their dispute was turned into the absorbing play and a movie by Michael Frayn, *Copenhagen*. Heisenberg died on 1 February 1976, but his son, Jochen, began posting letters and Heisenberg's diary on the internet in 2002 to show his humanity, and contradict the claims by his critics, including those accusing him of being a hypocrite who wanted to build the atomic bomb but was incapable of doing so.[7]

The letters written by Heisenberg to his wife 'Li' during the disputed visit to Copenhagen certainly reveal a softer side to the man. They show Heisenberg met Bohr socially at least three times during his visit in the week of 15–21 September 1941. There are convivial evenings at the Bohrs' house at which Heisenberg plays Mozart on the piano and Bohr reads aloud. The implication is that this is hardly the behaviour of someone who is offended by his conversations with Heisenberg.

The Bohrs' occupied the 'honour house' at the Carlsberg brewery site. Even there it was difficult to escape reminders of the presence of their German overlords; the stone gates feature two elephants carrying a good luck symbol from India – the swastika.

In his letters home, Heisenberg painted a romantic picture to 'Li' of life in their old haunts in Copenhagen, where young people appeared happy despite the German warships in the harbour:

> This morning I was at the pier with von Weizsäcker, you know, there along the harbour where the Langelinie is [the pier, park and promenade where the Little Mermaid statue is situated]. Now there are German warships anchored there, torpedo boats, auxiliary cruisers and the like. It was the first warm day, the harbour and the sky above it tinted in a very bright, light blue. At the first light buoy near the end of the pier we stayed for a long look at life in the harbour.
>
> Two large freighters departed in the direction of Elsinore; a coal ship arrived, probably from Germany; two sailboats, about the size of the one we used to sail here in the past, were leaving the harbour, apparently on an afternoon excursion. At the pavilion on the Langelinie we ate a meal, all around us there were essentially only happy, cheerful people, at least it appeared that way to us. In general, people do look so happy here. At night in the streets one sees all these radiantly happy young couples, apparently going out for a night of dancing, not thinking of anything else. It is difficult to imagine anything more different than the street life over here and in Leipzig.

Being back in the city he had known fifteen years ago and hearing the bells from the tower of the Copenhagen city hall had reminded him of his youth. After arriving on Tuesday, he had addressed the Bohr Institute in Danish and had walked to the Bohrs' home late at night under a clear and starry sky. Mrs Bohr asked about Elisabeth and their children, and after midnight Bohr had walked with him to the tram accompanied by Bohr's son, Hans.

On Wednesday, the event Heisenberg had come to Copenhagen for – a lecture to the German Scientific Institute – took place. Heisenberg mentions that, sadly, the members of the Bohr Institute would not attend 'for political reasons' (he meant in protest at the German occupation) because after its founding 'a number of brisk militarist speeches on the New Order in Europe were given'.

On Thursday, Heisenberg returned to the Bohr home. The Bohrs had taken in a young English woman because she could not return to England. 'It is somewhat weird to talk with an English woman these days. During the unavoidable political conversations, where it naturally and automatically became my assigned part to defend our system, she retired, and I thought that was actually quite nice of her.'

On his last day in Copenhagen, Heisenberg went to a reception at the German embassy and then went on with von Weizsäcker to the Bohrs' home: 'In many ways, this was especially nice, the conversation revolved for a large part of the evening around purely human concerns, Bohr was reading aloud, I played a Mozart Sonata (A major). On the way home, the night sky was again star-studded. Two nights ago, a wonderful northern light was visible, the whole sky was covered with green, rapidly changing veils.'

Heisenberg avoided the censor reading his letters by not posting them until he got to Berlin. It can be assumed therefore that they are a fairly honest account of his visit to see Bohr, though you have to read between the lines to see Heisenberg signalling he was not signed up to Hitler's Nazi Party.

He was not deluded about the mood in the country. It was amazing, he said, given that the Danes were living totally unrestricted and exceptionally well, 'how much hatred or fear has been galvanized here, so that even a rapprochement in the cultural arena – where it used to be automatic in earlier times – has become almost impossible'. Bohr too did not conceal his hatred of the Nazi regime from his former colleague. 'I find it difficult that even a great man like Bohr cannot separate out thinking, feeling, and hating entirely,' said Heisenberg, 'But probably one ought not to separate these ever.'

The release of their letters in 2002 did not settle the argument; they added more fuel to the fire.

Von Weizsäcker later backed Heisenberg, saying their motive was peace: 'We had the common idea it would be good to prepare a talk to Bohr on the question of whether physicists all over the world might be able to agree not to make the bomb or at least not to hurry it during the war. We said there is one scientist who has the moral and intellectual authority for achieving such a thing and that is Bohr.'

Von Weizsäcker added: 'Quarter of an hour after the walk, Heisenberg saw me and said it was a complete failure. "When I spoke about the possibility of making nuclear weapons Bohr became so excited that he was not able to listen any more so what I really wanted to say never got uttered."'

Bohr saw the conversation completely differently. He became alarmed that Heisenberg was trying recruit him for the Nazi cause. Jens Bang of the Niels Bohr Institute said in 1992: 'We had been occupied for a year – we didn't want cooperation with Germany. Heisenberg was coming here seeking cooperation. We thought it was tactless.' Bang added: 'Bohr told me his impression was that Heisenberg was threatening not necessarily Bohr, but coming with threats. But mainly he [Heisenberg] said he was convinced Germany would win the war and that they were able to make this terrible bomb.'

This was partly corroborated by von Weizsäcker in 1992 in a television documentary. Von Weizsäcker said Heisenberg was convinced in 1939 that Hitler would lose the war: 'The war will not last very long. Hitler has got a game of chess with one castle less than the other side. He will lose the war and he will lose it within one year.'[8] He said it was therefore 'not dangerous' to engage in atomic research, because the war would be over before a bomb could be built. Von Weizsäcker said that, by late 1941, when most of Europe was under Hitler's control, Heisenberg changed his mind. He was convinced that Hitler would win, and quickly, but the prospects for atomic research were the same: Heisenberg thought the war would come to an end before a bomb could be produced. Heisenberg told von Weizsäcker: 'We will need the result of the work after the war especially on what we called the uranium machine, the reactor.'

Long after Bohr and Heisenberg were dead, their families issued more evidence to refute the other side's account and justify their own. The spur to set the record straight was the 1956 publication of a book by Swiss journalist Robert Jungk, *Brighter Than a Thousand Suns,* which supported Heisenberg's account, although Jungk later distanced himself from it.

Bohr, who died on 18 November 1962, was upset by the letters Heisenberg wrote to Jungk underlining his peaceful motives. In 2002, Bohr's family hit back by releasing letters Bohr had written to Heisenberg but had never sent. In one of his unposted letters, Bohr wrote to Heisenberg:

[I] got a completely different impression of the visit than the one you have described in Jungk's book. I remember quite definitely the course of these conversations, during which I naturally took a very cautious position, when (without preparation, immediately) you informed me that it was your conviction that the war, if it lasted sufficiently long, would be decided with atomic weapons, and [I did] not sense even the slightest hint that you and your friends were making efforts in another direction ... Weizsäcker expressed your definite conviction that Germany would win and that it was therefore quite foolish for us to maintain the hope of a different outcome of the war and to be reticent as regards all German offers of cooperation.[9]

Heisenberg had built an experimental pile – a cylindrical vessel containing layers of uranium and paraffin at his Leipzig laboratory – and, in the spring of 1941, a few months before their meeting, Heisenberg's research team had obtained evidence of neutron multiplication in a reactor that a chain reaction was possible. Despite Heisenberg's later insistence he was only interested in developing a nuclear reactor for energy production, German researchers established that it was possible that plutonium could be produced from a reactor, and that could provide the breakthrough to a nuclear bomb.[10]

Given that they were two of the sharpest brains in the world, it is perhaps surprising Bohr and Heisenberg could not agree on what was said at their meeting, but there were pressing reasons to keep their views vague. Heisenberg claimed he was frightened for his life. 'Because I knew Bohr was under surveillance by German political operatives and that statements Bohr made about me would most likely be reported back to Germany, I tried to keep the conversation at a level of allusions that would not immediately endanger my life.'

He said the key talk with Bohr took place on an evening walk in the city district near Ny-Carlsberg. It is easy to imagine the memory of the year-long inquiry by the SS into his activities still haunted him:

The conversation probably started by me asking somewhat casually whether it was justifiable that physicists were devoting themselves to the uranium problem right now during times of war, when one had to at least consider the possibility that progress in this field might lead to very grave consequences. Bohr immediately grasped the meaning of this question I gathered from his somewhat startled reaction.

He answered as far as I can remember with a counter question: 'Do you really believe one can utilise uranium fission for the construction of weapons?' I may have replied, 'I know that this is possible in principle, but a terrific technical effort might be necessary, which one can hope, will not be realised anymore in this war.' Bohr was apparently so shocked by this answer that he assumed I was trying to tell him Germany had made great progress towards manufacturing atomic weapons.

There was one more puzzling thing about their meeting: it is claimed by Bohr that Heisenberg gave him a sketch of 'a squarish box with sticks on top'. When it was studied, it was interpreted as a nuclear reactor with control rods, roughly resembling the pile he had built in Leipzig a few months before. Even the sketch has caused continuing controversy: some claimed Heisenberg was passing Bohr a crucial nuclear secret to warn the Allies that Germany was pursuing a nuclear weapon; others that he was trying to convince Bohr they were making substantial progress in Germany and it was futile to resist.

In his final letter home, Heisenberg wondered how the world would have changed when he returned to Copenhagen. 'That everything in the meantime will continue just the same, that the bells in the tower of the city hall will toll every hour and play the little melody at noon and midnight is so weird to me. Yet the people, when I return, will be older, the fate of each one will have changed, and I do not know how I myself will fare.'

The scientist Arnold Kramish, Paul Rosbaud's biographer, dismissed this rosy picture. He said that Heisenberg and von Wiezsacker had gone there to 'pick Bohr's brains' for the German atomic bomb.[11] Bohr appears to have been traumatised by their meeting. He was horrified that the technology he had helped create was now likely to be used to create a bomb of unimaginable destructive power.

A week after Bohr arrived in England, he was joined by his son Aage. They went on together to America, where they lived under aliases, as Nicholas and James Baker. Bohr Senior was warmly embraced by General Groves as the father of atomic science and shown the work of the Manhattan Project. He was praised for inspiring the team at Los Alamos and saw the fissile material being made at the Oak Ridge plant.

He lived up to the image of the absent-minded professor, puffing on his pipe, spraying matches, and damping down the dottle when he wanted to speak; he was amused and a little irritated to have a secret service agent as a bodyguard who slept next door, and was upset when he caused a minor security flap after he mislaid his briefcase and his wallet – there were no secrets in the bag, but Bohr's concern was that he was left with no dollars.

Bohr returned to London a year later, and wandered into a political minefield. Bohr had become alarmed – like many other scientists – at the prospect of the atomic bomb triggering a nuclear arms race between Russia and America. He discussed his anxieties with Lord Halifax, the British Ambassador to Washington, Sir Ronald Campbell, a senior staffer at the British Embassy, and a pre-war friend, US Supreme Court Judge, Mr Justice Frankfurter, who was also a friend of President Roosevelt. Bohr was encouraged to believe that the President shared Bohr's anxieties, something that was later confirmed in person when he met Roosevelt.

When he returned to London, Bohr believed he was on a mission with the backing of the President to persuade Churchill to agree to discuss an agreement with the President and Stalin to achieve international arms control over this frightening new generation of weapons. He had a powerful lobby supporting him including the Prime Minister of South Africa, Jan Smuts, who was an old friend of Churchill – he had been co-opted onto the war cabinet and was Churchill's choice to replace him, if he was killed in the war; Sir John Anderson who had ministerial responsibility for Tube Alloys; and Sir Henry Dale, the President of the Royal Society, who was a member of the Tube Alloys board and 'in' on the secret of the atomic bomb.

Smuts, who had been made a field marshal by Churchill, wrote to the Prime Minister from the South African Embassy saying Sir John Anderson and 'the Prof' – Lord Cherwell – had raised with him the issue of sharing the nuclear secret. 'I think you are quite right in not raising the matter with Stalin, at any rate at present,' Smuts wrote. But he warned the Prime Minister that the Manhattan Project could 'start the most destructive competition in the world' and urged Churchill to discuss the issue again with Roosevelt, 'especially the question whether Stalin should be taken into the secret'.

Sir Henry Dale wrote a letter in the most portentous terms to Churchill. Marked in ink 'Top Secret', on the red-headed notepaper of the Royal Society, Sir Henry wrote:

> I cannot avoid the conviction that science is even now approaching the realisation of a project which may bring either disaster

or benefit, on a scale hitherto unimaginable, to the future of mankind ... The devastating weapon of which the early realisation is now almost in view, must apparently put the power of world mastery into the hands having a one-side control of its use ... It may be in your power, even in the next six months, to take decisions which will determine the future course of human history.

R. V. Jones persuaded the 'Prof' to badger Churchill, who agreed to the meeting. Cherwell minuted Churchill:

You will recall that, at the suggestion of Field Marshal Smuts, you asked me to arrange for you to see Professor Niels Bohr, the eminent Danish Physicist. As Professor Bohr is due to leave for America on Tuesday night or Wednesday morning, this has been provisionally arranged for Tuesday at 3 o'clock.

You may recall that Professor Bohr was a leading pioneer on the theoretical scientific side of Tube Alloys. We brought him out of Denmark last year. For the last few months, he has been in the USA in connection with Tube Alloys and is very well informed about the whole project.

Churchill may have been misled by Lord Cherwell's note into thinking that the main reason for the meeting was so that Bohr could brief him on the Anglo-American bomb project. However, the files I uncovered in the National Archives in Kew show Bohr's agenda was purely about future international arms control.

Bohr and his son had been put up in a flat at St James's Court in Buckingham Gate, and were allowed contact with no one outside a small group of people. He was looked after by R. V. Jones, who tried to coach Bohr before the meeting on how to put his case to the Prime Minister, that the Russians would inevitably discover the secret of nuclear energy and it would be better for world peace if the Americans shared the secret of atomic power with them, so that it could be controlled.

R. V. Jones took Bohr to the office of Lord Cherwell, who went with Bohr to Downing Street for the meeting on 16 May 1944. It was just a month before the invasion of France with the Normandy landings. Churchill, who had plenty on his mind, was already in a bad mood – he famously suffered from depression that he referred to as the Black Dog – and the meeting went badly from the start. Churchill began bickering with Lord Cherwell about his criticism for signing the Quebec Agreement with President Roosevelt under which Britain gave up any claim to the commercial use of Tube Alloys – nuclear power – after the war in return for continued cooperation with America over the Manhattan Project. Bohr was unable to get his message across. What made matters worse was that Bohr was inclined to speak in whispers and made his set-speech diffidently, with qualifications and provisos that sapped Churchill's patience. Churchill gained the impression that Bohr was a muddle-headed liberal, only interested in Britain and America giving up all their nuclear secrets to the Russians.

Jones was walking along King Charles Street from the Air Ministry to MI6 headquarters at 54 Broadway when he saw Niels Bohr coming in the opposite direction, apparently in a daze. 'It was terrible!' Bohr told Jones. 'He scolded us like two schoolboys.'

In the resulting fallout from his meeting with Churchill, Bohr's allies blamed each other for the disaster. Jones blamed Lord Cherwell for inadequately briefing Churchill, because Lord Cherwell was not convinced nuclear energy would ever be released; Churchill was angry with his old friend for setting the meeting up.

Churchill wrote an intemperate note to Lord Cherwell saying he and the President were 'much worried about Professor Bohr ... He made an unauthorised disclosure to Chief Justice Frankfurter who startled the President by telling him he knew all the details.' Worse, said Churchill, Bohr had been in touch with a Russian physicist, Peter Kapitza, in London – Kapitza had sent Bohr a friendly letter via the Russian Embassy in London, urging him escape to Russia with his family. 'What is all this about?' Churchill asked the Prof. 'It seems to me Bohr ought to be confined or at any rate made to see that he is very near the edge of mortal crimes.'

Churchill also saw Bohr's intervention as a direct attack on the accord he had signed with Roosevelt in Quebec, which banned the disclosure of TA secrets to a third party. Churchill was anxious to hold the Americans to the Quebec Agreement because it promised long-term collaboration with the UK on atomic energy, and he did not want anything to disturb it. Bohr was now threatening to disrupt the agreement that Churchill had sweated to achieve.

Churchill had played heavily on the 'special relationship' between Britain and America to secure vital support from Roosevelt in the summer of 1940. RAF Spitfires and Luftwaffe Me 109s created vapour trails in dogfights in the skies over Kent as Sir Henry Tizard, the head of aeronautical science at the Air Ministry, sailed to America from Liverpool to secure armaments – US warships and bombers, fighters and tanks – from the Roosevelt administration to ensure the survival of Britain as an independent country. In return, Churchill was prepared to offer Roosevelt a treasure trove of secret gadgets from Britain's 'boffins'. Tizard carried Britain's secrets in a black metal deed box. Tizard's 'little black box' contained blueprints and circuit diagrams for rockets, explosives, superchargers, gyroscopic gun sights, submarine detection devices, self-sealing fuel tanks and theoretical ideas that would lead to the jet engine and the atomic bomb.[12]

The box and its priceless contents were looked after by another member of the Tizard mission, Edward Bowen, who watched helplessly at Euston Station when it was carried off by a helpful railway porter for the boat train to Liverpool. To his relief, it was delivered safely and given an armed guard from Liverpool Lime Street station to the Liverpool docks, where they embarked for Halifax, Canada, before travelling on to Washington.

By far the most important of the contents of Tizard's 'black box' was a cavity magnetron, which was hailed as the second most important discovery of the war after the atomic bomb. It had been developed almost by accident by two Birmingham scientists, John Randall and Henry Boot. They had produced a small valve that could emit powerful pulses of microwaves – the same technology used today in microwave ovens – which provided the key to developing airborne radar small enough to place in aeroplanes. One US historian said it was the 'most valuable cargo ever brought to our shores'. Tizard's black box of tricks helped to open the door to Anglo-American cooperation on the bomb.

But cooperation with Britain broke down after the Americans realised they had quickly overtaken the British, who appeared to some – led by General Groves, the head of the US Manhattan Project – to be hitching a free ride for the exploitation of nuclear power after the war at America's expense. The British had been reluctant to surrender the work on the bomb to America, despite being keen on cooperation. Lord Cherwell had written a complacent note to Churchill saying: 'However much I may trust my neighbour and depend on him, I am very much averse to putting myself completely at his mercy and would therefore not press the Americans to undertake this work; I would just continue exchanging information and get into production over here without raising the question of whether they should do it or not.'

There was a period of silence from the Americans on cooperation, as Groves threw America's industrial weight behind the nuclear bomb project. The British became alarmed that America would go ahead without them. Sir John Anderson advised Churchill to support the building of a pilot diffusion plant for separating enriched uranium in America using British research: 'We must face the fact that the pioneer work done in this country is a dwindling asset and that, unless we capitalise it quickly, we shall be rapidly outstripped.'[13] Groves was instrumental in resisting sharing secrets with British scientists in the UK on the grounds of the need for security, urging a 'need to know' basis, and it was to cause a lasting rift with the British.

According to his biographer Robert S. Norris, Groves was an 'Anglophobe' who was suspicious of British motives. This was a view the young Leslie Richard Groves had inherited from his father, a US Chaplain, who was a witness of British imperialism in Peking in the 'Boxer Rebellion' of 1900. Dick – as the general was known to his family – grew up believing everything the British did was for selfish reasons, to gain advantage for the British Empire.[14]

When it came to cooperation with the British on the atomic bomb, 'Dick' Groves followed his father and did not trust most of them an inch. Groves believed the Brits' contribution to the atomic bomb was minuscule compared to the massive amount of money and materiel invested in the development of the bomb by the United States, and they could not expect to be treated as equal partners. He was also convinced they wanted to gain a commercial advantage in atomic reactors when the war was over.

General Groves believed Churchill was trying to protect ICI and British commercial interests after the war, fuelled by the fact that both Wallace Akers and Michael Perrin were from ICI. They even had a map of ICI offices around Britain on the wall when Tube Alloys opened in Old Queen Street. Groves objected to Akers going to the States in a British delegation because he was an ICI man before the war.

To put those suspicions to bed and restore cooperation, Churchill effectively signed a blank cheque to the Americans, giving up Britain's interests in the commercial use of atomic energy. The Quebec agreement said: 'The Prime Minister expressly disclaims any interest in these industrial and commercial aspects beyond what may be considered fair and just and in harmony with the economic welfare of the world.'

R. V. Jones was aghast when he learned the terms of the agreement. He said Churchill had 'given away our birthright in the post-war development of nuclear energy' to the Americans. He immediately called on Lord Cherwell to upbraid him for giving Churchill such bad advice. It was over this that Churchill and the Prof argued when Bohr went to Downing Street.

Churchill himself recognised that history might judge him harshly. In a memorandum I found in the Prime Minister's Cabinet papers, he admitted: 'In after years this may be judged to have been too confiding on our part. Only those who know the circumstances and moods prevailing beneath the Presidential level will be able to understand why I have made this agreement … I have no fear that they will maltreat us or cheat us.'[15]

On 31 May 1944, a few days before D-Day, a Top Secret memo was sent by Sir Ronald Campbell from the British Embassy in Washington to Sir John Anderson, the Chancellor of the Exchequer and chief negotiator on TA with the Americans, raising concern that Groves was insisting that none of the 'final military product' – weapons-grade enriched uranium or plutonium – should be sent to the UK, because of the risk of attack from Germany, and it should be restricted instead to Canada where the French team under von Halban had gone.

'In addition to overt arguments arising from security and worry about congressional investigations, we note a natural but increasing sense of American self-confidence and buoyancy as to their ability to carry through this project,' wrote Campbell. Some Americans had a growing sense of anxiety about their ability to play their 'just role' in international affairs, he added, but on the part of the others, 'There is certainly evidence of a thought that this weapon can be kept [in] a tight monopoly and can thus give the maximum protection to America.' He was clearly referring to General Groves.

To clear the air, a year after the Quebec conference, Churchill and Roosevelt held another meeting on 18 September 1944 at the President's Federal-style residence at Hyde Park, on the Springwood estate in New York State. It is the house where Roosevelt was born and is now the FDR Museum.

Emphasising the friendly nature of the meeting, the President and the Prime Minister got down to business in a private tête-à-tête without note-takers before a convivial lunch. The lunch party included Churchill's wife Clementine and his private physician Lord Moran. Edward, Duke of Windsor, the former king who had abdicated over his love for the American divorcée Mrs Simpson, was also there. A Nazi sympathiser, the duke had been packed off by Churchill to act as governor of Bermuda to avoid further embarrassment for Britain over his contacts with the Third Reich, but he was a fascinating celebrity in the US and Churchill knew he was popular with the Americans.

There was no official record, and no formal 'agreement', but an aide-memoire was circulated later by Churchill's office. Groves and Henry Stimson, the US Secretary of War, later disputed the British account of the meeting until their copy was found among US naval papers where it had been misfiled because someone thought 'Tube Alloys' concerned the navy. The Premier's papers in the National Archives at Kew include the original British version of their conversation. They rejected Bohr's appeal for the nuclear secret to be shared with the Soviet Union and reaffirmed America's and Britain's continued cooperation after the war on nuclear energy:

1. The suggestion, that the world should be informed regarding Tube Alloys [nuclear weapons] with a view to an international agreement regarding its control and use, is not accepted. The matter should continue to be regarded as of the utmost secrecy but when a bomb is finally available it might perhaps, after mature consideration, be used against the Japanese who should be warned that this bombardment will be repeated until they surrender.

2. Full collaboration between the United States and the British Government in developing Tube Alloys for military and commercial purposes should continue after the defeat of Japan unless and until terminated by joint agreement.[16]

Under item number three, they added: 'Enquiries should be made regarding the activities of Professor Bohr and steps taken to ensure that he is responsible for no leakage of information, particularly to the Russians.'[17]

9

The Bastard Mission

Colonel Boris T. Pash watched the sinking sun casting its glow over the Golden Gate Bridge from the windows of his office in Presidio, San Francisco, with a heavy heart.

It was 19 November 1943, seven days off Thanksgiving, and his wife Lydia had suggested having some friends over for the traditional turkey roast. The day before, he had received a telephone call from Washington, saying he was being ordered overseas with immediate effect.

Pash, aged forty-five, was one of the most senior intelligence officers involved in the American atomic bomb programme and, a year ago, he had missed Thanksgiving because he had been battling gales in the frozen wastes of Alaska on another mission. He had yet to break the news to Lydia that he was going to miss another Thanksgiving supper.

He had just returned from Washington where he had been appointed by Major General George V. Strong, chief of Army Intelligence, and General Leslie Richard Groves, head of the Manhattan Project, to command a new intelligence unit in Europe when the invasion took place. He would be in charge of a small, highly mobile military and scientific task force with a Top Secret mission: to seize Hitler's atomic scientists and their nuclear secrets. It was code-named the Alsos Mission because in Greek, *alsos* means a grove. The humour was lost on General Groves, and Pash, anxious not to give any clues about the nature of the mission on the Nazi atomic programme, also disapproved of its punning reference to his boss. He would have to live with it. Major General Strong sent a memorandum to General George C. Marshall, the US Army Chief of Staff, setting out the mission: 'The scope of inquiry should cover all principal scientific military developments, and the investigations should be conducted in a manner to gain knowledge of enemy progress without disclosing our interest in any particular field.'

Pash had one other reservation he would have to live with. The mission's objectives were set in Washington, but its logistics were dictated by commanders in the field. As such, he said, it was a 'bastard' mission that he knew nobody liked. He knew he would encounter stiff resistance once he got to France, and it would not all be coming from the Nazis.

Groves was giving the job to someone he knew he could trust. Pash was FBI-trained and had won a reputation among the intelligence fraternity as a 'Commie' hunter; he had just led a successful counter-espionage investigation for Groves to uncover a Soviet spy ring involved in the Manhattan Project in Ernest Lawrence's Radiation Laboratory at the University of California in Berkeley. As part of his investigation, Pash interrogated J. Robert Oppenheimer, the scientific genius at the head of the Manhattan Project. Pash cleared Oppenheimer of spying but left lasting doubts about his Communist sympathies – and a clandestine recording of his damaging evasions, which came back to haunt Oppenheimer during the witch-hunts for 'Commies' in the 1950s led by Republican Senator Joseph McCarthy.

Pash was a man after Groves's heart. Groves was the son of a Presbyterian minister in the US Army. Pash was the son of a Russian Orthodox priest. Both Pash and Groves were tough, uncompromising, no-nonsense army men with a phobia of Soviet-style Communism. Pash was born Boris Theodorovich Pashkovsky in San Francisco on 20 June 1900. His father, the Metropolitan bishop of the Eastern Orthodox Church in North America, was recalled to Russia and in 1912, as Russia headed for revolution, Pash sailed with his family for the mother country to join his father. He was educated at a Russian seminary, graduating at seventeen just a few months before the October Revolution, and joined the navy on the side of the White Russians against the Bolsheviks. Three years later, he married Lydia Vladimirovna Ivanov while working for the American Red Cross in Sevastopol. He escaped to Germany with his wife as the Bolsheviks consolidated their power and got a job with the YMCA in Berlin, where his son, Edgar Constantine Boris Pashkovsky, was born in 1921. He returned to America with his wife and son in 1923 and went back to college at

Springfield, Massachusetts, where he gained a Bachelor of Arts in physical education and shortened his name to Pash.

He became a physical training instructor at the Hollywood High School in Los Angeles where he remained for almost two decades. When he was called up for active duty in June 1940, he was already an officer in the Military Intelligence Reserve, having been involved in the internment of Japanese nationals as enemy aliens which deprived Hollywood of its gardeners. By the time America entered the war, Pash had become head of counter-intelligence at the Army Ninth Corps Area headquarters in Presidio, responsible for the Western defence of America from Alaska to California. He was athletic, bespectacled, and sharp. At the start, Pash was determined to keep the Alsos team like himself, small and nimble – not more than six scientists, six Counter-Intelligence Corps (CIC) agents, six interpreters. Pash was allowed to take with him his trusted executive officer, George Eckman, a former newspaper man, and he was given four scientists picked by Dr Bush at OSRD: Dr James Fisk of Bell Telephone Company, a physicist; Dr John Johnson of Cornell University; Navy Commander Bruce Olds who had been at the Massachusetts Institute of Technology and was serving with the Office of Naval Research and Development; and Army Major William Allis, another MIT professor serving with the War Department's scientific staff.

The Alsos team would be lightly armed with pistols and machine guns, travelling mostly in Jeeps for speed of response to changing circumstances. It also became known as 'Lightning A' after a wisecrack by one of Pash's Jeep drivers, Gerry Beatson, about the speed with which they hit Paris. By March 1945, however, the team in Paris had been expanded to thirty-three with an enlarged scientific support team.[1]

The first Alsos mission to Italy, following the liberation of Rome in June 1944, was a failure. Pash and the Alsos team found nothing of importance about German scientific advances, apart from a German glider-bomb. It was not entirely a wasted time for Pash, however, who returned to London with four enterprising CIC agents he had met at a raucous Christmas party in Naples: Ralph Cerame from Rochester, New York, who was fluent in Italian; Carl Fiebig of Sebewing, Michigan, a German linguist; Gerry Beatson, from Rockford, Illinois who was made Pash's 'trigger man' because he had experience in combat; and Perry Bailey, a tall blond easy-going agent who Pash described as an 'energetic American boy – a fine product of our education and our way of life'.[2] They would be useful when the Alsos mission joined the Allied invasion of France.

To prepare for the next lap of the race to beat the Germans, Pash returned to Washington where he was introduced to Samuel A. Goudsmit – a Dutch-American atomic physicist approved by Groves – at a meeting in Vannevar Bush's office. Pash was told Goudsmit, who had been trained in forensic policing, was going to be the new head of the scientific team when Alsos moved into Europe. Goudsmit joked to Groves that parachuting behind enemy lines or facing enemy fire at the age of forty-one was not his idea of recreation; at forty-three, a similar thought had occurred to Pash and they hit it off. Pash told Groves he could work with Goudsmit.[3]

Goudsmit, another MIT man, had a personal reason for wanting to do all he could to destroy Hitler's Nazi Third Reich: in the past few months, he had received a letter from his Jewish parents, saying they were being rounded up from the family home in the Netherlands and transported to a concentration camp. He never saw them again. He did not know it at that time, but they were to be exterminated in a Nazi gas chamber.

Within days of his appointment, Goudsmit sent a memorandum to the army intelligence chief, Colonel C. P. Nicholas, a professor of mathematics who would later become a director of the CIA, setting out his thoughts on his mission. He supplied a target list of scientists already in the US who 'must possess valuable intelligence' about atomic research, including Niels Bohr, then in New York, and said a list of more names of scientists in enemy territory was being drawn up by the Harvard Defense Group. Key industrial targets in Europe for the Alsos team included the Dutch Philips Lamp Works and Dutch Shell.

Underlining Groves's distrust of the British, Pash was given specific orders by Groves not to disclose the information they collected to anyone – including the British – except for General Eisenhower or his Chief of Staff, General W. Bedell Smith.

In late 1943, Groves sent one of his most trusted intelligence officers, Major Robert R. Furman, to London to set up a liaison office with British intelligence officers connected with the British atomic bomb programme for cooperation on the forthcoming Alsos mission.

At his first meeting with Lieutenant Commander Eric Welsh and Michael Perrin, the two leading British intelligence men attached to Tube Alloys, Furman gave the impression the Americans were a long way behind British intelligence on the German bomb programme. Welsh and Perrin were so pleased they were going to be the senior partners, they shook hands after Furman left.

That impression ended in January 1944, when Furman returned to Washington to act as General Groves's personal assistant for the Alsos mission and Groves sent Horace K. 'Tony' Calvert as his replacement in London. Calvert was Groves's Chief of Intelligence and Security at Oak Ridge, Tennessee, where the Top Secret uranium refining plants for the Manhattan Project were based. He was told to prepare the ground for the Alsos mission in London with Captain George C. Davis, three WACs and two Counter-Intelligence Corps (CIC) agents.

Calvert's task was to draw together all the known intelligence on German uranium research from the British using the links established by Furman with Perrin and Welsh. It soon became clear to Welsh and Perrin that the Americans were going to be firmly in the driving seat, and the British intelligence team would have to lobby to join the Alsos mission as junior partners. R. V. Jones later accused Welsh of seeking influence with the Americans by rolling over before them.

In May 1944, 'C', Sir Stewart Menzies, appointed Welsh to take the lead at MI6 on scientific intelligence on TA, relegating R. V. Jones to a support role on atomic research. Welsh's determination to elbow Jones and his assistant, the scientist Sir Charles Frank, aside led to lasting animosity with Jones, who later complained the true reason for separating off atomic intelligence had more to do with 'personal motives and ambitions of those who jumped on the atomic bandwagon and who wanted to keep everybody else off. Maybe they thought they alone were fit enough to be entrusted with the awesome responsibility of atomic developments or maybe they had less worthy motives.'[4] He clearly meant Welsh.

Unlike the more direct Jones, Welsh was an astute player of power games in Whitehall. He had 'the ear' of 'C' and was also credited with a sort of 'feminine intuition' that allowed him to rely on his hunches.[5] After the war, Welsh eclipsed Jones and took the lead on atomic intelligence in Britain as head of D.At.En. (In) (Directorate of Atomic Energy Intelligence) in charge of a small, highly secret team of analysts with ready access to 'C' and the Joint Intelligence Committee. His unit was housed on the fourth floor of the Ministry of Supply in the Shell-Mex building in the Strand and surrounded in mystique. Its office was known as 'the Cage', because entry from the elevator was through an entry gate manned by an armed guard.

Calvert's first call was on Colonel George Conrad, head of US army intelligence for ETOUSA (European Theatre of Operations,

United States of America) in London. Calvert, an oilman and a lawyer in peacetime, was not used to military 'bull' and shook Conrad by the hand instead of saluting him. Despite this lack of military formality, Conrad – who had been roommates with Groves at West Point – arranged for Calvert to have a desk in his office at 31 Davies Street behind the US Embassy.

He was given diplomatic cover by John Gilbert Winant, the US Ambassador to London, as an Assistant Military Attaché with a desk at the US Embassy, where he could see raw intelligence data crossing the US desk. Winant is credited with shifting the US stance in London from broadly pro-appeasement by his predecessor Joe Kennedy to solid support for Churchill's war strategy. He committed suicide by shooting himself in the head in his office in 1947 after suffering depression over debts, a broken marriage, and an alleged affair with Sarah Churchill, the Prime Minister's daughter.

Calvert was also given a desk at the Tube Alloys office in Old Queen Street, around the corner from the MI6 headquarters in Broadway Buildings, to encourage him to share intelligence reports with the British when they were sent to Washington. One of his key British contacts was the aforementioned Sir Charles Hambro, the former head of SOE, and Churchill's go-between on intelligence on TA with the Americans.

Calvert's cable messages to and from Washington were in a Top Secret code – 'New York' was uranium, 'Indiana' was plutonium, 'Nevada' was British Intelligence. He reported back that 'Nevada' had no hard evidence about plants where the Germans could be manufacturing 'Indiana' or the progress they had made. Welsh and R. V. Jones at MI6 judged the paucity of intelligence on a Nazi bomb was proof Hitler's Uranium Club had made little progress. Groves was unimpressed. 'We were truly in the dark then about their progress in atomic development,' said Groves.[7]

Groves was particularly worried about rumours circulating occupied Europe that Hitler had a secret weapon that he would unleash against the invaders when D-Day got underway. A German paper that came into allied hands indicated that nuclear reactors might be used to spread radioactivity. Groves knew the Germans could produce a 'dirty bomb' without the mighty industrial effort he had overseen in the Manhattan Project. It would take a primitive reactor, some uranium-235, and a couple of capable chemists to produce plutonium, which could be laid down in front of the US and Allied forces to stop them breaking out of the bridgehead.

I found similar fears had secretly been raised with Churchill as early as 10 January 1944. The Prime Minister minuted Lord Cherwell:

> In conversation yesterday General [Jacob] Devers [later chief of the US Sixth Army Group] spoke to me about the possibilities of a German bomb which emitted some liquid starting radioactivity over an area which might be two miles square, causing nausea and death and making the area unapproachable. He said the Americans had made many experiments in this direction and that perhaps the Germans had now achieved success ... All this seemed very fruity. I do not know whether he is mixing up the possible after-effects of an explosion on the lines of [John] Anderson's affair (I have forgotten the code-name). Anyhow I mention it to you in case you have heard anything about it.'[8]

Cherwell replied to Churchill on 21 January with a note headed 'Tube Alloys' – the code name which Churchill had forgotten:

> Some months ago, the Americans warned us that they thought that, although the Germans were probably not yet in sight of getting 25 or 49 [code numbers for nuclear materials], they might have obtained highly radioactive products [plutonium] which would be much easier to produce and which could be spread as a sort of super-poison gas. I imagine General Devers' anxieties refer to this.
>
> Sir John Anderson and his advisers went into this and came to the conclusion that it was most improbable that the Germans were working along these lines. Field Marshal Dill was asked on 6 January to explain this to the Americans.
>
> Incidentally C.I.G.S. [Chief of the Imperial General Staff, Field Marshal Sir Alan Brooke] told me that General Eisenhower had mentioned something of the same sort to him and I suggest he might talk to the Chancellor [Sir John Anderson] about it.

Churchill scribbled a note in red ink on the memorandum saying: 'Watch it, and tell me.'[9] It was no wonder Churchill was concerned. He had been prepared ruthlessly to unleash poison gas on the beaches of England against Hitler's forces if they had invaded in 1940. His shocked private secretary, John Colville, noted in his diary: 'He considers that gas warfare would be justified in such an event. The other day, he said to General Thorne (commanding forces south of the

Thames) "I have no scruples except not to do anything dishonourable" and I suppose he does not consider gassing Germans dishonourable.'[10]

Field Marshall Sir John Dill, the British defence chief in Washington, penned a sceptical note on behalf of the British Government expressing doubts based on SIS intelligence about the plutonium threat to Groves; but Groves was still unimpressed by British intelligence. He fired back his riposte to Dill on 17 January 1944:

> We agree that the use of a T.A. weapon is unlikely. The indirect and negative evidence developed by your agencies to date is in support of this conclusion. But we also feel that as long as definite possibilities exist which question the correctness of this opinion in its entirety or in part we cannot afford to accept it as a final conclusion. Repeated reports that the enemy has sufficient raw material and the fact of the early interest of enemy scientists in the problem must be explained away before we can safely disregard the possible use of this weapon.[11]

Groves took his concerns to General George C. Marshall, the US Chief of Staff at the War Department in Washington, on 22 March 1944. It was Groves's usual practice to encapsulate his thoughts in a memorandum, and he handed it to Marshall as he sat down. There were two blunt points:

1. Radioactive materials are extremely effective contaminating agents; are known to the Germans; can be produced by them and could be employed as a military weapon. These materials could be used without prior warning in combating an allied invasion of the Western European Coast.
2. It is the opinion of those most familiar with the potentialities of these materials that they are not apt to be used, but a serious situation would occur should any units of an invading Army be subjected to the tarrying effects of radioactive materials.[12]

Marshall agreed with Groves they had to alert the Allied Supreme Commander in England, Dwight D. Eisenhower – 'Ike' – about the risk, but decided the warning would have to be delivered in person. They sent a senior officer from the Manhattan Project to inform Ike face-to-face. The Supreme Commandeer took the advice and decided to keep it secret. Ike told Marshall: 'Owing to the importance of maintaining secrecy to avoid a possible scare, I have passed this information to a very limited number of persons;

moreover, I have not taken those precautionary steps which would be necessary adequately to counter enemy action of this nature.'[13]

Ike was taking a huge gamble with Overlord, the battle plan for the Normandy invasion, if it had gone wrong. Groves took the precaution of issuing some units with Geiger counters but it was a huge relief to the US high command that, when they hit the beaches on 6 June 1944, their troops encountered no clouds of radioactive poison.

The relief was short-lived. On 10 June 1944, at Prisoner of War camp No. 11 England (a stately home called Trent Park, at Enfield, North London) the following conversation between two captured German officers, *Generalmajor* A 1201 (in charge of Air Defences Tunis, captured in Tunisia on 9 May 1943) and Oberst M 513 (Regimental Commander of the 954 GR, 362 Division, captured in Italy on 23 May 1944) was overheard by the 'listeners' – the British intelligence team of MI19 eavesdroppers under Colonel Thomas Kendrick, who had bugged the house where they were being held from a listening post called the M Room:

A 1201: Are people's hopes still primed to an imaginary 'secret weapon' of some kind or another?

M 513: There is a lot of talk about it. It is a tremendously discussed topic. It was that everlasting talk of retaliation. 'Retaliation' is the most often used word in Germany. Wherever you go you hear: 'Retaliation', nothing but 'Retaliation'. I believe it was a great psychological mistake to use that word. It spread like wildfire and now everyone is expecting the retaliation.

A 1201: What is it to consist of?

M 513: Well, the wildest rumours are circulating.

A 1201: For instance, what?

M 513: Rockets, the splitting of the atom –

A 1201: Remote ignition and all those Jules Verne stories?

M 513: Yes, Jules Verne, good and proper.

M 514: I take it that it will come as a secret form of retaliation, and will be in connection with the invasion. It won't take place before then.[14]

The bugged conversation was transmitted to Major Robert Furman, Groves's top intelligence officer at the War Department in Washington, by British intelligence on 22 June. It fuelled Groves's nightmare that the Germans could use a plutonium 'dirty' bomb at any stage of their retreat. It was to haunt him until the war in Europe was won.

10

The Wild Bunch

The rumour mill about the Nazi atomic bomb was in overdrive in 1944 as US and Allied forces smashed their way out of the Normandy bridgehead in Operation Overlord. Among Pash's papers at the Hoover Institution Archives in Stanford, California, I found a cutting from the *Daily Mail Continental Edition* published in Paris on 4 October 1944 carrying the headline: 'Atom Bomb is Hitler's Latest V Weapon'.[1] Atomic bombs had already been tested by the Nazis, claimed the newspaper. 'Mysterious explosions which have been seen 80 miles away from the Danish island of Bornholm are now fairly conclusively established as being caused by atom-bombs.'

Two days later, the same newspaper ran a headline: 'Germans Decide V-2 has failed, Dutch-based weapon "too inaccurate", Atom-Bomb is their next hope …' The report underneath said: 'Germany's V-2 weapon has been in operation and has proved a complete failure. A neutral observer who has served in the German Army and has just arrived in Sweden told me this today. Its failure, he added, has caused Hitler to issue fresh instructions to his scientists to speed up their efforts to perfect V-3 – the atomic bomb.'

Groves and Pash must have been unsettled by such wild reports. The Alsos team checked out the claims of 'mysterious explosions' and found them to be false. As early as December 1943, Pash had sent to Colonel John Lansdale at the Pentagon building a copy of a Newsweek editorial posing the question: 'Can the Nazis "Blow up half the globe"?' A year later, they could still not answer the question posed by Newsweek. The plutonium scare before D-Day served to highlight a gaping hole in US and British intelligence – they still had little hard intelligence about how far Hitler's scientists had progressed with the atom bomb. It was now down to Pash and his mission to provide the answers.

Pash carried with him a letter from Henry Stimson, the US Secretary of War, addressed to Dwight D. Eisenhower, Commanding General US Army Forces, European Theatre of Operations, London, stating that Pash's mission was of extreme urgency and overriding priority, with the clear emphasis that it had the backing of the President.

Dated 11 May 1944, Stimson told 'Ike': 'Lt. Colonel Boris T. Pash who will deliver this letter has been designated Chief of the Scientific Intelligence Mission organised by G-2 [military intelligence] of the War Department to procure intelligence of the enemies' scientific developments ... I consider it to be of the highest importance to the war effort ... your assistance is essential and I hope that you will give Colonel Pash every facility and assistance at your disposal which will be necessary and helpful in the successful operation of this mission.'

It was accompanied by a detailed memorandum, also marked secret, giving Pash and the head of a separate scientific team carte blanche to travel in Europe, once the Normandy invasion had taken place: 'The mission will proceed to various theatres at times to be determined by A. C. of S. G-2 [Assistant Chief of Staff, Army Intelligence, Major General Kenneth Strong] with the advice of the Advisory Committee. The mission will follow the advance of Allied forces who occupied the territory, remaining the necessary time after the enemy's defeat and making necessary visits and contacts in order to collect intelligence of the enemy's scientific developments.'

Pash was designated 'chief of the mission' with the final say over determining targets by Major General Strong, a senior British army intelligence chief at Eisenhower's Allied Force HQ, and an advisory committee comprising the Director of Naval Intelligence (Rear Admiral Roscoe E. Schuirmann), the Director of the Office of Scientific Research and Development (Vannevar Bush), and the Commanding General Army Service Forces in charge of logistics (Lieutentant General Brehon B. Somervell).

He brought Eckman, Beatson and Fiebig to London with Major Richard 'Dick' C. Ham, his chief investigative officer from his US headquarters, and Captain Robert Blake as his operations manager. Lieutenant Reginald Augustine was drafted in from an Air Corps base in Arkansas for his linguistic skills in French and German.

Pash's priority as the Allies rolled back the German occupation of northern France was to track down the French scientist Frederic Joliot and his laboratory at the College de France in Paris. He hoped Joliot would be able to shed some light on the Nazi atomic research programme because it was known that scientists from Hitler's Uranium Club had been working at his laboratory through the German occupation of Paris. General Groves and Pash were highly suspicious of Joliot because he was a known Communist. Pash had received intelligence reports stating that Joliot was seen recently at his summer home near l'Arcouest, on the Brittany coast of France, within striking distance of the invasion. Pash pinpointed the town on a borrowed British map. It was a small coastal town on the bulge of Brittany jutting into the English Channel and over 300 kilometres from the bridgehead beaches.

Pash had to wait through the rest of June and the whole of July after the Normandy landings before he was able to put his plans into effect. At last, on 9 August 1944, just over two months after Overlord started, Pash landed with Gerry Beatson in a courier plane at an improvised landing strip at Omaha Beach, where the 1st and 29th US Infantry Divisions and the Rangers had taken heavy casualties.

They headed towards their target in a Jeep through a landscape that bore the scars of battle. French civilians appeared to be in shock, still wandering aimlessly weeks after the battle. The fighting was raging inland as General Patton's Third Army pushed south towards Rennes and west towards Dinan. With Beatson at the wheel of their Jeep, Pash and Beatson drove thirty miles to the Twelfth Army Group (Forward), where they found Brigadier General Eddie Sibert in a G-2 US Army intelligence van concealed in a forest, leaning over a map. Sibert was listening to a report from one of his officers. When he received Pash's request for help to reach the Joliot house, Sibert said they would have to go through Oscar Koch at Third Army Headquarters and scribbled Pash a note. It said: 'Lt. Col. Pash, Infantry, AGO Card A-126044, is travelling for G-2, War Department, in the interests of technical developments. It is requested that he be given every assistance and freedom of action within the areas under the control of your headquarters. Signed: E. L. Sibert.'

Before dawn the next day, Pash and Beatson headed for Avranches. They could not miss the signs of General Patton's advance among the deadly bocage of Normandy, the narrow lanes with steep banks topped by hedges that became a killing ground for Patton's tanks; they came across the hulks of burnt-out American Sherman tanks and half-tracks and then the German 88 mm gun – an anti-aircraft gun that was converted into an anti-tank weapon – or the feared heavy Tiger Panzer tank that had been used in the ambush, before it too was destroyed by Patton's implacable advance.

It was heavy going and dangerous for Pash and Beatson; the roads were slippery with rain, and when they encountered Patten's Seventh Armoured Division heading towards the combat zone, Beatson had to drive the Jeep up the muddy banks to avoid the tracked vehicles. The journalist Bob Traynor of the *Los Angeles Times* had been killed a few weeks before when his Jeep was dragged under the slipping tracks of a tank. At night they could barely see the road because of the need to use 'cat's eyes' covers over their headlights, leaving just a slit of light on each. Sometimes it was only the hedges that kept them from sliding off the road.

When they reached Koch's headquarters at Lucky Forward, they were told that the way to the coast of Brittany had not yet been cleared. The Germans still held strong points at Brest and St Malo, and the bulge in the north of Brittany, where they were headed, was still in German hands. It would take several days before the coast was clear, so Pash returned to London where the team was expanded with more military specialists, including Colonel Martin C. Chittick of the Chemical Warfare Service. He had been Director of Research for Sun Oil in civilian life.

While in London, Pash found British intelligence led by Welsh and Perrin 'were trying to grab the initiative' over the pursuit of the German nuclear programme, but he put up resistance and left George Eckman, his office manager, to fight the corner for Alsos in the Combined Intelligence Objectives Subcommittee (CIOS) which set out the key intelligence targets.

When he returned to Valognes in France on 14 August, Pash found Beatson eager to get going in the Jeep because he had secured enough petrol in jerry cans and wanted to move before it could be pilfered. They moved out at 4 a.m. the next day and pushed once more through the detritus of war towards Major General Ernest's Task Force A, which was tasked with clearing German resistance from the north coast of Brittany. They found Ernest near Lezardieux as German resistance began to crumble, allowing the armour to push forward. They paused overnight in an orchard and early the next day joined the armoured push for Paimpol, near their target area. Pash was astonished by the apathy of the local men, who showed no interest in joining the fight against the

Germans, but the mood quickly changed at Paimpol, where Task Force A was greeted by jubilant French townspeople and Pash's Jeep was decorated with flowers by women, old men and children.

L'Arcouest was a small village above a fishing port, which came to a dead end with a large stone house by the sea. On the east side of the wild headland resembling Cornwall, there was a church and a cemetery enclosed by a stone wall, a few stores and a wine cellar. A wide lane led down to the rocky shore where the Germans were holed up behind a make-shift fortification. US soldiers were keeping the Germans pinned down with fire and Pash took cover in an armoured half-track with Gerry Beatson. Then they saw a tall elderly gentleman, a local civilian, strolling down the road towards them, indifferent to the zip of the bullets flying around. It turned out to be a relative of Joliot, who took them to an inlet below the village on the fringe of a wooded area. He pointed to a track through weeds and brush to the house, and said: 'Voilà, mes amis ...'

Nearby was another holiday home belonging to Francis Perrin, one of Joliot's scientists. The US forces warned Pash that there were rumours that the houses were surrounded by mines. Beatson went first, gingerly pushing forward, fearing the path would be booby-trapped with trip-wires. They found the stone house in the open, but the moment they made a move towards it, they came under fire from both sides in the firefight that had been going on before. They took cover and waited until the firing died down, then they drew their carbines – light semi-automatic rifles – and cautiously went into the house, but found it stripped bare. They had been on a wild goose chase.

Pash returned to London to plan the next move. He wanted Goudsmit to come with him, but Goudsmit stayed behind until the laboratory had been safely captured. Tony Calvert, who had worked with Goudsmit on the intelligence evidence, went with the Alsos team. Pash laid out the plan of attack on the Joliot-Curie laboratory at the College de France in Paris. They would go in two Jeeps: Pash, Beatson (who had been left in France), Calvert and Agent Nathaniel W. Leonard, a new recruit from CIC (US Army Counterintelligence Corps) in France, would be in the first; the CIC special agent, Carl Fiebig, physicist Nick Dolida and Captain Blake, the operations officer, would be in the second. Once they had safely secured Joliot, Goudsmit would be called in with his scientific team.

Pash told Eckman, who was left in London in charge of liaising with Washington, to assume command of the Alsos mission if he was killed, which was a real possibility. Washington had again impressed on Eckman the high priority it attached to capturing Joliot and his laboratory within twenty-four hours of Paris being liberated. Pash felt under greater pressure to get going.

The breakout from Normandy came in August 1944, as the US Third Army under General George Patten swept south. The German Seventh Army and Fifth Panzer Group were pinned into the Falaise pocket near Caen where they were enveloped by General Omar Bradley's US Army Group and XV Corps to the west, the British Second Army under the overall command of General Bernard Montgomery in the centre and the Canadians in the north. German Field Marshall Gunter von Kluge was ordered by an increasingly hysterical Hitler not to retreat with his Panzers, despite being reduced to four depleted Panzer divisions. The German Panzers were forced to retreat at a huge cost, allowing the allies to liberate Paris and cross the Seine. It was the final battle of Operation Overlord. A furious Hitler sacked von Kluge, who was suspected by the Gestapo of being involved in the failed 20 July bomb plot to assassinate the Führer, and ordered him back to Berlin. Seeing it as a death sentence, von Kluge killed himself with a cyanide tablet in his car on the long drive back to Berlin rather than face arrest by the SS.

On 19 August German tanks and half tracks loaded with troops appeared to be pulling out down the Champs-Élysees as the Free French leaders called on an armed uprising in Paris against the invaders. The same day, Pash travelled with Major Calvert to Portsmouth, because they had been unable to secure a cross-Channel flight. They boarded a Navy patrol boat and had a rough crossing; Pash spent the night on deck, trying to avoid being seasick by taking in lungfuls of fresh sea air. They found Gerry Beatson with Nat Leonard, armed with a Tommy gun, in Valognes. Beatson told Pash he had loaded the two Jeeps with ammo, rations, and 'gas' (petrol). Their plan was to hook up with the Twelfth Army Group near Rennes, seize any documents they could find in the city's university, and press on to Paris.

Pash's problem was that Eisenhower had not given priority to the liberation of Paris, focusing instead on the prime objective of forcing the German forces into a general retreat. They learned that a US T-Force – like Alsos, a special operation task force to seize key assets – was to rendezvous sixty miles west of Paris at Châteauneuf-en-Thim on 23 August. That day, German tanks blasted barricades in the streets of Paris and a resistance stronghold at the Grand Palais. By 24 August Pash and Calvert were still driving across the bumpy lanes of rural France west of Paris in their two Jeeps

1. Farm Hall. Erich Bagge climbed over the wall to the right of the door to 'escape' to the local pub.

2. Professor Marcial Echenique, owner of Farm Hall.

3. Werner Heisenberg, von Laue and Otto Hahn in Göttingen in 1946.

5. Werner Heisenberg.

4. Werner Heisenberg (right) and his wife Elisabeth with Niels Bohr in 1936.

6. Erich Bagge.

7. Kurt Diebner.

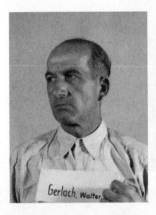

8. Walter Gerlach.

9. Paul Harteck.

10. Otto Hahn.

11. Carl Friedrich von Weizsäcker.

12. *Left*: MI6 headquarters at 54 Broadway Buildings.

13. *Below*: Headquarters of the British nuclear bomb programme, codenamed Tube Alloys, at Old Queen Street.

The undersigned, His Majesty's Ambassador at Paris
presents his compliments to the Chief Officer of Customs at
port of landing and hereby recommends to his good offices
The Earl of Suffolk & Berkshire
Major A.V.Golding, R.T.R.
and their mission,
who have in their charge supplies and documents of importance
to His Majesty's Government,
the bearers of the present letter, for the grant of all such
facilities as may be consistent with the Regulations in force.

His Majesty's Ambassador)
Secretary of His Majesty's Embassy

British Embassy to France
at Bordeaux.
June 18th 1940.

14. *Right*: Major Golding's passport for a priceless cargo landed at Falmouth in 1940.

15. *Below*: SS *Broompark*.

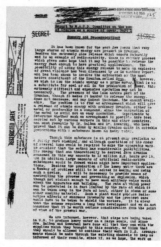

16. *Left*: Gaynes Hall SOE Special Training School 61, where the Gunnerside team waited for their mission.

17. *Above*: The Maud Report found that atomic bombs could be made with just 11 kg of uranium.

18. *Below*: Radio message telling MI6 about the disaster of Operation Freshman from Agent George in Norway.

LOCAL NR. 62/SRL 866.
CIPHER MESSAGE FROM SWAN.

DESP. 1424 11.12.42.
RECD. 1640 11.12.42.

TRANSLATION.

GEORGE SK.

GLIDER PLANE FELL DOWN AT SELLELAND CHURCH STOP.

FIVE MEN STOP.

TWO KILLED CERTAINLY SOME WOUNDED STOP.

ALL TAKEN PRISONER INTERROGATED FOR TWO HOURS STOP.

ALL GAVE RJUKAN POWER STATION AS TARGET STOP.

THEY WERE ALL SUBSEQUENTLY SHOT.

GEORGE.

58° 31' 4" N.
6° 7' 25" E

19. *Above*: Alsos Council of War at Hechingen.

20. *Below left*: Robert Oppenheimer led the Manhattan Project team but had his security clearance withdrawn.

21. *Below right*: General Leslie R. Groves, known as the 'biggest son-of-a-bitch', ran the Manhattan Project.

22. *Above left*: The Big Three at Potsdam: Churchill, Truman and Stalin.

23. *Middle left*: The Alsos team reviewing documents seized at Walter Gerlach's lab at Thuringen.

24. *Below:* Sam Goudsmit (right) and Lieutenant Toepel driving a military jeep during the Alsos Mission in Stadtilm 16 April 1945.

25. *Above*: Colonel Boris T. Pash (right) on Operation Big in Hechingen with Sergeant Holt (middle) and Corporal Brown (left).

26. *Right*: The Jackpot, the message from SHAEF to Marshall and Eisenhower saying Pash has 'hit the jackpot'.

SHAEF MESSAGE FORM

ORIGINATOR'S FILE No.

| CALL | CIRCUIT No. | PRIORITY | TRANSMISSION INSTRUCTIONS |

SPACES WITHIN HEAVY LINES FOR SIGNALS USE ONLY

FROM (A) SHAEF FWD   ORIGINATOR   WES/rmb   DATE-TIME OF ORIGIN AIR 271015Z

TO FOR ACTION AGWAR

TO (W) FOR INFORMATION (INFO)   EYES ONLY   GR

(REF.NO.) FWD - 19991   (CLASSIFICATION) EYES ONLY

THE SPECIAL ALSOS REPEAT ALSOS MISSION HEADED BY BORIS PASH CMA WORKING WITH THE TASK FORCE OF SIX ARMY GROUP HAVE HIT THE JACKPOT IN THE HECHINGEN AREA PAREN FOR THE EYES ONLY OF GENERAL MARSHALL AND THE SECRETARY OF WAR FROM EISENHOWER UNPAREN CMA AND HAVE SECURED PERSONNEL CMA INFORMATION AND MATERIEL EXCEEDING THEIR WILDEST EXPECTATIONS PD FULL DETAILS WILL BE REPORTED LATER THROUGH THE USUAL SECRET CHANNELS CMA BUT WE NOW UNQUESTIONABLY HAVE EVERYTHING AND NONE OF THIS INFORMATION HAS LEAKED OUT

EYES ONLY

DECLASSIFIED
DOD Dir. 5200.9, Sept. 27, 1958
NARA by [signature] date [illegible]

DISTRIBUTION: COORDINATED WITH:

THIS MESSAGE MUST BE SENT IN CYPHER IF LIABLE TO INTERCEPTION   Precedence   URGENT   URGENT   THLor IOR   Opr.

ORIGINATING DIVISION   Chief of Staff

INITIALS   NAME AND RANK TYPED. TEL. NO.

THIS MESSAGE MAY BE SENT IN CLEAR BY ANY MEANS   LT COL J B MOORE III 6582 AUTHENTICATING SIGNATURE

INITIALS

27. The cave at Hagierloch, where the Alsos team found the German atomic reactor. It now houses the Atomkeller Museum.

28. American trucks assembled outside the Haigerloch cave.

29. The Alsos team dismantling the German atomic pile at Haigerloch – portly Lieutenant Commander Eric Welsh stands on the rim handing out graphite blocks. Wing Commander Rupert Cecil is in the foreground.

30. Hagierloch. The cave where the Alsos team found the German atomic reactor.

31. A reconstruction of the German atomic pile in the Atomkeller Museum at Haigerloch.

32. Members of the Alsos team digging up uranium cubes buried near Haigerloch.

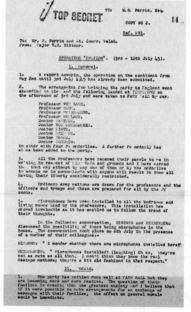

33. *Above left*: Major Thomas Hardwick Rittner wrote secret reports on bugged conversations of Hitler's Uranium Club.

34. *Above right*: The brief of Operation Epsilon, the first of Rittner's secret reports on bugged German scientists.

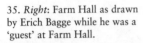

35. *Right*: Farm Hall as drawn by Erich Bagge while he was a 'guest' at Farm Hall.

36. *Below*: Farm Hall in 1945, as photographed by Werner Heisenberg.

37. *Above*: Gibraltar Barn remains Britain's most poignant memorial to the SOE and MI6 agents who gave their lives for king and country.

38. *Below*: The drawing room at Farm Hall where the scientists heard the news about the detonation at Hiroshima.

searching for the US T-Force. They tracked the T-Force down to the town of Rambouillet, between Chartres and Versailles, west of Paris, and were told by its commander, Colonel Tommy Tompkins, that two Allied groups would be hitting Paris from the south, an American unit currently at Palaiseau, about forty kilometres away, with the main French force heading up the Orléans road, the N20.

The handwritten note by Tompkins authorising Pash to cross the US lines is still in the Pash papers at the Hoover Institution Archives in Stanford, California: 'T Force near Rombouillet Lt Col B T Pash Inf Comdg ALSOS Mission a component of T Force 12th Army Gr is authorised to proceed on his special mission subject to the tactical situation T P Tompkins Col GSE Comdg T Force.'[2] Tompkins had hurriedly scribbled it on a scrap of lined paper, torn out of his notepad, as he gave orders to his team. The note appears to be still carrying two blobs of French mud. It speaks volumes across the years about the urgency of Pash's mission in the field.

When they reached the US unit, they were surrounded by cheering French men and women and showered with bunting and gifts of bottles of wine, but they found their route north blocked by a 2,000-strong German unit; it was cut off but dug in. In spite of the assurances Hitler had given to Speer about wanting to save the treasures of Paris, the Führer had ordered General Dietrich von Choltitz, the German commander of Paris, to stand and fight. Paris, said Hitler, 'must not fall into the enemy's hands except in ruins'. Hitler wanted to turn Paris into another Leningrad and is alleged to have screamed down the line to his commander: 'Is Paris burning?'

Pash learned that the French 2nd Armoured Division was to be given the honour of being the first into Paris. Pash had no alternative; he had to find the French force. Pash turned the Jeeps around, causing a panic that the Americans were pulling out, and headed for the Deuxième Division Blindée Française (French 2nd Armoured Division). It had fought with distinction in North Africa, and had been shipped from Southampton for Operation Crossbow to neutralise the V-1 rocket sites in France. Its ranks included Moroccans, Algerians, a few Spanish republicans, and Parisians who had escaped from occupied France.

There was a pause while arrangements were made for the French to retake the city, and for General de Gaulle, leader of the Free French, to lead the French troops into the heart of Paris. The arrival of General de Gaulle carried immense symbolic importance for the French, and for de Gaulle's future. De Gaulle insisted on being allowed to liberate his own people, which secured his place in French history. He did not want the Americans stealing a march into the city. That proved a problem for Pash, who had orders from Groves to get to Joliot's laboratory on the Parisian Left Bank before secret papers and materiel could be removed or destroyed.

Pash decided to join de Gaulle's liberation procession when it went forward. A small French force from the Second Armoured Division mainly made up of Spanish republicans took up position around midnight on 24 August outside the Hôtel de Ville, the city hall, about a mile east of the Louvre. Von Choltitz claimed he believed Hitler was insane and on 25 August surrendered the city at the Hotel Meurice, though French partisans – whose friends had been executed by machine gun by von Choltitz's forces in the hours before the surrender – were furious at his claims to humanitarian motives.

Before sunrise on 25 August Pash's small force of Jeeps reached the long lines of armoured vehicles and troop carriers waiting for the order to go forward; they were just north of Arpajon, thirty-two kilometres to the south of the city. Pash discovered it was the French Second Division that was to be given the honour of leading the liberation parade into the centre of Paris. As the sun rose, the French armour showed no sign of moving forward and Pash was impatient to press on. He waited until 7.30 a.m. when, with still no sign of movement by the Second Division, Pash ordered his Jeeps to roll forward. They went as far as a road block where he got Nat Leonard, a fluent French speaker, to tell the moustachioed French officer commanding the guards that a small group of US tanks was driving into Paris ahead of the French column and Pash's Jeeps had orders to stop them. It was a lie, but the subterfuge to save the honour of the French worked; the barrier was lifted and Pash's Jeeps drove on.

Pash and his team were thus the first American troops to enter Paris. Some die hard Nazi units, however, supported by Nazi collaborators who were facing death from the mob, were determined to fight on. Pash continued cautiously through the streets in the suburbs of Paris thronged with excited Parisians expecting the arrival of the French troops, not US soldiers in Jeeps. Pash's pair of Jeeps carried on until about 8.30 a.m. when they reached a square a few miles to the south of the Seine called La Place de la Porte d'Orléans. There were cafés and shops below handsome apartment buildings with small balconies, and there was a carnival atmosphere on the streets. The Parisians had already turned out in their thousands around the square to celebrate the arrival of the victorious French division, with tanks and soldiers marching to liberate Paris after four years of occupation by the Germans. They were surprised to see two US Army Jeeps carrying four soldiers in American uniforms with a small puppy dog called Alsos that had been picked up on the way.

Pash suddenly heard an American voice on the street. It was a US airman who had been shot down and, having been hidden by the Resistance, had been brought into the city for the liberation to rejoin his unit. He came up to them to give Pash a warning. He told Pash that a force of Germans with two Tiger tanks was installed at the Luxembourg Gardens, blocking their route to the university. His force was too small to get involved in street fighting with Tiger tanks, nor could he call for back up because he feared that Washington would order his detention if it found he had advanced so far.

Pash had to head around the obstacle using side roads, but it proved impossible. He was forced to wait until the French Second Division was approaching and then he decided to improvise. Pash waited for five French combat vehicles to pass, then ordered his US Jeeps to join the column rumbling towards the bridges over the Seine to the Champs-Élysees and the Arc de Triomphe. The column came under heavy machine gun and small-arms fire when it reached Boulevard Du Montparnasse, by the Luxembourg Gardens, which underlined the risk Pash was taking in pushing into areas where Nazi fanatics were still holding out. Pash decided it was time to leave the main column and make a dash for Joliot's laboratory along the tree-lined Boulevarde Saint-Michel near the Sorbonne, a traditional centre of student dissent in the Latin Quarter of Paris. Within thirty yards, they came under heavy sniper fire.

Incredibly, it was all captured by Calvert on black and white movie film. It shows Pash's team running for cover and returning fire at snipers in the apartments lining the street. Pash and Major Calvert took cover behind their Jeep while Gerry Beatson, who was more used to being under fire, ran to take cover in a doorway. As Parisian partisans joined in the firefight, Nat Leonard sprayed the rooftops and windows with his Tommy gun and Calvert fired his carbine at windows on balconies to keep the snipers at bay. When the firing subsided, they jumped back in their Jeeps and accelerated away, turning off to the right, into Rue Saint-Jacques, a long road running north towards the university area where they knew the Curie-Joliot laboratory was located. They were warned by Parisians that the crossroads ahead was covered by one of the Tiger tanks located at the corner of the Luxembourg Gardens. The enemy tank was about two blocks away, but the Tiger's shells could destroy anything trying to cross the Rue de l'Abbé.

Pash knew they had no way round it. He ordered the two Jeeps to line up, side by side, to run at the crossroads at their maximum speed. The drivers floored the accelerators and raced across the junction, two abreast to limit the chances of being hit. They heard a gun blast, but kept going, and after a few more blocks Pash saw the elegant pillared buildings of the College de France where Joliot had his laboratory in the basement. It was about 4 p.m. and Frederic Joliot was waiting for them.

The scientist was relieved when they arrived; it was well-known locally he had been providing the partisans with home-made Molotov cocktails and he feared reprisals by Nazi sympathisers. They relaxed that night with a makeshift dinner party with some of Juliot's students, five attractive young ladies, and two bottles of champagne, which had been handed to the Americans by jubilant well-wishers in the street while de Gaulle took possession of his country's capital. That night General Charles de Gaulle returned in triumph; he walked to the Place de Concorde and established his headquarters in Paris.

The BBC reported: 'At 1900 local time, General Charles de Gaulle – leader of the Free French who has been living in exile in London since the Fall of France in 1940 – entered the city.'

Lieutenant Colonel George Eckman reported: 'Col. Pash and party proceeded to cut across country to Highway 20 and joined the 2nd elements of a French Armoured Division. The ALSOS mission thus proceeded into the South of Paris on 25 August 1944 in the rear of the first five French vehicles to enter. So being the first American unit to enter Paris. The first target was taken during that day, though the party was turned back four times by sniper fire.'[3]

Joliot was flown back to London by Major Calvert and interrogated by Calvert and Sam Goudsmit in early September. The story that emerged left unanswered questions about Joliot's role. After the heavy water had been evacuated at Bordeaux, Joliot and his wife went to a small village nearby to let things settle down; then he had been pressed for former university colleagues to return to the College de France. When he did so, the Germans took an interest in his cyclotron and sent a young scientist, Wolfgang Gentner, from Bothe's laboratory in Heidelberg to act as an interpreter. Gentner had been a student of Joliot's and met him secretly in one of the student cafés in the Boulevarde Saint-Michel to warn him that the Germans intended to seize the cyclotron. Joliot decided it was better to ask the Germans to use it in place; Bothe happily agreed to this arrangement. Joliot succeeded in reaching a promise that he would remain director of his laboratory provided the only projects would be pure research and not war work for the Germans. Before the end of 1940, four German scientists including Gentner began work on the cyclotron. Otto Hahn worked at the laboratory but complained that he could get more radiation out of a gram of radium than the cyclotron. One reason for its poor results was sabotage – the chief mechanic would turn off the water feeding the cooling system and it would overheat, forcing it to be shut down. Bothe, as the operator, would take the blame. 'Such little failures together with poor progress in the laboratories in Germany had a large significance,' said one expert.[4] 'In retrospect, it might appear that Joliot came dangerously near to outright cooperation with the German fission programme. But he would not have recognised any danger for like the Germans, he remained convinced that a nuclear bomb could not be built during the war. He and Gentner, who became firm friends, went so far as to talk over whether a bomb could be made. They concluded that it could not. Joliot still held this view when he was interrogated, shortly after the liberation of Paris in 1944 by an American intelligence team.'

His interrogation is preserved in a secret report, held among the Pash papers at the Hoover Institution Archives in California. 'J' (Joliot) was questioned on 30 August 1944:

SUMMARY: no important information, except for some more details or names.

REPORT: Military visitors to the laboratory of 'J'.

General Schumann, Chief of Army Scientific research, physicist interested in theory of music.

Bieder, his deputy, formerly professor of musicology at Heidelberg.

Diebner, his scientific expert. Physicist with thorough knowledge of TA [Tube Alloys, atomic bomb] Returned to Paris frequently.

Gentner, definitely anti-Nazi.

Danzer, circuit man.

Hartvig, astrophysicist.

The above scientists arrived soon after the occupation and stayed for about one year, being replaced by the following:

Bagge, pupil of Heisenberg, stayed for about six months in 1942. Interested in cosmic radiation only.

Maurer, second rate physicist, liked by nobody. Gentner returned especially to Paris to warn J against him. Maurer stayed until the very end.[5]

In addition, Joliot told them that occasional visitors included Bothe, who was 'more or less in charge of the men sent to Paris', Abraham Esau, present director of the PTR (German Bureau of Standards), and von Weizsäcker, who gave a lecture in Paris, which was boycotted by the French as was a luncheon in his honour. 'J talked to him, but not on physics, merely about the bad taste of accepting a lecture engagement in Paris, to which von Weizsäcker answered that he had been forced to accept. J believes von Weizsäcker to be anti-Nazi and trustworthy.'

Joliot described Bothe as a 'hostile visitor' who gave the impression he knew a lot about the Americans' atomic research. If the Germans were developing a bomb, said Joliot, it would involve Bothe and Diebner. The report adds – contrary to later reports – that Hahn had been asked by the Germans to go to Paris but he refused 'not wishing to confront J as victor'. Joliot wondered why von Weizsäcker could not have refused too. It concluded that Joliot had no factual clues at all which might give information on German 'TA' (Tube Alloys) work. 'His personal opinion is that little or no war work is done by scientists in Germany, it is all done by specialists of the type of industrial engineers. The Germans never asked J to perform specific experiments or measurements. He was free to do his own work.' It was signed by Sam Goudsmit, scientific chief.

Joliot also told his interrogators how he had sent 8 tons of uranium oxide to Morocco, and two of his men, 'K.' (Kowarski) and 'V. H.' (von Halban), had gone to England with a stock of heavy water to carry on work on TA (Tube Alloys) – the escape from Bordeaux by the Earl of Suffolk and Major Golding on board the SS *Broompark*. Goudsmit said attempts were made to save the stockpile of uranium at Oolen, near Antwerp; some of the freight cars were discovered near Le Havre; the trail of the rest was lost, and all of it was probably taken to Germany.

Diebner had interrogated Joliot and seemed to Joliot to have a thorough knowledge of the TA problems. Goudsmit noted: 'If the Germans do any work on TA, J expects Diebner to be a key man.'

Joliot's information about the German lack of progress may have been reassuring, but the Alsos team doubted its accuracy. The memorandum says it was evident his knowledge extended only over the early occupation of France by the Germans. Joliot's alertness to TA work by the Germans had faded, it suggested, because he had a preconceived notion that the Germans 'were unable to solve the problems involved'.

Joliot seemed to the Alsos team to be carrying the 'idealistic view' that no scientist would do good work on cracking the atomic problem if their aim was purely destructive, to create a bomb. They were clearly mystified by his attitude, ending their note with the observation that his basic interest appeared to be in the peaceful use of atomic power as a 'super source of energy, not as an explosive'. They came away with the impression that Joliot thought the German scientists wanted to be in the lead in the use of atomic power after the war, even it meant a German defeat.

Goudsmit and Calvert did not share Joliot's idealism and in Groves's view Joliot was a dangerous Communist, one who could not be trusted not to pass atomic secrets to the Russians. Groves's distrust of Joliot was to have far-reaching consequences for Britain when Groves learned that von Halban had been allowed to visit Joliot in Paris in late 1944 and had told him about the Manhattan Project, in breach of the terms of an Anglo-American agreement signed between Roosevelt and Churchill in Quebec. Groves, who did not trust the British, helped to block co operation with Britain after the war.

Having achieved the first objective on Calvert's target list, Pash and his team had to look elsewhere for leads. The Alsos mission made its temporary headquarters at 2 Place de l'Opera, a vast intersection of wide boulevards near the Champs-Élysées. Pash had now amassed an intelligence, security and scientific force of eighteen men and said he spent days admiring the legs of the Parisian girls as they cycled joyfully around Paris.

The pause in Paris did not last long. Despite von Kluge's heavy losses – estimated at 344 tanks, 250 guns, and around 70,000 men captured or killed and injured – up to 50,000 German troops escaped the encirclement, fell back, and fought even harder to stop the Allies reaching the Fatherland. The defeated German forces regrouped and Hitler threw in reserves, using Luftwaffe reserves as ground troops. Now the battle for Europe was to be engaged with a new fury.

The British 21st Army Group (under the recently promoted Field Marshal Bernard Montgomery) in the north, the US 12th Army

Group (under General Omar Bradley) in the centre, and the Franco-American Southern Group of Armies (under Lieutenant General Jacob L. Devers) in the south, were facing an enemy with its back to its own borders. By the middle of September 1944, the three Western Allied Army groups formed a broad front under Eisenhower and SHAEF (Supreme Headquarters, Allied Expeditionary Force), facing the retreating German forces in France.

Groves ordered Major Robert Furman, his most trusted intelligence officer, back to Europe as soon as he learned about the large amount of uranium ore that was still unaccounted for. He set Pash a new priority: to seize the uranium refining plant of Union Minière De Haut-Katanga near Oolen, to the north-west of Brussels, and its headquarters, the Société Générale Métallurgique de Hoboken in Antwerp. They were right in the middle of the British sector and Pash was under orders from General Groves to secure the support of the British 21st Army Group 'without revealing to the British the name or purpose of the material being sought'.

That spelled trouble for Pash: he knew if he tried to break through to the plants, the British would try to stop him, unless he gave a full explanation. He explained the problem to the man he called his 'fairy Godfather': Colonel G. Bryan Conrad, Assistant Chief of Staff, G-2 at European Theatre of Operations USA (ETOUSA) in Paris. Conrad decided the only way to explain it to the British was to go in person with Pash; he would have to go to Amiens, the last-known location for the British 21st Army Group, to clear the way by speaking in person to Brigadier Edgar 'Bill' Williams, Montgomery's bespectacled, academic-looking head of intelligence.

At 7 a.m. on 6 September, Colonel Conrad holstered a .45 pistol and joined Pash, Reg Augustine, Carl Fiebig, Gerry Beatson, and Nick Dolida for the 140-kilometre journey by Jeep to Amiens. Failing to locate the British group, they went on to Brussels, but still failed to track them down. Conrad told Colonel Strangeways, the commander of the British R-Force – the British equivalent of the US T-Force – that Pash and his team were on an important classified mission and needed to get to Antwerp without delay. Antwerp was in the British sector and still partly in German control.

Conrad returned to Paris, but at 8.30 a.m. on 7 September 1944, Pash's Jeeps rolled into the liberated sector of Antwerp past hundreds of British 'Tommies' trudging through the streets, and headed for their target, Union Minière. There were no cheering crowds. The Germans were still in control of the north of the city.

As they neared the port area, they saw British troops everywhere, but they were moving forward cautiously. Amid the sound of gunfire in the north of the city, Pash found the port staff still at their desks, and willing to be of service. The port director turned over his plans of the port and assured Pash that the Germans were preparing to quit without blowing up the facilities.

Pash later visited Antwerp Zoo, where Belgian Quislings – collaborators – were caged like wild animals by partisans looking for revenge. The sight of caged prisoners revolted him, and he went off with his men to the Palace Hotel where they spent the night. In the morning, they located the head office of Union Minière in Antwerp. Riffling through the files at the offices, Reg Augustine discovered records showing 1,000 tons of refined uranium had been shipped to Germany, but a further 150 tons was reported at the Oolen plant, twenty-eight miles to the east along the Albert Canal.

The Alsos Mission sped out of town on the Oolen road in two Jeeps until a group of British 'Tommies' manning an anti-tank gun behind a house at a crossroads frantically waved them down – a few more yards would have brought them into the line of fire of German guns. Pash figured out he could manoeuvre round to the plant from the south using side roads, but they came to a British captain who had a detailed map showing the plant was in no-man's land between British and German forces. To reach it, they would have to drive over a raised railway crossing, which was in the sights of the German guns.

Pash ordered the two Jeeps to halt about sixty yards from the crossing; they would have to jump the railway and surprise the German guns. Drivers in both Jeeps revved their engines. Then at a signal from Pash, they floored the accelerator pedals, and gunned the vehicles to the ramp over the railway line. They hit the crossing at more than 50 mph and took off on the ramp like a ski jump before crashing to earth with two solid thumps across the tracks. They sprinted for the factory as fast as they could and tumbled inside the plant.

A few employees were still at work. As Pash's men checked the paperwork, the rattle of small arms fire started up outside. The Germans fired mortars, but the heavy fire from British troops forced them back. Office records confirmed that the Germans had removed around 1,000 tons of uranium, but 70 tons of refined uranium ore were still at the plant. A detailed bill of lading dated 4 June 1940 showed a further 80 tons had been shipped to France, just before the German invasion. The document contained identity numbers for the freight trucks that carried the uranium in more than 150 barrels. They had to be traced, even though after four years the trail was likely to have gone cold. Their only hope was that French record-keeping would allow them to defy the odds.

Before they could seize the uranium ore, the Alsos team came under renewed heavy fire and were forced to retreat. They went back to Paris to regroup, and to await Eindhoven being cleared. Goudsmit returned from Brussels with disturbing intelligence that their rivals on the Combined Intelligence Objective Subcommittee were sending their own teams to Eindhoven, where the Philips Works was a high priority target for all Allied technical intelligence teams. The Germans were putting up stiff resistance along the Albert Canal between Antwerp and Liège in Belgium and Pash was concerned that they would re-cross the canal, learn about the Americans' interest in uranium stocks, and ship them out. They had to go back as soon as possible.[6]

The chance came after 17 September when the Allies launched the ill-conceived Operation Market Garden, the largest airborne operation of the war at that stage, to try to drive an armoured thrust through the Low Countries like a dagger into the industrial heart of the German industrial zone, the Ruhr. Montgomery was behind the strategy to end the war in autumn 1944, enabling the West to enter Berlin first, before the Russians. Churchill supported it, but Eisenhower, the Supreme Commander, thought it was risky and insisted on a 'broad front' advance, which meant that the war continued into the spring of 1945, and that the Russians were the first to reach Berlin, bringing Prague and Budapest under Soviet domination. Churchill's biographer, Paul Johnson, said, 'Montgomery wrote sadly: "The Americans could not understand that it was of little avail to win the war strategically if we lost it politically." That was exactly Churchill's view.'[7]

Market Garden failed because it was too ambitious. It required parachute troops to seize bridges in a series of carefully co ordinated attacks over miles of ground held by the Germans (Market) to allow the armour of the British Second Army (Garden) to smash through the German defences; it would only work if everything went right. It famously proved a 'bridge too far', as the SS Panzer divisions under Field Marshal Walther Model fought tenaciously against the British 1st Airborne Division to hold on to the last bridge in the battle plan – Arnhem. Model's forces gained the advantage when they captured a copy of the battle plan from the body of a US officer. The push through Eindhoven, however, gave Pash and his secret mission the chance to reach Alsos targets in the Belgian city. At 4 a.m. on the day after the Allied offensive was launched, Pash and his team moved out of Paris and headed for Brussels once more. They covered the 190 miles in four hours, a bone-shaking average speed of 47 mph in the Jeeps. Pash called into the British headquarters of the 21st Army Group in Brussels, and obtained a pass note from Brigadier Williams, Monty's intelligence chief, asking all British troops to assist Pash in his undisclosed mission.

Pash anxiously asked the British Brigadier, 'What about Eindhoven?'

'Your chaps dropped there yesterday,' said Williams.

The US 101st Airborne Division – the Screaming Eagles – had parachuted into Holland near Eindhoven as part of the offensive. The fighting was intense and bloody. Pash's Jeeps pressed forward past the burnt-out wrecks of tanks and tracked vehicles, ambulances, and the haggard troops, some of whom were the US Airborne troops who had hardly had a rest since their parachute drops four days earlier. The Alsos team succeeded in reaching the Oolen plant again on 21 September, the same day the Germans regained control of the Arnhem Bridge. British airborne troops suffered 70 per cent casualties around the bridge at Arnhem, as Colonel Pash and Major Furman raced in their Jeeps for Oolen to recover the stocks of uranium.

Once more Pash had to make the dash across the railway lines, but this time it was Major Furman who felt his spine had been pushed through his skull. His driver, Fiebig, shouted to 'hang on', but Furman nearly fell out and was annoyed. Furman understood why they had raced at such speed, however, when the German mortars opened up as they reached the plant. Furman flattened himself against a building, while Pash jumped into a doorway. Once inside, they removed some barrels for samples to take back to Brussels, where the British TA scientist David Gattiker would carry out tests in a makeshift laboratory in a hospital to make sure it was uranium.

Pash confided to his own notebook that, after returning to Paris, George Eckman told him the British army chiefs had made an official complaint through the Combined Intelligence Objectives Subcommittee (CIOS) about the behaviour of the Alsos team in riding roughshod over other T-Force missions; George Eckman, his office chief, complained to Pash that his 'wild west approach to fighting a war' was not making it easier to smooth things over with the British.

Eckman escorted Pash to the 'Alsos House' at the Royal Monceau hotel, laid a British letter of protest down on the table and said, 'You handle this. I have enough problems trying to explain you to Bryan Conrad.'

Pash's readiness to race into areas which were still being cleared to beat rival intelligence teams would be a continuing source of irritation both to the British, French and American task forces, but he refused to have his hands tied by red tape. His priority was to carry out his orders from Groves to get the names on his target list, no matter whom he upset.

Gattiker's tests on the Oolen samples showed it was uranium ore. With the help of British transport, they shipped the captured uranium ore back to the United States, and Pash was told it was used in the bomb dropped on Hiroshima. Pash and Furman took into custody two Dutch scientists who gave them their biggest breakthrough: they disclosed that Nazi atomic research was being conducted in Strasbourg. Sam Goudsmit had already had his suspicions raised about the importance of Strasbourg to the Nazi atomic effort by the discovery of a 1944 catalogue of Strasbourg University that showed several scientists on his wanted list were located in the city. Confirmation that the city on the Rhine in Alsace, 480 kilometres away, was being used for atomic research made it a key strategic target.

Meanwhile, the Alsos detectives in Paris had traced the rail cars carrying the shipment of uranium ore from the Oolen plant to Toulouse, over 1,000 kilometres away in the south of France. That meant a 670-kilometre race in their Jeeps across war-battered France. German forces were not likely to be confronted south of the Loire, but it was still uncertain territory. It was also in breach of a SHAEF directive prohibiting Allied units from crossing to the south bank of the Loire. Pash had to seek special permission from 'Ike's' Chief of Staff, General Walter Bedell Smith at the Trianon Hotel in Versailles.

Once he had obtained approval for the next stage of his mission, Pash called up support and was given a convoy of eight Jeeps packing mounted machine guns, each with a three-man team from a US military intelligence battalion. On 9 October they were joined by the fabled US transport corps known as the Red Ball Express. The men and their trucks were addressed the night before launching their mission by Lieutenant Edell, Commanding Officer of the RBE, who left them in doubt that the operation would be dangerous.

'Men, we have been selected for a special mission,' Edell told them. 'It's so secret that you will not discuss it even among yourselves. I want every truck in perfect running condition and that's an order. Those with mounts will draw .50-calibre guns. Light mortars will be issued to every other truck. Each man will see that his rifle or carbine is in working order. You will draw ammunition and hand grenades.'

The next morning at 3.30 a.m., this extraordinary convoy headed out to meet up with Pash's Military Intelligence units at Rambouillet. At an overnight stop in a clearing the next evening, Pash told the drivers they were going about thirty-six miles further on to Toulouse the next day, to a French government arsenal where certain vital material was stored. It was a French partisan stronghold, he said, and while he did not believe they would object, the truckers were under orders to fire if they showed any violent resistance.

At 8.30 a.m. on 11 October, Pash walked into the arsenal office in Toulouse. The chief engineer asked Pash if he had a paper to show his authorisation.

'Monsieur, I have orders!' said Pash.

There was a bridge across a moat leading to a big solid gate to the arsenal. The engineer ordered the gate to be opened, and the trucks of the Red Ball Express thundered in, turned in a semi-circle and came to a stop with perfect timing, in a line facing the exit.

They found what they were looking for in one of the warehouses: a stockpile of barrels whose markings indicated they had come from Belgium.

Reg Augustine got out a Geiger counter and the needle immediately jumped. There were about 31 tons of uranium there, and the truckers, all black Americans with a white officer, were given little protection for handling their cargo. They were issued with gloves with instructions to return them for disposal after the loading had finished. They quickly realised that the small barrels were extraordinarily heavy, and some found their hands covered in yellow dust. The rumour started that they were secretly shipping out a cargo of gold dust. Believing they were carrying a priceless cargo, the men checked their weapons and rolled out of the base on a 400-kilometre journey to Marseilles, where it was to be shipped to the United States aboard a US Navy transport ship.

Furman commandeered the ship using a letter he had been given by Major General Kenneth Strong, the same British army intelligence officer named in the pass for Boris Pash, attached to Eisenhower's Allied Force Headquarters (AFHQ), telling anyone he asked for assistance, in Major Furman's words, to 'help him or drop dead'. Major Furman said he carried it throughout the war and that is how he got the Navy to put the uranium on board a transport for the US.

It would help Groves with another objective. He had hoped that by sending Furman to join the Alsos team in the field, Groves could 'calm down' the scientists on the Manhattan Project, who feared the Germans were years ahead of the US and would bomb America. Furman said later:

> I should say that you might say the whole project, the Manhattan Project, was built on fear: fear that the enemy had the bomb, or would have it before we could develop it. And this they knew to be the case, the scientists did, because they were refugees from Germany, a large number of them, and they had studied under the Germans before the war broke out.[8]

There was just one mishap in loading the ore; as the load was being lifted into the ship's hold, a barrel slipped through the loading net and splashed into the sea. A navy diver recovered it a few days later but, as it sank faster than a rock, the incident added weight to the rumours the barrels contained French gold dust.

The 'gold' from France was used with the uranium ore from the Oolen factory less than a year later in the bomb dropped on the Japanese city of Hiroshima.

At the Philips Lamp Company in Eindhoven, Goudsmit and his scientific team learned that the Strasbourg University had ordered equipment for nuclear research and had enlarged its staff. This strand of evidence, together with other clues being pieced together by Goudsmit in the Alsos headquarters in Paris, suggested Strasbourg was a vitally important piece of the jigsaw. Goudsmit had learned from a routine visit to a French scientific optical plant that Dr Rudolf Fleischmann, a German physicist known to be working in the nuclear field, had been teaching at Strasbourg University. It was thought that the German physicist Carl Friedrich von Weizsäcker was also at the Strasbourg University. Another on the Strasbourg target list was Dr Eugen von Haagen, a Nazi biological warfare specialist.

Strasbourg, on the Alsace border between France and Germany, was world-famous for its canals, pâté de foie gras, Rieslings and fine restaurants. It had been under German control since June 1940, and its institutions had been Nazified for years. All the evidence now pointed to Strasbourg being a prime target for the Alsos Mission. After returning from Toulouse, Pash ordered his Jeeps to drive to Strasbourg, closely following the French Second Armoured Division that they had met in Paris.

The Alsos team followed the French armoured force through the hills over the Dabo Pass to Wasselonne and Strasbourg, hoping to bypass fighting to clear the Saverne Gap. But they quickly realised the French were up against a fierce rearguard action by the Germans when they encountered a number of burned-out French tanks that bore witness to the bitter fighting to stop the French crossing the Rhine. The journey using back roads was nerve-racking. After a burned-out French tank, Pash and his team found another French tank that had taken direct hits, before they came across a heavily-camouflaged German 88 millimetre gun concealed behind a hedge, which had carried out the ambush before it too was hit, probably by a third French tank.

They pressed ahead but suddenly stopped when Bob Blake and Carl Fiebig braked and took cover. Up ahead, Pash saw what had caused their panic – the steel barrel of an 88 gun jutting out of a hedge, ready to fire at anything approaching along the road. They dismounted and carefully walked towards the gun with their weapons drawn and hearts pumping hard. They found it was surrounded by the bodies of its German gun-crew, cut down by French infantry before the 88 could open fire.

It came as an enormous relief when the Alsos team entered Strasbourg and saw the magnificent façade of Strasbourg University in the centre of the city, with its colonnade and wide stone steps leading to the entrance. Their first target was Fleischmann's house, which they had located with their detailed intelligence for the mission. The house had been damaged by a bomb, but it was still partly occupied by a housekeeper. She denied at first that Fleischmann was still in the city, but Pash noticed a fresh loaf and an egg. He had a hunch that Fleischmann was still using the house and confirmed it when he broke the egg into a saucer: it was still fresh. They moved on to the house of another scientist on their target list. Pash became suspicious when the scientist asked for permission to go to the local hospital. The man explained he was not ill; he did a little work at the hospital.

Pash immediately realised that this was the breakthrough he had been hoping for. The Germans were using the hospital as cover for their atomic research. He ripped out the telephone wires to stop the scientist alerting his colleagues at the hospital, and hurriedly arranged a raid at dawn on the Strasbourg Hospital. Fighting was still going on in the streets and the French feared they would have to retreat if there was a German counter-attack. That night, Pash saw German patrols edging forward, but they did not come in large numbers and quickly retreated. Early the next morning, 26 November, Pash drove to the hospital with military support from members of the intelligence Task Force he had been allocated and marched in through the front door.

He was challenged by the hospital director who protested that Pash was flouting the Geneva Convention by seizing a hospital, but Pash persisted. His hunch paid off: he discovered Fleischmann in a separate building in the grounds of the hospital, where he had established a secret laboratory under the cover of carrying out medical research. Pash identified Fleischmann from a photograph he had found in his house. His team of German physicists tried to pass themselves off as medical doctors in white coats, and Fleischmann was unco operative. Pash learned that von Weizsäcker and von Haagen, the virus expert, had left town some time before the French troops liberated the city, but a pile of paperwork gave the Alsos team all they wanted to know.

Goudsmit and Pash took over von Haagen's comfortable flat in Strasbourg as a billet and sifted through the papers they had scooped up at Fleischmann's laboratory. They tucked into an improvised dinner of K-rations in von Haagen's flat, then slumped into some easy chairs to read the papers over a few candles and a gas lamp while the Germans shelled the city from across the river.

They read for two days and nights, until their eyes hurt. They were amazed to discover that the Germans had taken no measures to conceal their whereabouts: letterheads on the letters sent to Fleischmann carried the addresses of the most secret atomic laboratories in a district near Stuttgart called Hechingen. The addresses pointed to two towns they had never heard of before: Haigerloch and Tailfingen. Goudsmit also found letters addressed to 'Lieber Werner', and memos about the difficulty they were having in obtaining 'special metal', which Goudsmit assumed was uranium.[9] They even included a telephone number for Heisenberg's office. Goudsmit joked that he could just ring him up.

Their careful search for evidence pointed to the German atomic research programme being housed in a textile factory and a nearby cave under a picturesque castle in Haigerloch in the Swabian Alps. Otto Hahn's laboratory was nearby at Tailfingen.

Goudsmit traced Carl Friedrich von Weizsäcker's home, but he was not there. It had been stripped bare. They found von Weizsäcker had taken everything of importance with him, but a pot-bellied stove had an awkward metal chimney which, when dismantled, proved to contain fragments of papers he had tried to burn. They also found evidence of the Nazi horrors yet to be exposed to the world. They uncovered an angry letter from von Haagen to an official representative of Himmler's SS called Hirt, who was supposed to supply von Haagen with prisoners from concentration camps for his biological experiments with viruses. In one, von Haagen complained that, of 100 prisoners he had been sent, twelve had died and only twelve were in a condition suitable for his biological experiments.

They threw a mini-banquet in the apartment owned by the Nazi biological warfare expert, with extra rations rustled up by the CIC man, Carl Fiebig, and prepared by Frau Rilda, von Haagen's elderly housekeeper. They drank cocktails and made toasts of Cognac to their success. The next day, Goudsmit and Pash drove by car to Paris with the papers and Fleischmann in their custody with a couple of his colleagues in another car; the German physicists were later flown to internment in the United States until being freed in 1946 to return to Germany.

Fleischmann maintained a defiant attitude of superiority to the Americans who had taken over his laboratory. Goudsmit and the intelligence officers pored over the papers in Paris. They were in no rush. They were not going anywhere until the Allies had dealt with the German counter-offensive by Hitler's Panzers through the heavily forested Ardennes region that became known as the Battle of the Bulge.

In a detailed report on his findings, Goudsmit wrote to Richard Tolman at the National Defense Research Council in Washington: 'The Kaiser Wilhelm Institut for Physics has been in part moved to Hechingen, Hohenzollern, No 1 Weiherstrasse. The telephone No. is 405 ...' Among the personnel known to be working there, Goudsmit added, were Heisenberg, von Weizsäcker, Hocker, Jules Hiby, G. Moliere, Wirtz, Dr B. Gysae (the librarian). 'As far as could be discovered the Hechingen group is entirely concerned with theoretical nuclear physics. No definite evidence was found at Strasburg of experimental work at Hechingen but reports received from OSS in Switzerland have indicated that this may have been going on in nearby Bisingen, where a new cyclotron is being built.'

Goudsmit's report confirmed what Lieutenant Commander Eric Welsh and British intelligence already knew from their agent in Berlin, Paul Rosbaud, *Griffin*. The spy chief for the Office of Strategic Services (OSS) in Bern, Switzerland, was Allen Dulles, who later became head of OSS's successor, the CIA. He had also reported to Washington that a Swiss scientist and professor had said Werner Heisenberg, one of the top names on the Alsos 'wanted' list, was living near a place called Hechingen on the edge of the Black Forest in southern Germany.

That had caused great excitement in Washington. Lieutenant General Leslie Groves went to the Pentagon for a meeting in the office of Secretary for War, Henry Stimson, with General George Marshall, the US Army Chief of Staff, to find Hechingen on a map of Germany. It was so far to the south, they finished up on their knees, looking at the town at the bottom of the map.

Tony Calvert, Groves's liaison man in London, had also identified Haigerloch as another key name on their target list which was nearby. It was a small town on a bend in the River Eyach. It was one of a number of towns among the dramatic limestone gorges cut by the tributaries of the River Neckar that laced the area about twenty-five miles east of the Rhine. Eric Welsh had located a vicar in England who had been the vicar of Bisingen south of Stuttgart before the war, and he was able to pinpoint buildings and factories in the narrow valleys.

Calvert had suggested sending in an unlikely spy, Moe Berg, the former catcher of the Washington Senators and the Boston Red Sox, as a Swiss student. Berg had worked for the OSS before, but Groves vetoed the plan, fearing Berg would give the game away if captured by the Germans. Air photo-reconnaissance using purpose-built PR Mark XI Spitfires carried out several runs over Hechingen. The resulting pictures caused a flap when the analysts at RAF Medmenham, located at Danesfield House on the Thames in Buckinghamshire, thought they had found anomalies that looked like new factories. It turned out to be German shale oil works, showing how desperate Germany had become to find oil.

But the OSS had another job for Berg. In December 1944, William 'Wild Bill' Donovan, director of the OSS, authorised a plan to decapitate Hitler's atomic team at a stroke. Dulles had noticed that Werner Heisenberg was due to give a lecture in the

Swiss city of Zurich. Donovan approved a plan put up by Dulles to assassinate Heisenberg at the lecture.

The unlikely assassin was Berg, who had carried out OSS Special Operations in the Balkans and Europe. Berg went to Heisenberg's lecture posing as a tourist. He had a gun in his pocket and a cyanide capsule for himself, to be used if he was caught by the Nazis. He had orders to shoot Heisenberg if he gave any hint that the Nazis were ready to use an atomic bomb against America or Britain. Heisenberg gave no such indication in his lecture, and Berg later met the physicist in a relaxed mood at a dinner party hosted by Paul Scherrer, the director of the Swiss Physics Institute and an OSS spy code-named Flute.

Berg had no specialist knowledge of atomic research, but reported back to his OSS handlers that, having spoken to Heisenberg over dinner and as they strolled through the streets of Zurich, the Nazis seemed far away from making an atomic bomb and, if anything, Heisenberg might be ready to defect.[10]

Killing Heisenberg was a crass idea on a number of levels: it flouted international conventions regarding Switzerland that even Hitler had observed; if Berg had committed suicide with his cyanide pill there could have been no hiding the fact that Heisenberg had been murdered by an American agent in a neutral country; and the 'decapitation' of Heisenberg would not have stopped atomic research in Germany. It is little wonder that neither Groves nor Pash mentioned his assassination plot in their memoirs.

Dulles was later to lead the CIA into dark practices in the Cold War, using burglary in Washington to protect the CIA from criticism and using violent coups in places such as Iran for 'regime change' to further American foreign policy. He was 'retired' by President Kennedy after presiding over the Bay of Pigs fiasco in Cuba in 1961.

Pash returned with Goudsmit to Washington to prepare for the final push. Pash was later having lunch with Colonel 'Mickey' Moses from the Pentagon when the question of the Alsos scientists cropped up. 'I'm glad you're getting along with those longhairs,' said Colonel Moses.

'Longhairs, hell!' cried Pash. 'Those guys are longhairs with crew-cuts. They can work, scheme, bitch, finagle and ride a jumping Jeep right along with the best of our field officers ... we now have an even wilder bunch.'[11]

11

Operation Big

The German winter was bitter. In January 1945 the temperatures dropped to minus 20 degrees Celsius in the small towns in Württemberg on Pash's target list. In Hechingen, Werner Heisenberg, Germany's leading theoretical physicist, had joined the People's Defence League, and had done his duty in the freezing cold at night.

They had learned the patriotic songs '*Die Wacht am Rhein*' (The Watch on the Rhine) and '*Deutschland hoch in Ehren*' (Germany in High Esteem), though he wondered what use they would be if they saw action. During the day, he had no heating in the institute, and he was forced to wear two vests to keep warm.

He complained about the 'barbaric' cold in letters to his wife, 'Li'. He had sent Li with their six children and Heisenberg's mother three years earlier to their mountain chalet in Urfeld in the Bavarian Alps to escape the war. They were still separated by 450 kilometres and the war was closing in for both of them.

Heisenberg wrote to Li on 21 January describing the Allied bombing of nearby towns: 'Reutlingen was hit heavily, in Tubingen the railroad station and surrounding area are affected. Today there were again about 800 planes above our region, but I do not know yet where the attacks took place.'[1]

He made light of the Allied attacks on local towns compared to the sweeping advances by the Soviets: 'Actually, this kind of warfare of the Anglo-Saxons has something dismal about it compared to that of the Russians; at a time when the Russians are conquering large parts of Europe, they are bombarding villages in Württemberg.'

But he was not despondent. 'Next to all these immense events there still is blossoming in Hechingen a little bit of life from more peaceful times: this morning, when the People's Defence League was cancelled, we went on a ski trip to the Zeller Horn, and tonight there will be a quartet playing here.'

Heisenberg revealed in his letters to Li that a long-running dispute between his Berlin-Dahlem operation and Kurt Diebner's Berlin-Gottow group had flared up again over the share-out of the scarce supplies of heavy water and uranium metal. Diebner complained to Esau, the plenipotentiary for atomic research, that his laboratory was losing out after Heisenberg became director of the Berlin operations. Esau backed Diebner by ordering 600 litres of heavy water to be given to Diebner in Gottow. Speer, backing Heisenberg, had tried to resolve the dispute by getting Goering to replace Esau with Walther Gerlach. The dispute, however, continued and Diebner was highly reluctant to share his stocks of heavy water and uranium with Heisenberg.

In Berlin, there was growing panic that the city and its nuclear installations would be overrun by the Russians. The Red Army was racing through Poland and a new breach through the German lines was expected. On 30 January 1945, Gerlach ordered the Berlin-Dahlem atomic pile to be dismantled and loaded on trucks for the journey south from Berlin to Diebner's laboratory in Stadtilm, Thuringia, where Diebner had been forced to move from Gottow in the late summer of 1944. He telephoned his friend, Paul Rosbaud, and told him he was taking the 'heavy stuff' out of Berlin. Gerlach telephoned the local gauleiter, Fritz Sauckel, to tell him to expect a convoy of lorries carrying the equipment from the laboratory in Dahlem. Sauckel asked him what he wanted to do with these things, and Gerlach told him: 'The politician who is in possession of such an engine can achieve anything he wants.'

The next day, Gerlach, pale, on edge and depressed, left Dahlem in a convoy of cars with Diebner, who was wearing his uniform, and Wirtz and Gerlach's secretary, Miss Guderian.

On 2 February, Heisenberg vented some of his anxiety to Li: 'In our nuclear physics group the internal battle (Diebner vs. K.W.I.) has broken out anew, probably as a result of the new wave of conscription and the threatening danger in the East. Maybe I will have to travel in the next days to Thuringia [Stadtilm] on account of this; I don't really like this, but perhaps it is necessary, and besides, I might on the way back travel via Munich. As long as I am healthy,

I will cope with the problems, and the fact that things are showing movement is just giving me new courage.'

Heisenberg undertook a perilous journey with von Weizsäcker by bicycle, train and car to see Gerlach in Stadtilm in Thuringia and – with the Russian threat increasing – persuaded him to move the atomic pile further south to Haigerloch. Erich Bagge was given the job of escorting the lorries to pick up the Top Secret freight in Stadtilm. Bagge noted in his diary: 'Dramatic journey. Fighter bombers, bomber formations. Journey mostly by night.' The return journey to Haigerloch was just as nerve-racking, with black ice adding to their worries; one lorry crashed into a ditch.

Heisenberg was becoming increasingly alarmed at the fate of his family in their alpine retreat in Urfeld, and urged Elisabeth to take cover with the children in the basement of their mountain cabin if there was any sign of air attacks. On March 4, he wrote: 'Unexpectedly, by car from Berlin, Dr Telschow and Diebner have arrived. Tomorrow morning Gerlach will come from Tubingen [north of Haigerloch]. That is good, as there are many important things to be discussed.'

Heisenberg's team prepared for their final experiment, code-named B-VIII which had been ready at Berlin-Dahlem until they had to evacuate the laboratory there. They had assembled 1.5 tons of heavy water, 10 tons of graphite blocks to line the vessel and 1.5 tons of uranium for the core. Heisenberg had accepted Diebner's design for the pile using cubes of uranium, rather than layers of uranium plates. In total, they lowered 664 uranium cubes into the reactor, suspended in groups of eight or nine on seventy-eight fine-alloy wires from the lid of the vessel. Heisenberg, Wirtz, who was directing the operation, and their colleagues nervously grouped around the reactor as it was carefully prepared. The lid was bolted in place and the heavy water was slowly pumped in. Measurements of the neutrons were taken as the level of the heavy water in the reactor began to rise. Occasionally, the pumping would be stopped to check on the data. The readings increased; Heisenberg and Wirtz suppressed their excitement as the readings showed the neutrons were multiplying, like the 'population' increase he had predicted to the Reich Research Council. At last, more neutrons were 'giving birth' than were 'dying'. They were heading for criticality.

As the number of neutrons climbed, Wirtz realised they were vulnerable if anything went wrong. But then the explosive increase in the neutrons began to tail off, and their hopes of a chain reaction being sustained crashed. Erich Bagge, interviewed in 1992, said:

'Neutrons were measured from stage to stage. The number of neutrons was rising, nearly linearly. There was a chance when the cylinder was filled fully perhaps we would have criticality. In fact, it was not so – [the graph] rose, and then went horizontal. We were in a situation of sub-criticality. It was not so far [away]. It was about seventy five per cent.'[2]

Heisenberg studied the figures and concluded that he needed to increase the size of the pile by 50 per cent to achieve sustained nuclear fission. It would be difficult to do so with American Allied forces pouring across the border into Germany from the west and the Red Army surging towards Berlin from the east, but he had to keep trying.

Heisenberg telephoned Gerlach in Berlin to say that they were on the brink of achieving nuclear fission; they just needed more heavy water and more uranium. Gerlach was excited by the news. He rang his friend Rosbaud – unaware that Rosbaud was in contact with British intelligence – and told him to come round to his office. At 1 p.m. on 24 March, Rosbaud arrived at Gerlach's office and Gerlach said: 'It works!' Rosbaud was sceptical and asked Gerlach how he knew. Gerlach replied the good news had come from Haigerloch; it was possible they would get the first chain reaction in six or seven months.

Rosbaud interrupted him: 'Don't you see that at least in two months the Russians will be in Berlin and the whole of Germany occupied by Allied troops, perhaps with the exception of a small part near *Berchtesgaden* [site of Hitler's Eagle's Nest], which means a delay of a couple of weeks till the definitive fumigation of the Nazis in their caverns. And you don't really expect the work on the machine would be continued in Hitler's *Bergfestung* [mountain fortress].'[3]

Gerlach became more and more excitable; Gerlach said he wanted the Allies to stay where they were and the Nazis to go to hell. Rosbaud said he acted like a naughty child who did not want his toys taken away.

'This is a great triumph,' Gerlach cried. 'Think of the consequences. You don't need radium or petrol.'

Rosbaud was more concerned about Hitler acquiring the atomic bomb than atomic-powered VWs after the war. He replied: 'Thank God it is too late.'

Gerlach hinted that the Third Reich could use their atomic research as leverage when Hitler was forced to surrender: 'A wise government, conscious of its responsibility, could perhaps get better conditions ... we know something of extreme importance which others don't.' Then he added sadly: 'But we have a government, which is neither wise nor had ever any feeling of responsibility.'

*

Groves's main concern now was to stop Hitler's Uranium Club and its raw materials falling into the hands of the Russians sweeping in from the east. The Third Reich still had 1,000 tons of refined uranium ore shipped out of Belgium from the Oolen plant.

In a secret memorandum on 15 September 1944, Goudsmit had reported back to Groves that at least 60 tons of refined uranium was shipped from the Oolen plant between June 1940 and August 1941 to the German Auer-Gesellschaft plant in Orianienberg near Berlin. The Auer-Gesellschaft plant's main source was the Joachimsthal uranium ore mine in Czechoslovakia, which had shipped ore to the works in Oranienburg about fifteen miles to the north of Berlin. This was a cause of serious concern in Washington because it was in the area zoned for Soviet occupation after the fall of Berlin. The plant was clearly of importance to the German atomic programme – it supplied metal uranium sheets and cubes for the experimental reactors being tested by Heisenberg and Diebner.

The Alsos team could not reach the plant, but Groves decided it had to be destroyed before it fell into Russian hands. Groves wanted to bomb the Auer plant to yellow dust. It is a measure of Groves's power that, once he wanted an air strike, it was 'job done'. A coded message was sent to Groves on 13 March 1945 confirming the raid on Oranienburg (code name Gary) would go ahead: 'Reception by Salem [Major General Carl Spaatz, Commander of the US Eighth Air Force] was excellent and he was delighted to undertake the contract which he guarantees will be carried through to full satisfaction ... Due to the smallness of Gary, however, the work must be done by sight without aid of instruments.'

On 15 March 1945, a massive force of 1,347 US Flying Fortresses and Liberators escorted by 732 fighters of the Eighth Air Force dropped 1,684 tons of high explosives and 178 tons of incendiary bombs on the plant and associated railway marshalling yards. A small nearby town, Zossen, was also heavily bombed by the US Air Force with 1,373 tons of bombs at the same time. Zossen, like most German towns, contained a German Army headquarters which served to justify the raid, but the real reason it was bombed was to conceal from the Russians that the

Americans' intended target was the Oranienburg uranium plant. Zossen was merely a decoy.

On 19 March, Major General Spaatz reported to General George C. Marshall, the US Army Chief of Staff: 'The attack on Zossen drew most of the attention and in itself presented a plausible cover plan for the Oranienburg operation ... Virtual destruction of this target is confirmed by reconnaissance flown on 16 March 1945, from which it appears that substantially all of the buildings within the special target area are gutted or burned out.'

Groves noted in his memoirs that a bonus of the raid on Zossen was that General Heinz Guderian, Chief of the German General Staff and a tank expert who was one of the architects of the Blitzkrieg, was injured. The operation failed to fool the Russians, who had their own Alsos mission scouring eastern Germany for precious remains of the German nuclear programme.

Groves was also determined to deny the Russians a major stock of uranium ore at a salt mine called the *Wirtschaftliche Forschungs Gesellschaft* (WIFO) near Stassfurt, about 200 kilometres south of Berlin. The Alsos team was so stretched that a separate American–British task force hurriedly had to be assembled to investigate it. The US team included Tony Calvert and Lieutenant Colonel John Lansdale, Lieutenant General Groves's security chief; the British team comprised Sir Charles Hambro, Michael Perrin and David Gattiker of Tube Alloys. The Stassfurt mine was directly between the sectors to be occupied by the American and Soviet armies. Brigadier General E. L. Sibert, head of intelligence of the Twelfth Army Group, hesitated to upset the Russians but he was tersely overruled by General Bradley who said, 'to hell with the Russians'.

The Alsos team joined the 83rd Division and quickly achieved their first objective without a shot being fired. Hidden in the manager's house was an inventory of the plant's stocks, which showed 1,100 tons of uranium ore were stored in barrels in open sheds above ground at the salt mines. Most of the barrels were either broken or rotten and the ore would have to be repacked before it could be shipped out.

By a stroke of luck, they discovered a factory producing fruit barrels nearby. They commandeered the plant to make over 10,000 barrels, and called in the army's Red Ball Express to ship them out. Groves recalled: 'Trucks were in great demand at this period and the men, all Negroes with one white lieutenant, were exhausted from lack of sleep ... Nevertheless, they performed splendidly.'[4]

They used forced labour from the plant to load the ore in the barrels over three days and nights. It was taken to an airport hangar located by Lansdale at Hildesheim, near Hanover. From Hanover the barrels of ore were flown to England, while the remainder were carried by train to Antwerp, where the ore was taken by ship to England. From England, the ore was sent over to the United States, where it was used in the building of the bombs destined for Japan. Groves sent a memorandum to the chief of the US defence staff, General Marshall:

In 1940, the German Army in Belgium confiscated and removed to Germany about 1200 tons of uranium ore. So long as this material remained hidden under the control of the enemy, we could not be sure that he might be preparing to use atomic weapons.

Yesterday I was notified by cable that personnel of my office had located this material near Stassfurt, Germany, and that it was now being removed to a safe place outside of Germany, where it would be under the complete control of American and British authorities.

The capture of this material, which was the bulk of uranium supplies available in Europe, would seem to remove definitely any possibility of the Germans making any use of an atomic bomb in this war.[5]

Pash feared the scientists could defect to the Russians with vital intelligence. Having crossed the Rhine a month before, Pash was ready to launch the final operation to capture Hitler's Uranium Club. But Groves was concerned that Haigerloch was in the sector recently allocated to the French. Germany was divided into three sectors of occupation by the Americans, Russians and British at the conference between 'The Big Three' – Roosevelt, Stalin and Churchill – at Yalta, but since then a fourth zone had been added for the French, and their sector included the area to the south of Stuttgart where Groves was now certain that the German nuclear bomb research was centred. He was determined to share nothing with the French. His experience with Joliot had convinced him that 'nothing that might be of interest to the Russians should ever be allowed to fall into French hands'. But that meant beating the French to Hechingen.

Groves conceived of a bold plan to do so. The Americans would divert a sizeable force from General Eisenhower's Sixth

Army Group – possibly as much as an airborne division and two armoured divisions – to carry out an airborne attack on Hechingen and Haigerloch to seize Hitler's atomic secrets and his scientists before the French arrived. Fortunately for Pash, who was not looking forward to a combat air drop at the age of forty-four, it was abandoned in favour of a land attack.

For Pash, it was the last lap of the race to stop Hitler acquiring the atomic bomb; it was the reason he had jolted and bounced hundreds of miles across France, Belgium and southern Germany by Jeep and armoured car. It would be given a suitably dramatic code name: it was called Operation Big. But, as Groves's paranoia about a German bomb subsided, the scale of the assault was also paired back.

Pash's small force was reinforced by two armoured cars, four more Jeeps with machine-gun mounts and a pair of .50-calibre machine guns to add to the German light machine guns they had already captured. The Alsos Mission now included those who had been to Stassfurt, such as Lieutenant Colonel John Lansdale, who was clearly there to act as Groves's eyes and ears, and the British officers who wanted to be in at the 'kill', led by Hambro, who was wearing the uniform of the Coldstream Guards, his First World War regiment, under a sand-coloured waterproof greatcoat. The British contingent included Lietenant Commander Eric Welsh, Percy Rothwell, an army intelligence officer, Michael Perrin and David Gattiker – wearing khaki army uniforms although they were civilians – and Wing Commander Rupert Cecil, an RAF bomber pilot already decorated for bravery, who had been sent by R. V. Jones to organise the airlift of equipment and documents to London. Hambro had a rival who tried to stop him joining the mission.

I discovered in the War Cabinet papers an unsigned hand-written draft memorandum – possibly by Welsh who was determined to keep the lead on TA intelligence – to the Prime Minister trying to stop Hambro joining the Alsos team:

> Sir Charles Hambro apparently intends to take part in the expedition and has in fact been over to Paris with one of my officers to arrange details of Anglo-American cooperation. He has, I am told, lent valuable weight to our side in the discussions, but I feel that there is a danger of embarrassing situations arising if he or the Americans should thereby be led to believe that either the Mission or T. A. [Tube Alloys] Intelligence in general is likely to become one of his responsibilities. I therefore think that it would

be better from a long term point of view if Sir Charles was not to take part in the Mission.[6]

If it was read by Churchill, it was ignored.

First, the Alsos team struck north to Stadtilm in Thuringia in the heart of Germany where Diebner's laboratory was said to be based. Pash took a twenty-man Alsos task force with two armoured cars and as many Jeeps as he could get and headed for Stadtilm on the heels of the retreating Germans. The inhabitants looked stunned by the sight of the Americans when they entered the town. Within minutes, Pash discovered Diebner's laboratory in an old school house.

The cellar looked like a natural cave. Pash noticed a black block of paraffin, an important element in aiding fission, lying outside. Then he saw some black briquettes. He asked a family who appeared to be squatting in the basement for safety what the black stuff was. They said it was nothing but coal.[7] Pash picked up one of the pieces and found it was heavier than coal. They were blocks of pressed uranium oxide used as the core of the pile. A deep pit had been dug in the middle of the cellar, where the blocks of uranium were to be flooded with heavy water. Next to it was a pit where the uranium was kept. They discovered the school basement had been used by Kurt Diebner, the chief co ordinator of the German atomic research project, and Walther Gerlach for what appeared to be a desperate last-ditch attempt at creating the basis for a nuclear bomb, before Hitler's Germany was overrun by the Americans, the British, the French and the Russians.

They were too late. Locals told Fred Wardenburg, a member of Goudsmit's scientific team, that a number of Gestapo men arrived on 8 April with the Führer's order to evacuate any vital research groups near enemy fronts to the Alpine Redoubt. Those who resisted would be shot. The SS had organised the removal of heavy water, uranium metal, radium and instruments by a convoy of lorries to Ronnenberg and headed for a secret location in the direction of Munich.

In fact, the material had gone to the Hechingen area, around 400 kilometers to the south. Pash and the Alsos Mission headed south, towards Stuttgart.

Walther Gerlach had first suggested to Schumann and Diebner that Hechingen, south of Stuttgart, would be a good place to hide their atomic laboratories when the bombing of Berlin became too great to continue there. He knew the area because he had studied physics at nearby Tubingen, where he became a professor. It was an area of steep limestone cliffs cut into gorges and beautiful narrow wooded valleys by the River Eyach, twisting into a serpentine 'S' at Haigerloch.

Gerlach said it would be easy to dig a secret bunker into the cliffs of the soft limestone where they could establish a network of laboratories safe from Allied bombers. During a recce of the area, they found a cave had already been hewn out of the sheer rock at the base of the cliff in Haigerloch, eighty feet below the church and the castle. It was being used as a beerkeller, and would suit their purposes perfectly. It would not need excavating and, being under the church, no one carrying out surveillance from the air would suspect Germany's main atomic reactor was there.

The cave was used by Johan Merz, the innkeeper of the nearby seventeenth-century inn, *Gastahus Schwanen* (the Swan Inn), to keep his barrels of beer cool.[8] German beer was to give way to a mixture of uranium, graphite and heavy water.

Townsfolk in Haigerloch saw the mysterious work start in September 1944. An official approached Johann Beck, who lived in *Pfluggasse*, the narrow lane leading to the cavern, to clear the cave because it was needed for another purpose. Lufthansa workers came from the Meyer factory in the Karistal to dig the reactor pit and complete the construction work. Access was banned to anyone who was not connected with the Kaiser Wilhelm Institute. Rooms were commandeered in the nearby *Oberstadtrasse* and *Unterstadt* for staff from the institute. One night, Beck was told not to allow anyone to leave his house because lorries would be arriving with a delivery. A few days later, Beck's son, Hans, was warned that he and his friends should keep clear of the former beerkeller and the people who worked there, but they were curious. 'A person with a white coat came out and had a glass tube of about 2.5 m in length upright in his hands. The man went down the *Pfluggasse*. We followed and his way terminated at the building of the District Court. A door opened and the man went inside. We learned that here in the District Court a laboratory was installed that would belong to the K. W. I.'

Despite the warnings curiosity got the better of young Hans Beck, who entered the mysterious cave during an air-raid alarm. He saw a furnace and a lavatory in the entrance to the cellar, while a second room contained the workshop with a workbench, drilling machines, a lathe and another furnace. There was a hole in the ground that was covered. Layers of graphite blocks were stacked between the hole and three aluminium containers. 'I asked a man for the purpose of so many briquettes. He told me that it would be graphite with which I could draw and he gave me a small piece.'[9]

The Reverend Marquard Guide, whose beautiful baroque church stood at the top of the limestone cliff, towering over the cave, was allowed to see inside the Atomkeller when the other scientists were away by Professor Fischer, a member of Heisenberg's team. Guide saw a large dome on the floor of the cave and a tangle of wires on the ceiling. 'I told Professor Fischer that this would be our doom. But he just said, "Just as you have in the church your *Sanctissimum*, this is our *Sanctissimum*".'[10]

As German resistance collapsed, Heisenberg, von Weizsäcker and Bagge decided to bury their stocks of uranium and heavy water and hide their research documents. Heisenberg noted in his diary for 17 April: 'In the morning trip with Wirtz, Bopp and Fischer to Haigerloch, to determine the place for the U-metal. At the Seehof a division troop is staying bound for the Alb [a plateau in the Swabian Alps] during the night. In the distance smoke clouds of burning villages; at the horizon for the first time detonations of grenades. The defeated German artillery has passed through Haigerloch during the night and went on in the direction of Balingen.'

Three days later, Pash left the forward headquarters at 3 p.m. on 20 April in one of the two armoured cars for the final lap of his mission. He was closely followed by nine men in three Jeeps.

Eddie Dolan, driving the first armoured car, was ready for combat against die hard Nazis, but their first obstacle was the French; they suspected the Americans wanted to advance into their zone to capture a group of Vichy French collaborators who were believed to be holed up in a town on the Danube called Sigmaringen.

The French had advanced much faster than expected towards Stuttgart, and had already taken Horb, a town to the south of the city; they were now ready to push on towards Haigerloch, despite orders to leave it to the Americans. Having advanced to Freudenstadt on the eastern slopes of the Black Forest, Pash now had to face a run of 130 miles in about five hours to secure his objectives, in darkness, with not only the Nazis to avoid, but also the French.

When they reached Horb on 21 April, they found it had been heavily damaged by the advancing French armour, but a beer garden had survived, where Pash set up his command post. They found a small unit of twenty French troops with two machine guns on the bridge in Horb and Pash demanded to see their commanding officer. A French major arrived, and Pash congratulated him on his swift progress, but told him to hold firm at the line of the river Necker.

Scouts returned with the news that Haigerloch appeared to be unoccupied. By the time Pash reached Haigerloch early on the next morning of 22 April, the fight had gone out of Heisenberg's People's Defence League. It had disbanded three days before and Pash was relieved to find the town surrendering with every form of white sheet they could find, hanging out of the windows of their houses from broom handles and garden poles, as his convoy of Jeeps and armoured cars wound down to the bridge across the river Eyach. They parked in the market place by the river, surrounded by medieval-style half-timbered houses including the *Gasthaus Schwanen,* which dated from before the Thirty Years War, with a façade showing the Fall of Man. Towering above the town, Pash saw the 800-year-old fairy-tale castle with its ancient church perched precariously on the edge of an 80-foot drop of sheer limestone rock. Hooded crows circled from the trees at the top of the cliff, protesting at the intrusion.

Marti Previti and Lawrence Feindt, Special Agents of the US Counter-Intelligence Corps, with Jack Ditesheim and Gus Toepel, two army lieutenants attached to the Alsos team, led teams in a rapid operation to find the Nazi atomic bomb laboratory. They quickly located the cave, directly below the church on top of the cliff, which Pash thought was an ingenious set-up to avoid detection from the air.

Hans Beck witnessed their search from his house in the *Pfluggasse.* 'The soldiers entered the *Gasthaus Schwanen* with their machine guns at the ready and came out again after a short time with the old inn keeper, Johann Merz. He led them to the cavern, which was occupied by the American soldiers and guarded.'[11]

The innkeeper led them down an alley, between the rock face and a short row of houses to a blockhouse that had been constructed over the entrance to the cavern with bricks and reinforced concrete. It was protected by a steel door that was padlocked. Contact details for the manager of the plant were on the door. When the manager appeared, Pash told him to open the door. When he hesitated, Pash told Beatson to shoot the lock off. 'If he gets in the way, shoot him,' added Pash.[13] The manager quickly produced a key, opened the padlock, and drew back the steel door.

At that moment, a Jeep pulled up to Pash. It was driven by Eddie Dolan, a young US soldier, who had been left with a broken arm in a field hospital run by the French. He had discharged himself to re join the Alsos Mission. A black-and-white cine film of the Alsos mission, taken by Tony Calvert for posterity, shows Dolan with his arm in plaster and a cheeky grin on his face.

Pash was not so pleased to see him.

'Dolan!'

'Sir,' Dolan replied, 'before you say anything, may I report that my arm was set, it is in good condition, and a French hospital is a hulluva place to be in … I even brought these gentlemen up forward, sir.'[12]

He had brought with him Fred Wardenberg and Jim Lane, who were also fluent German speakers. Dolan was lucky. Pash had other things to worry about; he had to dismantle whatever was in the cave.

Pash posted guards to seal off the narrow lane leading to the cavern while Wardenberg and Lane interrogated the German manager. He confirmed that this was the site of the Nazi 'uranium machine' that the Alsos Mission had spent ten months, and driven across France and southern Germany, to find. Wardenberg and Lane were jubilant, and their delight was echoed by the rest of the team waiting patiently in Horb. They raced the eighteen kilometres to Haigerloch when they heard the news. The giant figure of Hambro appeared almost as soon as the steel door to the Haigerloch cave had been thrown open. He led the British contingent with the SIS officer Eric Welsh. They wanted to go in immediately to inspect the main chamber, but Pash kept them waiting until after they had supper at the Hotel Post in Haigerloch.

When Hambro was at last allowed to see inside the cave, the British inspection team found it dark and dank. They wandered about, with the cave partly lit by candles, fascinated at what they found. Michael Perrin, probably the only member of the team who had seen a working nuclear reactor – Fermi's pile in Chicago – was appalled by the absence of radiation protection for the German scientists, who would have been made seriously ill if their pile had gone critical. One room was fitted out as a laboratory, another as a work room, and a third as a store where they found three tall cylindrical metal containers about thirty inches in diameter and forty inches high, mounted on concrete blocks, that had held the heavy water. They were connected by a pipe that ran into the large chamber. There were two electrical control boxes one on top of the other. On the lower one was written a name: Professor Gerlach. On the upper one was another name: Professor Diebner.

This was confirmation they had found Hitler's last atomic workshop. Compared to Groves's mini-cities for the Manhattan Project in America, it was a cottage industry. There was a small blackboard propped up in front of the cylinders. On it was chalked a message in German which, translated, said: 'Keep your Holy calm. Only fools are madly rushing.'[14]

Still pondering on the humour of German physicists, they moved into the main chamber, where they found what they were looking for: the German atomic reactor. In the centre of the main chamber they found a concrete-lined silo in the floor of the cave. Inside it was an aluminium container 210 centimetres in diameter and 210 centimetres high. It was empty. When it was working, it would have been surrounded by ordinary water for cooling purposes. An inner core contained an array of 664 cubes, each five centimetres in length; it would also have been suspended from a heavy metal lid lowered by electric winch from the ceiling. The space between the two vessels was filled with a forty-centimetre layer of graphite carbon bricks that provided an external shield, preventing the escape of neutrons generated during fission. It was just as Heisenberg and his colleagues had left it after their final attempt to reach criticality, except the heavy water and uranium cubes had been removed and hidden.

The next day, on 23 April, Hambro and Welsh got to work dismantling the German reactor. A US army photographer took the iconic photograph of the Alsos team as they began to remove the reactor in pieces: the portly Eric Welsh, in a British army uniform, stands above the hole in the ground, handing what appears to be a piece of graphite shield to an unnamed soldier. Wing Commander Rupert Cecil stands on top of the pile, dismantling more parts with Michael Perrin while Percy Rothwell kneels at the side, watching.

Hans Beck nervously watched as a convoy of American six-wheelers arrived and everything was loaded onto the trucks. 'When in the later afternoon, everything was loaded, we heard shooting and went to the window. We could see through the open front door of the cavern that soldiers shot with handguns into the three heavy water tanks in the cavern.'

A US soldier came to his parents and ordered them to leave their home in *Pfluggasse*. Down by the market square, an American colonel – probably Lansdale, as it was never mentioned by

Pash – appeared at the door of his manse. The officer told the priest he should open immediately all the windows in the manse.

Guide asked him, 'Why?'

The officer told Guide he had orders to blow up the church to cover the entrance to the cave below. Opening the windows of the manse would save them from being smashed by the pressure pulse from the explosion. The priest was horrified.

The beautiful baroque *Schlosskirche* had stood for nearly 500 years. It was attached to the 800-year-old Haigerloch castle that had been converted from an earlier fortress by Count Christoph, the first Count of Hohenzollern-Haigerloch, in the 1500s. The priest protested that blowing up his beautiful church would achieve nothing. He remonstrated with the US colonel that they had already removed the uranium and heavy water from the Atomkeller; there was no need to destroy his church.

That failed to sway the colonel: he was keen to obliterate all traces of the laboratory so that it would go unnoticed by the French when they occupied the town. The priest decided to appeal to the officer's humanity. He told the officer, 'Let us first visit the castle church so that you can see for yourself what would be destroyed.'

The church is up a flight of 145 stone steps. They made the long climb together up the stone stairway to the entrance. The officer and the priest stopped inside the ancient wooden doorway to regain their breath. They stepped inside and when their eyes began to adjust to the gloom of the dark interior, the US colonel began to see the beauty of the church. 'I explained to him the details,' said the priest. 'One artwork after the other – one more beautiful than the other.' Priceless treasures glittered through the shadows of the nave. Gilded icons glowed dimly in the dark, a glittering side altar, and a high altar dating from 1609 emerged from the gloom. Turning round, the officer saw a spectacular organ loft in white and gold over the entrance porch.

The colonel was won over. 'I have never seen anything so beautiful,' said the officer. Suitably impressed, he retraced his steps to the bottom of the stone stairway with the priest. As they walked down, the officer said: 'You really have had great luck here in Haigerloch. If the intelligence service had found out that nuclear research works had been carried out here, everything would have been destroyed. Carpet bombing by a few aircraft would have been sufficient...'[15]

At the foot of the steps, the priest stood back as the officer gave the order for the charges to be laid in the cave and the cavern to be cleared. From the marketplace, Hans Beck and his parents saw soldiers leaving the cavern. A short time later, 'there was an explosion and a cloud of smoke'.

After the smoke cleared the church was still standing, undamaged, eighty feet above the cavern. Though he records nothing of this in his memoirs, the locals say Pash ordered that the explosive charge to be reduced, so that it did not bring down the church above.

Wing Commander Cecil had been drafted into the Alsos team by the British with orders to organise the airlift of the Haigerloch reactor back to Britain, but Groves was having none of it. Groves ordered the pile to be flown back to the United States.[16]

The cave where Heisenberg and his colleagues built their atomic pile has been turned into a museum. A replica of the crude atomic pile that Heisenberg and von Weizsäcker worked on in the dying days of the war has been installed above the original pit. Lit with an eerie blue light, it resembles a chandelier or piece of modern art. The dummy core is suspended over the hole – 664 cubes of 'uranium' on strings of steel hanging from a stainless steel lid. In the back of the cave lies one of the original vessels that held heavy water and was shot full of holes by one of Pash's men.

An expert guide to the Atomkeller Museum, Egidius Fechter, tells the story of Heisenberg's nuclear reactor to a new generation of tourists. Most German visitors are still curious about why Hitler did not have the bomb: 'They know that fifty years ago the Germans did not have the bomb. They ask why? When I answer it was impossible to make the material for the bomb, they say: "OK".'[17]

Herr Fechter, who has extensively researched the subject, is convinced Heisenberg and his colleagues could have achieved a critical mass with their atomic pile at Haigerloch if they had possessed the raw materials. Whether they would have built a bomb remains an open question.

12

The Jackpot

Pash mounted his armoured car and headed for Hechingen, and, he hoped, the final chapter in the Alsos story: the capture of Heisenberg. He was reinforced by a company of the 1269th Engineer Combat Battalion and the head of intelligence at the US Sixth Army Group, General Eugene Harrison, who had been an aide to US Secretary of War, Henry Stimson, before the war.

Even so, Pash was worried more reinforcements would be needed. A patrol had reported that a village some way out of Haigerloch was being used as a collection point for over 2,000 German artillerymen, who were being retrained as infantry after abandoning their guns when the Siegfried Line was overrun and their SS officers had fled. They were now rumoured to be gathered around a former school in the village.

When they reached the village they came under small-arms fire from the school building. Pash ordered Gerry Beatson to take a note to the school under a white flag demanding they should surrender. Beatson said it was the toughest fifty yards he had ever walked, but when he returned, he was followed by 200 soldiers, who had surrendered.

Pash left four men with a Jeep as a prisoner-of-war collecting point, and pressed on toward Bisingen and Tailfingen, where he knew Hitler's Uranium Club had taken over a woollen mill as cover for more atomic research.

So far the prisoners had been unarmed, but it was only a matter of time before Pash feared he would run into serious opposition.

Pash sent an armoured car and two Jeeps to probe south towards Tailfingen, beyond Bisingen, the last known whereabouts of Otto Hahn and von Laue. It was late on 23 April, when Pash was getting ready to catch some sleep, that he received an urgent message from the Tailfingen team: the Alsos unit had been attacked by a Nazi last-ditch guerrilla force of youths, called the *Wehrwulf* – Werewolves – a name dreamt up by Josef Goebbels, the propaganda minister.[1]

The attack took place to the east of Bisingen on the road into a town called Thanheim. Gerry Beatson, who had been on the mission, arrived with more details: two German soldiers at a well had spotted the US team and run. A few moments later, all hell broke loose. 'The Krauts lobbed mortar shells, opened up with machine guns.'

Beatson screamed at Eddie Dolan, the driver, to turn the armoured car around, but it would not move. 'I yelled for Eddie to get the hell outa there.' Dolan told him that an engineer soldier they had taken on board had dropped down so low when the shooting started, Dolan could not get his feet on the pedals. He kicked the guy out of the way, reversed, and escaped, but Beatson said they then had a second fight with some of the local people.

Pash was told that another unit also had come under fire in Bisingen. The stakes were too high for Pash to be held up. Pash says in his memoirs of the Alsos Mission that he ordered the Bisingen *Burgomeister* to be taken into custody with a warning of reprisals if his men were attacked again.[2] But that is not the whole story.

According to a report filed by his aide Eckman in the Pash archives at the Hoover Institution Library, Stanford, a civilian leader was actually shot. 'The Burgomaster of the town tried to incite the *Folkstrom* against the Task Force. He was taken to prison and his assistant shot.' It may be judged harsh by today's standards, but it worked. The fight had gone out of the *Folkstrom* by the following morning when Pash returned in force.

At 6 a.m. on 24 April, Dolan called on Colonel Pash and General Harrison to take them to their field mess for breakfast before beginning their final lap of Operation Big. They moved out at 8 a.m. in two armoured cars, with four Jeeps, a supporting column of company strength from 1269th Combat Engineer Battalion and the headquarters platoon. A couple of miles outside Thanheim, Pash and Harrison halted their armoured cars at a

Bavarian *Gasthaus* with a beer garden to allow the rest of the force to catch up.

On entering the *Gasthaus,* Pash asked the owner if his telephone still worked. When told that it did, Pash asked the Thanheim operator for 'den *Burgomeister,* bitte'. A few seconds later, the *Burgomeister* of Thanheim was on the line. Pash told him that he was a colonel in the US Army and Lieutenant Fiebig would give him Pash's order. Fiebig told the *Burgomeister* in German that the US force would move into Thanheim at 11 a.m. and Pash would give him fifteen minutes to surrender. Without hesitating, the *Burgomeister* said: 'Thanheim surrenders!'

An hour later, with Company A of the 1269th Combat Engineer Battalion walking along the side of the road, Pash stepped out of his armoured car and walked with General Harrison the last few hundred yards to the town hall of Thanheim to accept the surrender. A photographer embedded with 'Lightning A' captured the moment; he took a photograph of bespectacled Pash marching in front of his armoured car, looking resolute, to take the town's surrender.

In the early afternoon of 24 April, Pash and 'Lightning A' pushed on to Hechingen through steep-sided, wooded valleys. Here he encountered a French unit, but they were intent on reaching the Vichy collaborators rumoured to be in Sigmaringen. Pash lied to them that he had called for heavy artillery to clear the way, and ordered the French commander to keep his men out of the area, which he did.

'Lightning A' captured the Grotz textile mill in Tailfingen without a fight. Within fifteen minutes, they had taken over the woollen mill and six nearby buildings, which had been used by Heisenberg, Otto Hahn and their team as a laboratory for the Berlin Kaiser Wilhelm Institute, in addition to storage for their stocks of uranium and heavy water. They also located Heisenberg's office but, just a week before, Heisenberg had gone to join his wife and family in their mountain cabin in Bavaria.

Pash noticed Heisenberg had left on his desk a framed photograph of himself taken with a friend before he boarded ship in New York for his return to Germany and the war in 1939. Pash instantly recognised the person standing by Heisenberg at the dockside: it was Sam Goudsmit.

In his diary for 17 April, Heisenberg noted:

> 7 p.m. institute meeting: Start of evacuation of the facilities, secrecy, I myself will be leaving. After 8 p.m. departure of the technical staff for Haigerloch, the uranium metal will be buried in the night. In the evening, visit from Miss Reinebeck's father in my apartment who most graciously brings me wine, cigarettes, and chocolate.

Pash's team rounded up twenty-five scientists, including von Weizsäcker and Bagge, and placed them under guard in separate rooms in the mill so that they had no chance to agree on a story. At first, they denied all knowledge of lab reports and important documents relating to their uranium research, but the interrogators beat down their resistance over the next four days using the receipts for documents they had captured in Strasbourg that carried their addresses on the letterheads, with a complete disregard for secrecy. Hahn was helpful, and volunteered what details he could about the whereabouts of documents and uranium.

Finally, the haughty von Weizsäcker broke, and told them he had not destroyed his files as he had earlier claimed; he had hidden the documents, wrapped in protective covering, in a drum that had been dropped into the cesspool. The uranium ingots had been buried in a field and three large drums of heavy water were buried by an old water-driven grist mill outside town.

Pash gave the messy job of retrieving the files to the British intelligence officers, Michael Perrin and Lieutenant Commander Welsh, and US scientist Jim Lane. On 26 April, Dolan drove them back to Haigerloch where they began the excavations in a nearby field. A German technician brought from Haigerloch was ordered to lead the digging to avoid the Allied men being caught by a booby trap; he quickly struck a wooden cover. When it was lifted, they uncovered nearly the entire core of the Nazi atomic pile in uranium cubes. They were loaded onto a truck by the US 1269th Engineer Combat Battalion. They appeared small but they weighed over 2 tons. Three drums of precious heavy water hidden in petrol cans were recovered from a cellar in the mill.

Perrin, Welsh and Jim Lane still had the unappetising task of retrieving von Weizsäcker's hoard of documents from a cesspool outside the home of one of von Weizsäcker's friends. They arrived with long poles, but quickly found the filthy task too much for them. They dropped the drum back into the slurry of human waste, while two US soldiers, armed with protective gloves and a stream of water, did their dirty work for them. Eventually, the documents were recovered. The seizures from the cesspit brought the official end to Operation Big.

A secret cable carrying the good news was sent from Eisenhower to General Marshall, the US Chief of the Defense Staff, and Henry Stimson, the Secretary of War. It was marked for their 'EYES ONLY':

> The special Alsos repeat Alsos Mission headed by Boris Pash, working with the task force of Six Army Group, have hit the Jackpot in the Hechingen area – for the eyes only of General Marshall and the Secretary of War from Eisenhower – and have secured personnel, information and materiel exceeding their wildest expectations. Full details will be reported later through the usual secret channels, but we now unquestionably have everything and none of this information has leaked out.[3]

Despite its jubilant tone, the hunt for Heisenberg was not over. Pash learned that Heisenberg had travelled 200 miles by bicycle and train – the only forms of transport he could rely on as Germany collapsed into chaos – to his mountain retreat in Urfeld, in the Bavarian Alps. Pash would have to follow his quarry east into the mountains of Bavaria, where Hitler's die hard supporters were rumoured to be gathering for one last stand. There was a nagging fear among the Allied high command that Hitler wanted to go out with a spectacular bang; that the Führer would finally unleash a secret weapon against the invading forces. It was fed by wild rumours that the Nazis were planning to mount their own version of Wagner's *Götterdämmerung* in a *Bergfestung* (mountain fortress), manned by thousands of fanatical SS troops wearing the death's head symbol, and willing to die for the fatherland in one last big suicidal stand.

The rumours were encouraged among Hitler's high command: Gerlach told Rosbaud after the Haigerloch test that their research would be evacuated to the Führer's Alpine Redoubt. Crack SS troops were reported to have been withdrawn from the Eastern Front against the Russians and moved into a vast underground Nazi fortress in the mountains in Bavaria. Allen Dulles, the OSS intelligence agent in Bern, Switzerland, who had put up the suggestion of an assassination plot to kill Heisenberg, dutifully passed on the rumours in his summary of available intelligence in mid-February 1945. It had enough circumstantial evidence to make it sound plausible: it was well known that Himmler, the head of the SS, and Hitler each had their own mountain retreats. If there were a Führer mega-bunker anywhere, surely it would be there. Diebner was rumoured to have been taken to Bavaria by the SS with orders to continue his research into uranium energy in a gigantic mountain bunker dug deep into the Bavarian Alps. Could Hitler be building a plutonium poison bomb in a secret Nazi fortress, just as Groves feared on D-Day?

Pash was worried he could be walking into an atomic disaster when he left Bisingen on Heisenberg's trail. Pash's feeling of foreboding was underlined by a final chapter of his Alsos memoirs, which he wrote by hand on foolscap sheets. It was called 'into the Alpine Redoubt'.

When he was planning his moves for the last lap of the mission, Pash had been alarmed to find that the main spearhead of the US 7th Army was not directed at the Hechingen area. The Hellcats, the US 12th Armoured Division, were trying to outpace the 10th Armoured Division, but they were ordered to strike east and northeast to an area between lakes Ammer and Starnberg. The combat command was to continue its thrust to the south. That left the areas of Kochel and Walchensee and Urfeld open with little US military back up. Pash was, however, promised the 36th (Texas) Division, who were last reported to be at Landsberg, some way behind. He had a choice – did he wait for the Texas infantry to catch up or should he continue with the 'Lightning A' rapid advance of the Alsos Mission as he had in the past? He decided to 'plunge ahead' without waiting for the reinforcements. He left orders for the Texas Division to rendezvous with him at Kochel, near Urfeld, and he moved out with the Alsos team. The journey by the convoy of Jeeps and armoured cars was captured on Calvert's black and white silent cine camera.[4]

His remarkable footage shows a sudden change in the weather. One minute the Jeeps are surrounded by trees bursting with spring blossom; the next, they are in a snow blizzard that blankets the men, the Jeeps, houses, the fir trees, and the road signs. Pash's Jeeps ran into snow a foot deep after Vailingen.

Pash and his men paused briefly to pose for Calvert's cine camera on the Disney-like battlements of the Hohellerengen Castle high on its own hill, with commanding views of the plains. As they push on, they come across a large hotel with Bavarian artwork on the gable wall in Bad Kochel on the approach to *Kochelsee* (Lake Kochel). It was about a mile before the main town where Pash had ordered the rendezvous with the Texas Division.

Pash and his task force were therefore delighted when they came across the US 36th Cavalry Reconnaissance Platoon under Lieutenant Frank C. Anderson Jnr, from Butler, Pennsylvania, waiting at the *Gasthof*. Pash assumed Anderson had been ordered to make the rendezvous here, but Anderson had no such orders.

Anderson told him they were on a recce for the main battle group; they had gone a short way up the mountain as far as a bridge but found it had been blown by 'some Nazi teenagers who considered themselves Werewolves (*Wehrwulf*).' They had decided to turn back at the point. Anderson told Pash 'There's no way to get vehicles across the gorge. It's a tough mountain to climb.'

One way or another, Pash replied, he was going to climb up the mountain. As he was puzzling how to do so, he received word that a German major general wanted to surrender. When he arrived, the German officer told Pash that a small SS unit had passed by, and a pro-Nazi writer, Colin Ross, who had toured America, was living in the village of Urfeld, six miles away. Pash found this disturbing, fearing the presence of a Nazi writer and diehard teenage storm troopers indicated they could encounter stiff resistance in the wooded mountains. Perhaps the rumours of a last stand were true.

It did not deter him, however. Calvert's film of 'Lightning A' shows Pash's Jeeps cautiously moving forward and the snow getting deeper as they climb up through the wooded foothills. The road to the bridge across a gorge is covered in snow. It gets deeper as the road enters a series of S-bends rising up the mountain. Eventually they come to a halt by the bridge. It had been blown.

Pash had to concede the *Wehrwulf* youths had done a good demolition job, dumping the bridge in the deep gorge it once spanned. He realised there was no option – if he was to capture Heisenberg before he went over to the Russians or was shot by die hard Nazis, he would have to abandon the armoured car and hike up the mountain through the woods in thigh-deep snow.

Carl Fiebig and three men reconnoitred the bridge area and found a steep path leading up the mountainside on the other side of the gorge. Anderson told Pash he could spare ten men to make the assault on the mountain. In all, Pash led nineteen men across the gorge and up the mountain path on the other side. They had taken off most of their gear and looked more like Pancho Villa and his bandits than Bavarian alpine climbers. As they climbed a few hundred feet through the soft snow, they flushed out two frightened German soldiers, who immediately surrendered. Before sending them down, they learned from the prisoners that there were small bands of German soldiers roaming the woods as Pash feared. Further up, they found three more deserters in a trail hut. Gerry Beatson ordered one of the men to strip to his underwear. When Pash returned to find out what was going on, Beatson explained that he thought the guy resembled Adolf Hitler, and had ordered him to strip so he could see his underwear; he reckoned the Führer would be wearing the most expensive underwear the Third Reich could offer, and he wanted to see if this was Hitler in disguise. As the underwear was as threadbare as everyone else's, he let shivering 'Adolf' put his clothes back on and climb down with the other prisoners.

Pash's lungs were heaving by the time they crested the ridge at 4.40 p.m. and saw the dark expanse of the *Walchensee* shining in the fading afternoon light, surrounded by the natural bowl of the mountains. At the foot of the lake was a small town. It was Urfeld.

As they fanned out and approached the village, the keeper of an inn and his wife came out onto the porch of their guesthouse to greet the American soldiers with a white table cloth attached to a pole as a sign of surrender. Before long, German troops learned that the Americans had reached the inn. Pash and his small force were soon confronted by the officers of 700 SS troops who were eager to surrender to American forces. Pash was worried that they would discover that he had a force with him of just a handful of men. Using subterfuge to convince the German officers he had a far greater force in the woods, Pash told them they would have to wait until the morning, and bluffed his way out of a tight corner. Pash had to get on with his priority – to capture Heisenberg.

The innkeeper told Pash that Heisenberg had arrived about ten days ago, and his family had spent the winter in their cabin.

It had taken Heisenberg three arduous days to reach Urfeld from Hechingen, and on his journey, he had witnessed the collapse of the Third Reich as a fighting force. Heisenberg had travelled miles on his bicycle. It was a dangerous enterprise because the

SS had posted guards to stop soldiers or members of *Volkssturm* like Heisenberg from running away from combat areas. They had held peremptory tribunals before hanging deserters. At one point, he had to bribe an SS guard with cigarettes to get through: 'I had basically prepared for this peril by getting an identity document from the institute. An SS man recognised, however, that such a document could be fashioned quite easily at the institute and told me he would have to bring me in front of his commanding officer. This dangerous turn I was able to prevent by bribing him with the package of Pall-Mall cigarettes.'

The railways were still running despite regular bombing, but the schedules – normally the pride of Germany – were shot to pieces, like the rolling stock. Sometimes he had to wait hours for trains to take him on to his next stop; and then they were abandoned without warning. He recorded it all in his diary: he saw huge plumes of smoke and felt the waves of detonation in the distance over the town of Memmingen, south-west of Munich, as it was hit by large convoys of American bombers accompanied by fighters. When he reached Schongau railway station, the waiting room was filled by a 'horde of half-grown boys in SS uniform, probably from the Balkans'. On the final leg of his journey he had reverted to cycling, and had his biggest scare when he encountered some cars carrying the insignia of the SS in front of the wooden bridge at the moor to Kochel. He saw the passengers were 'hiding weapons under mounds of hay' – they eyed him suspiciously, but let him go. Exhausted, he was met by Elisabeth and the children at their mountain retreat in the trees above the *Walchensee*. It was the antithesis of a Nazi *Bergfestung*.

The Heisenbergs' wooden cabin has breathtaking views over the *Walchensee*, and still has happy memories for the Heisenberg family. He spent seven days going on errands on his bicycle, fetching milk and shopping, but the war, and Colonel Boris T. Pash, were closing in. On 23 April – the day Pash left Haigerloch – Heisenberg noted in his diary: 'Berlin is surrounded, the Führer in Berlin.' Four days later, on 27 April, he writes that he ran into the Nazi writer Colin Ross and his wife shortly before the beach area in Urfeld. They are pushing a suitcase in a wheelbarrow. He jumps off his bicycle and happily greets them, saying they would probably see each other more often. Austrian-born Ross, author of a pro-Nazi tract, *Unser Amerika* (Our America), tells Heisenberg he is very happy that the professor has managed to get back to Urfeld after all. Heisenberg notes the Rosses both appear somewhat curt and quickly say goodbye.

On Sunday, 29 April 1945:

> The 29th was supposed to be our anniversary and I had hoped for some peace and quiet to celebrate but I have to go to Kochel to get provisions ... Kochel is an ant-hill. Soldiers, SS, foreign labourers. In the train station a cargo train is standing with prisoners from Dachau who look terribly starved and pale ... Elisabeth has learned suddenly that Colin Ross and his wife have shot themselves in the night. People are talking a lot about this; Colin Ross was popular, his action is considered decent. 'The decent Nazis are taking the consequences, the scoundrels are left behind.'

When Heisenberg and his wife arrive back in Urfeld, they are invited to the Rosses' funeral. He goes as he is dressed – in lederhosen and a backpack. The bodies of Ross and his wife are laid out in the living room, shrouded in tent cloth, only the faces uncovered. 'The face of Colin Ross looks very angular, yet calm and at peace. This face is making a rather profound impression on me, but generally speaking, this time is so fraught with tension and events that even death is no longer moving me a whole lot.'

They were buried in graves dug a few metres above the house and Lieutenant Schneider read a last letter from Ross: 'He did not want to survive the demise of Germany and the new idea. His wife, a companion on so many hikes, also wanted to accompany him on this hike.' Heisenberg confided to his diary: 'For the last time we use the Hitler salute.'

It started to snow on 30 April and Heisenberg went with a friend up to the mountain huts below the summit of the Herzogstand to find a place of refuge. Up there, however, he finds a complete unit of mountain troops; at 995 metres above sea level, above the anti-tank cannons, he finds troops cooking in front of the huts he hoped to use. They see fires burning down in Grossweil and Schlehdorf and suddenly the whole gravity of the situation hits him; he resolves to prepare the cellar at his cabin and stay put.

The Heisenbergs had survived some nerve-racking days, waiting for this moment. The snow had got worse, and their son Wolfgang had fallen ill, with vomiting and pain in his right side, so they took him through a snowstorm for medical help. When they got back, Mrs Linder called out to Heisenberg from the door: 'Hitler is dead!' It was 1 May.

The next day, 2 May, the Enigma codebreakers at Bletchley Park in England decoded an intercepted message to all U-boat commanders:

On 30/4 The Führer died in the heroic Battle for Germany in Berlin with his men. According to his orders Grand Admiral Doenitz has become his successor. The Grand Admiral's order of the day will follow. The Battle for our people is being carried on.

Dönitz wisely wanted no part of it. Martin Bormann, the head of the Nazi Party, had sent a message to Dönitz confirming Hitler's death. It read: 'Grand Admiral Doenitz (Top Secret! Only via officer) Führer deceased yesterday at 3.30 pm Testament of April 29 appoints you Reich President, Minister Goebbels Chancellor, Reichsleiter Bormann Party Minister …' Dönitz locked the signal in his safe, and kept it secret.

The squalid truth about Hitler's death was graphically described by Hermann Goering when he was interrogated by intelligence officers of the US 7th Army. He told his interrogators:

When the situation in Berlin had deteriorated beyond hope, Hitler allowed his personal physician, Dr Morell, to escape to the South of Germany. Morell had been administering a very large daily dose of hormones to the Führer. Source [Goering] believes it was the sudden absence of those hormones which caused Hitler's general break down and subsequent death.

Following 20 July 1944, [the assassination plot to kill Hitler – a bomb exploded but he escaped] the Führer's health had been declining. His right leg and arm trembled spasmodically and the smallest contradiction irritated him to a high degree. Only Bormann, Goebbels and Fegelein [Hermann, brother-in-law of Eva Braun and member of Hitler's inner circle] still had any influence on him. PW [Prisoner of War, Goering] says the atmosphere of Hitler's shelter was horrible. His secretary and his mistress could stand it only by being drunk all day.[5]

In the days leading up to Hitler's death in his Berlin bunker with Eva Braun, Goering revealed that Hitler had planned to denounce the Geneva Convention and exterminate all prisoners of war, including thousands of Allied POWs and all political prisoners, but Nazi Party officials were opposed to it – all except Goebbels, the fanatical propaganda minister of the Nazi Party. Goebbels committed suicide in Hitler's bunker with his wife and children by morphine injections, followed by cyanide capsules.

There is little doubt that Speer was right – Hitler would not have hesitated in using an atomic bomb on London, if he had possessed one. Goering claimed Hitler was restrained from the use of chemical warfare during the last period of the war only by his fear of Allied retaliation. He often admitted he had missed the chance to use chemical warfare at the right time – the Normandy landings. He had been convinced that a German victory would be certain with the use of conventional weapons.

Heisenberg still had to worry about the present. There were SS troops lurking in the woods in Urfeld. He noted that news of Hitler's death appeared to be met with total indifference. On 2 May, Heisenberg wrote in his diary: 'Around noon gun-fire on the way to Sachenbach. Shuster and I try to identify the shooters with binoculars ... In the afternoon, I go to Mama with Ria. While up in the house, Elisabeth and Schuster are sitting in their armchairs in the dining area when there suddenly appear three armed men on the terrace, who push open the door and come up to Schuster and Elisabeth with their automatic weapons drawn.'

They immediately thought the armed intruders were SS men but they quickly realised they were Americans. Pash and Larry Brown reached Heisenberg's cabin after another steep climb up the west slope. They asked Elisabeth for Werner Heisenberg and she explained he was out.

Elisabeth telephoned her husband to tell him to come back. When Heisenberg returned to his cabin, Colonel Pash said he wanted to speak to Heisenberg alone. While they were talking, shooting erupted outside. Heisenberg recorded it in his diary: 'As we are sitting in the armchairs together, a wild shooting erupts outside. Colonel Pash jumps up, the automatic rifle at the ready, goes out to the terrace ...' A senior officer reports to Pash that one SS man is dead, two wounded and arrested, and the rest escaped.

Heisenberg adds in his diary: 'I myself am still too caught up in the fact that now, finally, everything had come to pass that I had for many years expected, feared, and hoped.'

The hunt was over. Major Ham of the Alsos team arrested Gerlach in the physics laboratory at Munich University and Diebner was picked up in Schongeising in Bavaria, around twenty miles west of Munich.

The Engineers of Company A went on to the Berchtesgaden, Hitler's Bavarian retreat, in support of the 101st Airborne Division on 5 May and helped to recover the art treasures hidden in a cave near *Reichmarschall* Herman Goering's mansion.

Hitler's Uranium Club was taken into custody, first into a comfortable mansion, but then into the house US troops nicknamed the 'dustbin' on the outskirts of Paris, where they were forced to make do with prisoner of war rations. They complained about their treatment to their 'jailor', a major in the British intelligence service, called Thomas Hardwick Rittner. Rittner sympathised with their complaints, but in Washington, General Leslie Groves had lost patience with Hitler's Uranium Club. He was worried they would defect to the Russians if they were released. He suggested to the British scientist Dr James Chadwick that the best solution would be to shoot them.

The British decided the time had come to airlift Hitler's Uranium Club to England for their own safety.

13

Farm Hall at War

Wing Commander Bruce Bonsey, the SIS air liaison officer at Farm Hall, was packing up to leave the MI6 'safe house' in Godmanchester at the end of the war in the summer of 1945 when he was suddenly ordered to be ready to receive a 'load of human freight' at RAF Tempsford and take them back to Farm Hall.

The country mansion in the sleepy backwater of middle England was to become centre stage in a drama about Hitler and the atomic bomb. The mansion was turned upside down as a team of specialists in electronic surveillance swarmed all over the house, ripping up floorboards, bugging every room that was going to be used.

'We were beginning to wind down when in June we were suddenly alerted to be prepared to receive and house a highly secret load of human freight consisting of seven bodies and two officers. Farm Hall became the scene of feverish activity as men swarmed all over the house, bugging every room, which was going to be used,' Bonsey recalled.

The bugging operation was masterminded by Lieutenant Colonel Thomas Joseph Kendrick of the Military Intelligence unit MI19, who was highly experienced in eavesdropping techniques perfected at Trent Park, the intelligence base, where the private conversations of Nazi officers were transcribed by 'listeners' in the M Room.

Electronic 'bugs' were placed in the bedrooms, the living rooms and the dining room at Farm Hall. Kendrick, however, discovered that, despite the house having many rooms, there was nowhere in the house where the secret recording staff and equipment could be hidden without being noticed.

It has been assumed that Kendrick's 'listeners' were secretly housed in servants' quarters above the 1860 kitchen range at the back of the house, until now. There was plenty of space in the hidden upstairs rooms behind the 'green baize door' of the servants quarters but I discovered a letter from Bonsey to R. V. Jones that confirms the 'listeners' were housed in the stable block.

'There were no facilities on the premises for recording,' said Bonsey. 'So an approach was made to a local important and patriotic neighbour with a house across the road that immediately agreed to allow the recording apparatus to be set up in his stables. Some boards had been put on top of the gate leading out of the garden to the parking area to prevent anyone looking in or out.'[1] It still raises a puzzle, though. There is no house with stables directly 'across the road' from Farm Hall in West Street, Godmanchester. However, the house next door, 22A West Street, is a converted barn and stables, now called Farm Hall Barn, and it is almost certain that this is where Kendrick concealed his listening team.

The listeners were native German speakers including Professor Peter Ganz, and his colleagues Pulay, Lehmann, and Heilbron. Another myth is that the conversations were 'taped'; in fact, they were recorded on shellac-covered metal discs that could be reused once the conversations had been transcribed. Professor Ganz said they used up to eight recording machines but only the most important extracts of conversations were transcribed, about 10 per cent of the total. Most of the original German verbatim records have been lost or destroyed, but the English transcripts were kept secret in the archives in Kew and the Pentagon until it was judged safe to declassify them in 1992. They caused a furore when they were released that is still going on today because they challenged the West over its use of nuclear weapons, and showed that America's priority now was not simply the defeat of Japan, but winning the coming Cold War against the Soviet Union.

Bruce William Edmund Robert Bonsey was thirty-three and a young RAF staff officer of the recently formed Pathfinder force in 1942 when he was recruited by an old friend, Wing Commander Cautley Nasmyth-Shaw, to join MI6 and become his assistant at Farm Hall.

The rumours picked up by Ray Berry's mother turned out to be true. The mansion and its extensive grounds were compulsorily purchased for the war effort, along with 113,000 other properties and a total of 14.5 million acres, by the wartime Government under the Emergency Powers (Defence) Act 1939. Like many owners of large houses in the country, the Towgoods were paid compensation by the state and had to find accommodation elsewhere. Farm Hall's occupants, including the children, Mrs Berry, Mrs Towgood, her cook, her housemaids and Mr Cook, her chauffeur-cum-gardener, had to leave. It was all too much for Alderman Towgood, who died on 7 June 1942.

Little detail about what happened next to Farm Hall has been uncovered until now. It is frequently reported that Farm Hall was occupied by the Special Operations Executive, but it was never used by SOE, according to Bonsey. Farm Hall was the preserve of SIS as Number One Training Billet. It was run by the florid-faced RAF officer Wing Commander Cautley Nasmyth-Shaw, who had shown R. V. Jones the ropes at Bletchley Park shortly after the outbreak of war.

Nasmyth-Shaw had recruited his old friend Bonsey to help him run Farm Hall late one afternoon when he was having a drink in the bar of the Bridge Hotel, Huntingdon, and Bonsey walked in.

Bonsey, a duty flying control officer with Number Two Group Pathfinder force at their headquarters in Huntingdon, had spent a tedious day smoking, writing letters, and reading to fill time because there was no flying due to low cloud. He wrote in his diary: 'Oct 42. An overcast day and there was no activity possible by daylight bomber squadrons 2 Group. Depressed and bored, by the end of the watch, I decided to call in at the Bridge Hotel on my way back to the Mess at the Old Court House in Godmanchester.'[2]

George, the barman at the Bridge Hotel, 'had many an amusing tale to tell'. He was six foot, middle-aged, theatrical with quite long curly peroxide hair, and was what Bonsey described as 'uninhibited', which probably meant he was gay. George's 'somewhat flamboyant mannerisms were not approved of by the manly, beer-swilling hearties of which there are a number in the headquarters', said Bonsey.

On entering the bar, Bonsey was brought up short when he saw a chap wearing an RAF uniform sitting at a table with two ladies wearing khaki uniforms, blue tabs and hat bands, and two very fine looking men in khaki battle dress.

'Mutual recognition was almost immediate, though we had not met since 1938 when I was doing my reserve flying training at Filton, Bristol, and he was connected with the auxiliary squadron based there.'

Nasmyth-Shaw cried out: 'Bonzo!'

Bonzo instantly recognised his old friend Cautley Nasmyth-Shaw, or Pink Gin Percy – PGP for short. Bonsey said he was delighted to see him again.

Nasmyth-Shaw was about five feet nine inches in height, of sturdy build, ginger hair and a brushed ginger moustache under a nose that had been broken at some time. His somewhat florid complexion, in which his large cold blue eyes were a noticeable feature, may have been due to his penchant for pink gin, a popular wartime cocktail combining neat gin with Angostura bitters, which earned him his nickname.

Bonsey was over ten years his junior but during their time at Filton Aerodrome PGP and Bonzo went out several times partying together. Nasmyth-Shaw, forty-four, had a reputation as a ladies' man.

Nasmyth-Shaw had once regaled a visiting American intelligence chief over drinks with R. V. Jones at St Ermin's Hotel, London, about the time at Filton he had once bedded a girl who had a wooden leg, a detail he had not noticed until they undressed. For weeks afterwards, he would have wags in the mess bar asking him whether he still had splinters. According to Jones, the head of SIS's scientific wing, the story so entertained the American visitor that he told Washington he was getting along fine with the British.

Nasmyth-Shaw looked every inch an English RAF officer, with a regulation moustache and a laid-back English drawl to match, belying the fact that he was born in Camperdown, Australia. After serving as an officer in a British cavalry regiment, he took up flying in the 1930s, joined the RAF, and with his natural flair for adventure including spying as a tourist on German airfields which impressed British intelligence chiefs, he was recruited to the SIS as war approached. In the autumn of 1942, he was put in charge of SIS operations from Farm Hall, Huntingdonshire, despatching agents and bringing them back from the nearby clandestine airfield, RAF Tempsford.

After introductions, Bonsey noticed the two young men with PGP were not English and the two ladies were in the MTC (Mechanised Transport Corps), a uniformed civilian organisation providing drivers for Government departments during the war.

'Cautley suddenly turned to me and said: "Would you like to change your job? I need someone to lend me a hand." So without knowing what on earth I was letting myself in for, I said "yes".'[3] That is how Senior Flying Officer Bruce Bonsey joined MI6 as an air operations liaison officer, based at Farm Hall.

As they left the Bridge Hotel, Bonzo noticed that Cautley drove off in an old Austin 12 Shooting Brake, which had civilian number plates, and the two young men were driven off by the other MTC driver in a large khaki-painted Buick, also with civilian number plates. There was something fishy about that, thought Bonzo, and he wondered what the set-up was.

Nothing happened for a week or two, then one evening Cautley rang up and paid a visit to Bonsey's mess, the Old Court House, another large house that had been commandeered in Godmanchester not far from Farm Hall. As on other occasions, they went out to one or two country pubs.

No further mention was made about the suggested change in his job, nor did he learn any more about what Cautley was doing until a few days later. Cautley asked Bonsey to come and have tea with him at the house in nearby West Street where he worked called Farm Hall. Bonsey said:

I went along and rang the bell. After a minute or two, the door was opened by a member of the WRNS [Women's Royal Naval Service – known as the 'Wrens'] which was a surprise because although I had seen some Wrens from time to time in the town I had no idea where they came from nor what they did. I was shown into a comfortably familiar sitting room on the right just inside the front door … I had had little chance to see anything except the lawn through glass doors at the end of a passage which seemed to run straight through the house. Cautley soon joined me and with him came his civilian housekeeper – a large middle-aged lady of impressive personality. Conversation was easy and relaxed about nothing in particular. The tea and cakes were very good and then, just as I was about to leave, an RAF Sergeant asked Cautley about something or other. I found this all very odd – a squadron-leader in charge of the house, a civilian housekeeper, a staff of Wrens, an RAF sergeant, foreign men in khaki, and an M.T.C. driver in khaki with a civilian number plate. Things did not add up.'[4]

In early January 1943, Cautley asked Bonsey to come to London as he wanted to introduce him to his boss, Wing Commander V. J. 'Sofi' Sofiano (later Group Captain). 'Cautley and I met and had lunch at the Colonial Club at Shepherd Market and then went to the Cavalry Club to meet the Wing Commander and to have a glass of port. I found Sofi under which nickname I came to know him later with Squadron Leader Gilbert Frankau, the author who was in some section or other of RAF intelligence. Cautley talked to him while Sofi got to work on me.'

Sofiano questioned Bonsey about his past. 'He asked me all sorts of questions about what I had done in life and about my RAF service and so on. The party broke up and I went back to Huntingdon in a very thoughtful frame of mind. I had been deeply impressed by Sofi who was very striking-looking with a finely shaped head, vivid blue eyes, enormous charm and a very real laugh. I found he had wide intelligence and experience of the RAF in the Middle East.'[5]

Nasmyth-Shaw took his raw recruit to MI6 headquarters, opposite the St James's Park underground station, to officially 'sign on' as an SIS agent. Cautley had a pass for 54 Broadway Buildings but Bonsey had to fill in a temporary one at the desk with the help of a small, white-haired man who was clean shaven, had bright blue eyes, impeccable manners and the most charming smile.

Over the next two years, as Bonsey became a familiar face around Broadway Buildings, he discovered the doorman at the front desk had a positively encyclopedic memory for names and faces of the agents, officers and politicians who came there. Bonsey was shown around by Cautley and again met 'Sofi' Sofiano; DD (Air) Commodore L. G. S. 'Lousy' Payne, well-known as the air correspondent of the *Daily Telegraph*; and Flight Lieutenant Compton, a former actor, who was concerned with pinpoints and maps (he was lost in a cross-channel flight in a Lysander in 1944 after D-Day). In the outer office were Flight Officer 'Bunny' Dawkes, and Sergeant Gwen Weston, a member of the WAAF and a 'charming Canadian girl'. Cautley had his own office and a secretary, Miss Phyllis Pratt, who was most helpful over some of the paperwork with which Bonsey became involved. Next he was taken to be introduced to Wing Commander 'Fred' Winterbotham (later Group Captain and author of *The Ultra Secret*), head of Operational Intelligence.

Bonsey was then given a stringent lecture on security before being sent off to sign various documents for SIS passes, the Official Secrets Act, and to learn his new London address: PO Box 444, GPO, Howick Place, London SW, and a temporary phone number: Whitehall 7946. Quite unwittingly, Bonsey signed all the papers in the green ink that he normally used, little realising green-coloured ink had been for decades in the SIS the sole prerogative of C, the SIS Chief, Sir Stewart Menzies. Hardly had he made his way back to Cautley's office when telephones started buzzing in all directions and people started asking, 'Where is Bonsey? Send him to Security immediately.' Nobody knew what the flap was about, Bonsey included. 'With my knees knocking a bit, I found my way back to the security office where I was curtly informed that only the Chief used green ink to sign papers, that my fountain pen was to be emptied forthwith – supervised by a security officer – and never again was it to be filled with green ink, and it never was.'

A new set of papers was duly signed in suitably dark blue office ink. A short while later he was taken around to meet the heads of the country sections of SIS operations in occupied Europe and the MI9 Prisoners of War representatives in the War Office, whose headquarters were at Beaconsfield. They included Airey Neave, one of the few prisoners of war who had escaped from Colditz. Having escaped from the famous castle, the War Office and SIS thought he would be the ideal chap to help other POWs make a 'home run'; he was a frequent visitor to Farm Hall to brief SIS agents on escape techniques. Neave later became Margaret Thatcher's staunchest ally and her campaign manager when she defeated Sir Edward Heath for the leadership of the Conservative Party. I witnessed his murder by an Irish Republican terrorist group with a car bomb at the House of Commons on the eve of 1979 General Election, before Thatcher's election to office. I was working as a lobby correspondent in an office in the Press Gallery of the Commons overlooking Parliament Square when the bomb went off under his car. It was triggered by a tilt mechanism and exploded as he drove up the exit ramp from the members' car park. I ran downstairs to the courtyard and saw Airey Neave's blackened body in the driver's seat of the car with its roof arched by the power of the blast. A police officer put his hand to his neck to feel his pulse; he heaved a great sigh, and drew his last breath. It was a sickening way for a war hero to die. Airey Neave would have become Margaret Thatcher's Northern Ireland Secretary, and may have been able to stop her resigning in 1990 when her Cabinet stabbed her in the back. 'Treachery,' she said, 'with a smile on its face ...'[6]

The last of Bonsey's visits was to AI 2 (c) (Operations) in Monck Street, the section of SIS that dealt with special air operations under the command of Wing Commander Brooke. At this time the Deputy Director Intelligence (2) Air Ministry was Group Captain, later Commander, Jack Easton, with whom Bonsey had served at RAF Station Mountbatten in Plymouth in 1933. As director of air intelligence (research), Easton was involved in Operation Crossbow in 1944 to identify German V-rocket sites by using 3D techniques on aerial photographs, and, after the war, when he was assistant chief of the SIS, he was involved in the investigations of the Philby spying scandal.

What impressed Bonsey most on this round was the cordial welcome given to him, a newcomer to the 'Firm', without knowing whether he was going to be any good or not. 'I am sure this was due to the fact I had been recruited by PGP who was an old hand from pre-war days and had done some invaluable work. So they accepted me automatically as being all right.'

Cautley's exploits for British intelligence before the war included carrying out a daring spying mission, posing as a tourist in a light aircraft who had lost his way over Germany. He was grilled by the Gestapo, but he managed to smuggle out photographs of Fassberger airfield and the Me 109s stationed there as proof of Luftwaffe rearmament in breach of the Versailles Treaty that had forced Germany to disarm.

Back in the headquarters of Two Group, Senior Air Staff Officer Group Captain Alan Hesketh was putting pressure on Bonsey to take the post of Senior Flying Control Officer as a Squadron Leader but he did not want it, in view of pending posting to the SIS which was taking a long while to come through. Bonsey learned later the delay was caused by more extensive background security inquiries carried out about him in places where he had lived including Merioneth, Wales, and Staffordshire. Bruce Bonsey was born in Bristol into a wealthy family. His father, Arthur, described himself as living on private means in the 1911 census when he was living with his wife, Katherine, and two sons – Bruce had a brother called Nigel Arthur Philip Bonsey who was four years older – and three servants at the manor house in the village of Leonard Stanley near Stroud, Gloucestershire. Bruce joined the RAF and passed his pilot's licence at Filton. He was put on the RAF reserve list as a flying officer Class A in 1934. A few weeks after the war started in the autumn of 1939, he married Sylvia Whitbread in Paddington, but no further mention is made of her in his private memoirs held at the archives of the Imperial War Museum.

In February 1943, 'PGP' rang up 'Bonzo' to say the posting would be through quite soon. In view of the imminence of his posting, Cautley asked Bonsey to join him one night and go over to Tempsford Airfield where 138 and 161 Special Duties Squadrons were based to see what was involved. That night, he was arranging for two Dutchmen to be parachuted into Holland where they would set up an intelligence collecting point and radio to send reports back to London.

'I was invited to an evening meal at Farm Hall where I was introduced to the two agents known as "Joes"; their conducting officer, Captain Henry Druce; and the M.T.C. driver Mrs Audrey Tonge. We had a cheerful and well-cooked meal which included a special dish of fried eggs and bacon for the Joes so that they would remember a typical British meal after they had arrived in their own hard-pressed country.'

After dinner, they drove to the airfield with Cautley and Bonsey in the Austin Shooting Brake, the others following in the Buick. As they drove down the hill towards RAF Tempsford, Bonsey got his first view of the airfield. He could see the concrete runways, a few hangars and Nissen huts laid out at the bottom of a great bluff, Greensand Ridge, beyond the east boundary.

They headed first for the Ops Block where they met the Station Commander, Group Captain 'Mouse' Fielden (later Air Marshall Sir Edward) who later received his DFC (Distinguished Flying Cross) from the king in the anteroom of the officers' mess when King George VI and Queen Elizabeth visited RAF Tempsford. Squadron Leader Berys Harcourt-Wood was in charge of the Operations Block; the SOE intelligence liaison officer was Wing Commander John Corbie.

The mess was packed with young flyers, including Wing Commander Percy Charles Pickard, the Commander of 161 Squadron, and his navigator, Flight Lieutenant Alan 'Bill' Broadley, who were already international celebrities. Pickard, a six-foot-four RAF pilot with a mop of fair hair, was already famous on both sides of the Atlantic in 1941 after starring as Squadron Leader Dickson, the skipper of 'F for Freddie', a Wellington bomber, limping home after being hit in *Target for Tonight*, a remarkably honest propaganda film using real crews and wartime footage. Both Pickard, aged twenty-eight, and Broadley, twenty-three, were killed in February 1944 during Operation Jericho, a raid to free prisoners by 'blowing down the walls' of the prison at Amiens, France. They were attacked by two Focke-Wulf 190s as they circled looking for a straggler to shepherd home. The twin tail of their Mosquito was cut off in a single burst of enemy fire, the plane flipped over on its back and crashed in a ball of flame. Pickard's widow Dorothy said that his lovable pet, an Old English sheepdog called Ming, let out a howl at the moment he was killed.[7] The raid is still controversial because of the deaths of many inmates. Documents in the National Archive suggest Jericho was requested by SIS chiefs to free resistance fighters facing death, but French sceptics claim the raid was part of an elaborate deception to convince the Germans that the 1944 Allied landings would be through the Pas-de-Calais.[8]

Also in the mess that day were Squadron Leader Hodges (later Air Chief Marshal Sir Lewis Hodges), Squadron Leader Boxer (later Air Vice Marshal Sir Alan), Flight Lieutenant Hooper (later Sir Robin), Flight Lieutenant Vaughan-Fowler (later Group Captain), Wing Commander R. C. Hockey (later Group Captain), who flew special duties with 138 Squadron, and Squadron Leader Griffiths (later Group Captain) and 'an astonishing Frenchman', said Bonsey – Flight Lieutenant Philippe Livry-Level, later Squadron Leader and Legion d'Honneur, and his navigator Squadron Leader Hugh Verity (later Group Captain and author of *We Landed by Moonlight*). Livry-Level was forty-three, but had insisted on joining the RAF on active service and flew many missions dropping agents into occupied France for 161 Squadron with Verity.

When the war started, they had little idea about the right kit for agents. Philippe Schneidau, the first MI6 agent to be dropped in occupied France with the cover name of 'Philippson', had a knife and two pigeons for sending messages back to Britain stuffed in a pair of socks to keep them quiet inside his shirt. Fortunately, he had landed safely in a large sandpit in Fontainebleau Forest and survived with the pigeons.

The development of the agent kit was largely due to the initiative of SIS and SOE officers, including Cautley Nasmyth-Shaw, who devised a magnetic trouser button that could be used as a compass, which became standard issue to aircrew to help them in escaping. They also had lessons in make-up so that agents could disguise themselves.

The journey of seventeen miles from Farm Hall took about half an hour, as there was no traffic on the country lanes by which they travelled. There was a strict security check at the gate to the aerodrome, but the moment that Cautley was recognised, they were waved through. They drove down a steep hill and then onto a white building that showed up on the right. Bonsey recalled they meandered round all sorts of buildings until they stopped at what looked like a single-storey building called the Link Trainer Room, although it was not linked to anything and was too small for actual training. It was a shed.

Before long, the pilot, navigator and air gunner who acted as the despatcher arrived. After a discussion about the pinpoint on which the Joes were to be dropped, the Joes began dressing in their drop kit, with the assistance of the air gunner. The Conducting Officer checked on special items that might be required in a hurry. After about an hour, when all was ready, they drove round the perimeter track to the aircraft dispersal point. They stayed in the vicinity of the aircraft while the engines were started up and tested, during which a final drink was taken. At a signal from the pilot, sandwiches and coffee were given to the Joes who, after handshakes, boarded the waiting aircraft.

Cautley and Bonsey then drove off to a convenient spot to watch the take off. 'During all of this, I was in something of a daze because so much had happened in a comparatively short time and after the aircraft was on its way, I felt as flat as a pancake,' said Bonsey. 'However, a quick drink soon put me up and Cautley drove me to my billet in Godmanchester. I learned later he had gone back to Tempsford to await the return of the aircraft. Needless to say that next day and for some days afterwards I was very thoughtful as I began to realise I was on the verge of a tremendous experience in helping Joes to return to their countries, to work in conditions of extreme peril. I hoped I had the wherewithal to match up to this job in a strange new world.'

The posting to Air Ministry ATI (c), the air component of the SIS, at last came through in February 1943 to take effect from 6 March 1943. Bonsey left Pathfinder Force Number Two Group with the minimum of fuss.

At about 11 a.m. on 6 March 1943, a large khaki-painted Buick drew up outside his billet on the Godmanchester–Cambridge road with Mrs Tonge at the wheel, accompanied by Captain Druce. They took Bonsey and his luggage down the road to Farm Hall. It would be his home until the end of the war. Cautley welcomed him to Farm Hall and showed him to his room, one of the smaller bedrooms on the first floor.

Fortunately it was a non-moon period so no operations were taking place. This gave the new arrival the opportunity to look around. There was a fine kitchen garden tended by a first-class gardener who lived in a cottage adjoining the coach house area. There were two sitting rooms – one for permanent staff and the other for outsiders who might call; two dining rooms if necessary; plenty of bedrooms and a bathroom; the playroom in which there was a miniature billiards table, a dart board and card tables; a large equipment store room stocking everything available at the SIS store in Savile Row from guns to suicide pills; a kitchen at the back of the house, which was spacious though it was very old-fashioned, a good pantry and upstairs some satisfactory domestic quarters for the servants. Car parking was never a problem as there was space for at least six cars in front of the old coach house to the side of the main building.

The staff at Farm Hall were: Mrs Gwen Watchorn, who was from Barbados and had an extensive knowledge of catering; four housemaids, Philo and Green from London, and Ives and Penfold from Sussex; two cooks, Jones from Rochdale and Mackenzie from Perth; and a pantry/kitchen maid called Edmunds who was from Cardiff. In the autumn of 1943 they obtained the services of L. A. C. Webster as a helper to Flight Sergeant Chaborel in the gardens and around the house. Webster was a boxer with six sons in Colchester and was not someone to be crossed on nights out in Godmanchester.

At first it was quite odd moving into a country house existence with servants, cars and every amenity immediately available, and special rations after the ordinary fare in the mess. Bonsey admitted he felt slightly guilty at enjoying the new luxury when almost everyone else was on strict, austere rations. 'Cautley eased my conscience when he explained the reason for these special conditions was that it was considered highly important that the Joes' impressions and memories of life in England should be of high quality and maybe these would help to sustain them in bad times.'

Security in the area was quite a problem. Farm Hall was referred to as Number One Training Billet, but this did not satisfy some of the local 'nosey-parker' civilians who thought it most odd that Wrens should have anything to do with parachuting; and there was much coming and going of large comfortable cars, usually occupied by men in khaki uniforms driven by attractive-looking ladies who wore a uniform with blue hat bands and tabs. The fact that there was an RAF officer in charge was about the only thing that fitted in with the name. The local police were first class in the help they gave in fobbing off indiscreet inquiries or in cases where a Joe carrying out an exercise was picked up and his papers were not in order.

Soon after Bonsey joined, the SIS masters in London decided to change the name of Number One Training Billet to the Inter-Allied Inter-Services Foreign Liaison Unit, which seemed to satisfy everybody. To avoid drawing more attention to their clandestine operations, it was arranged that Joes would wear khaki outside the precincts of Farm Hall and at the airfield, except when going on operations. Even then they had to wear khaki mackintoshes over their travelling clothes and service caps on their way by car to RAF Tempsford.

On leaving London to return to Farm Hall, Nasmyth-Shaw and Bonsey motored north up the A1 and dropped in at RAF Henlow, where Bonsey was introduced to Flight Lieutenant Bunn who was in charge of the parachute section and who played an important part in parachute testing and development there. They lunched at Henlow and afterwards decided to call in at RAF Tempsford on the way back.

They had to use the Link Trainer Room as the dressing room for the Joes, a store for Joes' equipment and parcels and a rest room. Nasmyth-Shaw slept on the table in a sleeping bag, which he called his 'fleabag'.

'I had yet to learn what a ticklish problem it could be when four Joes had to be dressed – two each on separate operations – with two Conducting Officers and two drivers; then came two pilots, two navigators and two despatchers,' said Bonsey.

'They had to be sorted out and dealt with at the same time. This awful overcrowding with people getting in each-other's way sometimes caused irritation to be shown which, with nerves at very high tension, did not help Joes' morale. Except on very cold nights, the drivers had to stay outside.'

There was one other bouncy addition to the party most nights. Cautley Nasmyth-Shaw had a golden cocker spaniel called Cromwell, known as 'Crommie', who became a hit with the Joes. He was of unusual intelligence and happy nature, Bonsey recalled. The Joes sometimes sent back telegrams with a message saying 'Love to Crommie'. On one occasion, a Polish Joe on his return from an aborted drop was so upset with bad nerves that he grabbed Crommie and hugged him close on the journey back to Farm Hall. Crommie seemed to sense that the Joe needed him, and stayed with him overnight. In the morning, Crommie's calming influence had done the trick – the Joe's nerves were restored, and he went ahead with the drop.

A typical timetable for Joes to be dropped began with a call from the MI6 headquarters in London to Farm Hall; a luggage check was carried out to make sure it tallied with a form on which all details were carried out; they had to wait for another telephone call at 10.15 a.m. the next day from RAF Tempsford controllers saying they had accepted the flight. Nasmyth-Shaw then telephoned his section in London and the country section to say the operation was on. It was given a code name. At 11 a.m. on the day of the operation, Nasmyth-Shaw went to the airfield, arriving at about 11.30 a.m. The kit was laid out and the luggage rechecked. In London the Conducting Officer got everything loaded up into a large and comfortable car driven by an MTC driver. At noon the party arrived. After arrival, the type of aircraft to be used was looked over. If it was a Hudson, the technique to be used by the agents for exiting with parachutes was explained and there was a trial run-through on the ground. If leg bags were to be used, they too were included in the ground trial. The parachutes ranged from twenty-eight feet and thirty-two feet for an exceptionally heavy man to a mere twelve-feet for small parcels weighing fifty to sixty pounds. They returned to Farm Hall for lunch but with a stop on the way at one of the country inns on the route. They could listen to the 1 p.m. news on the wireless at the pub while they had another drink.

One of their favourite pubs was the Leeds Arms, opposite the cricket green in the pretty village of Eltisley in the open countryside halfway between Tempsford and Godmanchester. They stopped by on one occasion with two Belgian agents who had just been given a run-down at RAF Tempsford on their mission and were due to take off that night. The publican who served them with drinks was sufficiently astute to refer to 'the needs of our foreign friends' that impressed the Joes considerably.

On arrival at Farm Hall, the Wren in charge of the domestic side of the house showed the Joes to the rooms. Another drink was laid on and a good lunch was had by all, including the MTC driver who, besides being attractive, could also speak French to the Joes and put them at ease. The next priority was the time of take off, but as this rarely was announced before 3 p.m., they usually had an easy couple of hours after lunch during which they could rest or clear up the briefing details. Between three and half past, the take off time came through as 8.30 p.m. This meant the operational meal took place at half past five and the Joes had to leave the house at half past six. In the middle of lunch, London came through to say two operations had been submitted for the next night – two French and two Norwegian Joes, one of the latter being Oluf Reed Olsen (who later wrote about his all-but-catastrophic drop in his earlier mentioned memoirs, called *Two Eggs on the Plate*).[9]

After the aircraft was on its way the Conducting Officer went back to Farm Hall. Nasmyth-Shaw and Bonsey snatched some sleep in the Link Trainer shed until a call from Flying Control in the early hours of the morning alerted them that their aircraft was about to land on its return from the drop.

They drove out to the dispersal point to meet the aircraft and were told that everything had gone according to plan. They went to the Ops block and sat in on the briefing before driving back to Farm Hall where they managed to get a few hours of sleep. Bonsey had hardly closed his eyes when a Wren woke him up with a cup of tea at 8 a.m. After a quick bath and a good breakfast, he and Nasmyth-Shaw got ready for the telephone to start ringing. At 10 a.m. RAF Tempsford came on the line to say that the two operations for that night had been accepted so the routine was set in motion again – quarters, meals and kit were set in train and they drove back to RAF Tempsford to await the fresh arrivals of Joes.

At noon the cars carrying the Conducting Officer for the Norwegian Joes and a driver, at the same time as the Conducting Officer for the French Joes and their driver, arrived at the Link Training Room. The lack of space in the changing room left Bonsey hoping that the take-off times would not overlap.

This routine was repeated for the remainder of the 'moon period' – Joes coming and going, some returning because of bad weather over the drop zone, insufficient signalling over the pinpoint by the reception committee, or incorrect setting of the pinpoint lights, if a landing was attempted.

Bonsey recorded the Ops in a logbook with the date, code name of the Op, the number of Joes, containers carried, and remarks on the outcome. On 8 August 1944, he recorded an Op called Birch involving a drop for two Joes with leg bags; under 'Remarks', he wrote: 'NBG' (No Bloody Good) – 'Joe trble' (suggesting there was unspecified trouble with the agents). That same night, there was a similar outcome on another mission – six Joes were flown out on an Op code-named Ecollier and Bonsey's remarks were: 'NBG – No Recep' (the Reception Committee had failed to signal they were at the pinpoint).

Abortive sorties were a nuisance because the Conducting Officer and the driver had to return to Farm Hall as there was nowhere at RAF Tempsford for them to wait. They then had to return to pick up the Joes whose mission had been aborted. The waiting around while the cars returned to the airfield was not good for the Joes' morale, especially if they were feeling tired and dispirited in reaction to the build-up of tension on the outward journey.

Bonsey complained to Nasmyth-Shaw that the Link Trainer Room was very poor accommodation for what they were doing. Nasmyth-Shaw shrugged it off, saying it was the best the station could do for them. 'I was puzzled as to why this organisation [SOE] should have priority over accommodation but apparently their scale of operations was much larger than ours and there was nowhere else they could have used.'

SOE had the use of the roomy Gibraltar Farm by the runways at RAF Tempsford. Its weather-boarded barn became the last place in England many agents would see before boarding their aircraft for occupied Europe, never to return. It was here that they collected their kit and did their final checks, before walking through the barn doors to the waiting Lysander or bomber a few hundred yards away on the concrete strip. It still survives today as one of the most poignant monuments in Britain to the courage of the agents who passed through it during the war.

Gibraltar Barn

Gibraltar Barn stands alone among 650 acres of rolling farmland owned by the Erroll estate as mute witness to the heroism of the SOE agents and flyers who passed through it.

I joined a private party led by Lady Erroll to see a few huts and hangars where she has created a small museum dedicated to those who flew out of RAF Tempsford. We passed through a gate, just as Bruce Bonsey and Cautley Nasmyth-Shaw had done in the 1940s, and drove onto the airfield perimeter.

A few of the hangars they would have recognised are still in use; one of the Nissen huts that served as wartime offices for RAF Tempsford has been turned by Lady Erroll into a small museum. There are logbooks, faded photographs of flyers and bits of old aero engine; all evoking the past for the many relatives of those who worked here or passed through and are now researching their family histories.

Lady Erroll tells us, in a no-nonsense manner, about the history of RAF Tempsford. Then we scramble to the cars and head off to the barn. There's not much left of the old concrete runways. Bits keep appearing by the hedgerows in the fields. Then in the distance, we see Gibraltar Barn like a great stranded wooden ark among the flat farm fields. We draw up on a concrete drive, where Gibraltar Farm used to be. There is no sign of the farmhouse, which has long since been demolished and cleared away. The barn is brick and weather-boarded with one side open to the elements and the barn owls that nest here.

There is a barely visible strip of concrete by a hedge at the back of the barn. This is where a Lysander or Halifax bomber would have been waiting with its engines running to take the agents to occupied Europe.

Inside the barn, brick bays where the Joes' kit was stored are now unofficial shrines to those who gave their lives. They include Violette Szabo, whose faded photograph is surrounded by red poppies in one of the bays in the barn. The face in the photograph is achingly beautiful, as haunting as the movie star Ingrid Bergman. 'She was really very pretty. She was an entrancing creature to men and women alike. Everyone had wanted to see Violette off; she had bewitched the whole of Baker Street,' recalled Nancy Roberts, an assistant to Vera Atkins, who helped Maurice Buckmaster, the head of the F (French) Section in SOE in Baker Street.[10]

Violette was sent to France by Buckmaster as part of the SOE offensive for D-Day. She had two aborted flights before flying from RAF Harrington, a US bomber base. Nancy Roberts fondly remembered Violette in a thin summer dress, gaily chatting to another Joe, sitting on the lawn at Hasells Hall, an SOE minor stately home near Sandy, Bedfordshire. She was listening to records of wartime hits as if she had no cares. She was dropped near Limoges on 8 June, two days after D-Day, on a mission to help delay German tank reinforcements heading for Normandy. Two days later she was captured after a shoot-out in a road block by troops from the 2nd SS Panzer Division searching for a commander kidnapped by the French Resistance. She was tortured, transported by cattle truck to Ravensbrück, the notorious women's concentration camp where, on 5 February 1945, with two other female agents, she was dragged into the camp's execution alley, forced to kneel, and killed with a bullet in the back of the head. Violette Szabo was posthumously awarded the George Cross, which was sold by Tania at auction for £260,000 to Lord Ashcroft, a Conservative peer, for his collection of medals at the Imperial War Museum.[11]

As we left Gibraltar Barn, a pilot flew low over our heads in a small single-engine stunt plane, and started doing loop-the-loops in the blue sky over Cambridgeshire in preparation for an air show. It was the perfect salute to the courage of agents like Violette Szabo.

*

In August 1943, Wing Commander Nasmyth-Shaw left Farm Hall and Bonsey was put in charge of SIS operations there. A year later, in the autumn of 1944, Cautley married Jean Buchanan in

Huntingdon. After the war they retired to Southern Rhodesia (now Zimbabwe) as a tobacco farmer, where he died from cancer and cirrhosis in 1958. His son, Angus, an author, described his illness as part of the 'hazards of the colonial life'.[12] He told me:

> By all accounts, he was a decent, philanthropic man in later life. After WW II he came to Southern Rhodesia to farm tobacco but farmer he wasn't. He always had managers to run things as a gentleman farmer and bon viveur. His luncheon parties were legendary but of course his luncheon guests are all long dead. The barman at the Salisbury Club regaled me with stories of Cautley's wit and heroic drinking when I joined in the club in the early 1970s.

Cautley's departure meant Bonsey could have Cautley's large bedroom on the ground floor that had been used by Mr Towgood when he was an invalid, with its single luxury item – an en-suite bath. Around D-Day in 1944 the activity increased and the SIS took over Orwell Grange, a smaller house than Farm Hall, just off the Sandy–Cambridge road. He turned in the old Austin Shooting Brake as it was a 'bit dilapidated' in exchange for a new Austin Shooting Brake powered by a Ford V8 engine, which did 70,000 trouble-free miles until he handed that over in December 1945. His driver opened the throttle on its first journey from London to Farm Hall: 'We did not dawdle.' At RAF Tempsford, Bonzo was able to expand into a cottage and Shed 12. He was disgusted by the state of the cottage; it had been used by Irish navvies who had laid the airfield runways. It was cleaned up and used for dressing Joes and as the MTC drivers' rest room. He was also loaned Flight Sergeant E. Craddock-Gibbins, an armourer, and A. E. Driver, an aircraftsman and general handyman who was a former window-dresser at a Dolcis shop in Manchester. Bonsey said he was a concert singer but did not have a voice of 'Festival Hall quality'. By the summer of 1945, Bonsey's time at Farm Hall was over, and he was preparing to leave when he got the call to prepare for the 'human freight'. Lieutenant Commander Eric Welsh, MI6 officer in charge of Tube Alloys, arrived at Farm Hall to inspect the bugging arrangements and appeared to be satisfied. Then they waited for their guests to arrive.

14

Operation Epsilon

At 11.30 a.m. on 3 July 1945, Wing Commander Bruce Bonsey joined a convoy of large cars in his Austin Shooting Brake that moved off from the SIS Cottage at RAF Tempsford for a remote corner of the aerodrome. Then they waited, scanning the sky for a US transport plane.

Bonsey had been given the ETA (Expected Time of Arrival) as noon. He had driven the seventeen miles from Farm Hall to RAF Tempsford aerodrome in the V8 Austin, registered number GLH 439, wondering what it was all about. He had been told to pick up some human 'freight', but it was all very hush-hush. Shortly after 12 p.m., a Dakota transport plane carrying the precious human cargo appeared over the airstrip and touched down on one of the runways among the flat fields and headed for the dispersal site, well away from prying eyes.

Bonsey, an SIS air liaison officer, was used to dealing with fit young foreign SIS agents brought out of occupied Europe but he had not had an arrival like this. When the Dakota came to a standstill, out of it stepped a British military intelligence officer, Major Thomas Hardwick Rittner, followed by a group of civilians, including some elderly men. There were also two German prisoners who would act as their batmen, and lastly Captain P. L. C. Brodie of the Intelligence Corps. Brodie was to act as the administrative officer for the operation with the 'guests' at Farm Hall. Major Rittner was to act as their jailor, confidante and agony aunt. He became a central figure in the drama played out at Farm Hall.

Bonsey learned the 'freight' comprised Hitler's top atomic scientists: Otto Hahn, Werner Heisenberg, Carl Friedrich von

Weizsäcker, Max von Laue, Paul Harteck, Erich Bagge, Walther Gerlach and Kurt Diebner, along with Karl Wirtz and Horst Korsching, who had both joined the scientific staff of the *Kaiser-Wilhelm Institut für Physik* in 1937. Wirtz had been head of the experimental department when it moved to Hechingen in 1944.

The scientists were hurriedly put on board the waiting cars. Bonsey said he took Erich Bagge 'who had been a bit air sick so he did not want to talk which was just as well as I did not know a word of German'. With Bonsey's Austin leading the convoy, they set off for Farm Hall, arriving with plenty of time in hand for everyone to be shown their rooms and have a wash before lunch.

It was a relaxed style of living that they were to enjoy for the next six months. They even had five German prisoners to act as the professors' orderlies at their country retreat and all their meals were prepared by prisoner-of-war cooks. It was also designed by British intelligence to put the 'guests' at their ease so that they would be lulled into giving away all their secrets. Every word they uttered in the living room, the dining room and their bedrooms was faithfully recorded by the 'listeners' eavesdropping on their conversations in the nearby stables.

The subterfuge worked. Three days after their arrival, the 'listeners' in the stables across from the main house were amused to hear over their headphones the following exchange between Diebner and Heisenberg:

DIEBNER: I wonder whether there are microphones installed here?

HEISENBERG: Microphones installed? (laughing) Oh no, they're not as cute as all that. I don't think they know the real Gestapo methods; they're old-fashioned in that respect.

Their first meal was a bit strained at first as neither Mrs Watchorn, the housekeeper, nor Bonsey spoke German but Major Rittner and Captain Brodie kept the conversation going. Those Germans who knew a few words of English tried them out. Bonsey said they all seemed prepared to settle in peacefully except one, Kurt Diebner, whom Bonsey had heard was a 'died-in-the-wool Nazi' and who had directed Hitler's nuclear programme.

Bonsey said Diebner was 'sullen, cantankerous and aggressive'. He was ignored and left to his own devices and, after a while, the peace of the house and gardens seemed to affect him, and he became more reasonable.

Major Rittner was to provide Welsh and Michael Perrin of Tube Alloys with regular reports of the bugged conversations. His reports and the transcripts they contained were kept secret for nearly half a century because of the controversy that the Allied governments feared they would cause. Reading them today, it is easy to see why.

On 14 July 1945, Rittner sent a report marked Top Secret on how the scientists were settling in, with a handy character sketch on each of the detainees:

Werner Heisenberg, forty-three, the chief German theoretical scientist: 'He has been very friendly and helpful and is, I believe, genuinely anxious to cooperate with British and American scientists, although he has spoken of going over to the Russians.'

Kurt Diebner, forty, director of German nuclear research programme and a Reich Planning Officer for the German Army: 'Outwardly very friendly but has an unpleasant personality and is not to be trusted. He is disliked by all the others except Bagge.'

Erich Bagge, thirty-two, Diebner's assistant: 'Serious and very hardworking young man. He is completely German and unlikely to cooperate. His friendship with Diebner lays him open to suspicion.'

Carl Friedrich von Weizsäcker, thirty-six, a German physicist and philosopher, from an aristocratic family of diplomats: 'A diplomat. He has always been very friendly and cooperative and I believe he is genuinely prepared to work with England and America but he is a good German.'

Max von Laue, sixty-five, a nuclear physicist: 'Shy mild-mannered man. He cannot understand the reason for his detention. He has been very friendly and is very well disposed to England and America.'

Otto Hahn, sixty-six, German chemist and Nobel laureate, 'father of nuclear chemistry': 'A man of the world. He has been the most helpful of the professors and his sense of humour and common sense has saved the day on many occasions.'

Paul Harteck, forty-two, a physical chemist, alerted the Reich Ministry of War to the military application of nuclear chain reactions: 'A charming personality and has never caused any trouble. His one wish is to get on with his work. As he is a bachelor, he is less worried than the others about conditions in Germany.'

Karl Wirtz, thirty-five, a physicist: 'An egoist. Very friendly on the surface but cannot be trusted. I doubt whether he will cooperate unless it is made worth his while.'

Walther Gerlach, fifty-six, a nuclear physicist: 'Has a very cheerful disposition and is easy to handle. He appears to be genuinely cooperative.'

Horst Korsching, thirty-two, a physicist, worked on isotope separation under Diebner: 'A complete enigma. He appears to be morose and surly. He very rarely opens his mouth.'

For the German professors, their evacuation from the European theatre of war brought an end to a troubling few months being moved from one detention centre to another in France, though they remained extremely worried about the fate of their families in Germany.

They complained about being treated as 'war criminals' but for some of them with families still in Germany, their main concern was for the safety of their wives and children, especially if they were threatened by occupation by the Russians or – with more than a hint of raw racism – black French colonial troops. Rittner told his superiors that Bagge 'came very near to tears when he described the fate worse than death which he pictured was that of his wife and children at the hands of the Moroccan troops' in the French forces who occupied the Hechingen area.

Rittner was a fluent German speaker and part of Kendrick's team of interrogators and eavesdroppers on Nazi prisoners at Latimer House near Amersham, when he was chosen for the special task of looking after Hitler's nuclear scientists.[1]

On 1 May 1945, Rittner had been ordered by Lieutenant Commander Welsh to proceed to Reims, where he would pick up a party of German scientists and take them to a house in Spa, Belgium. The next day, Rittner flew to Reims, headquarters of SHAEF (Supreme Headquarters Allied Expeditionary Force) where he met the US Army intelligence officer, Major Robert Furman, who, at the age of thirty, had been promoted by Groves to head the intelligence side of the Alsos operation. Furman was the shadowy intelligence officer referred to anonymously by Goudsmit in his memoirs as his 'mysterious major'. He told Rittner the house in Spa was no longer available. It was the first of Rittner's many disappointments. They would have to use a house 75 Rue Gambotta in Reims, and that evening they were joined there by the scientists Otto Hahn, Max von Laue, Carl Friedrich von Weizsäcker, Karl Wirtz, Erich Bagge and Horst Korsching. Heisenberg, Gerlach and Diebner had been taken to comfortable quarters in Heidelberg – the forward base for the 'Lightning A' team – after being taken into custody. Paul Harteck, the physicist who was picked up in Hamburg where he worked, said he was treated like a hotel guest because a black US soldier carried his bag to his room.

At Rue Gambotta, the scientists enjoyed the luxury of a large house with American 'A' rations – the most highly prized food rations that included fresh, refrigerated, or frozen food prepared in the kitchens. They had a staff of two British orderlies acting as batmen and an American cook put at their disposal.

Welsh told Rittner that 'no one repeat no one' was to be permitted to speak to the scientists except on the express instructions of his intelligence chiefs. He took those orders literally, even refusing to confirm the identity of the professors in his party to US officers. This gave rise to all sorts of rumours, including that he was concealing Nazi collaborators from the Vichy Government of Pétain. The scientists gave Rittner their personal parole not to escape or to speak to others outside their group. However, as the days passed they became more 'restive', particularly about the fate of their families, and Rittner took up their complaints with his superiors.

Commanders at SHAEF had no time to worry about the complaints of the British major and his party of German scientists, despite their importance. They were busy negotiating the surrender of the German high command. On 7 July, the same day that General Alfred Jodl signed the unconditional German surrender in Reims on behalf of the German high command, Rittner flew with his party of scientists to the Château de Chesnay at Versailles, Paris. 'A Dakota was put at our disposal and the party took off at 1700 hours in the expectation that at last the long-awaited contact with their British and American colleagues was about to take place.'

They were let down in their expectations. There were no meetings allowed with Allied scientists and Rittner clearly felt a sense of personal betrayal by his superiors. Despite the area's associations with the palace of Louis XVI and Marie Antoinette, he discovered the detention centre was known as the 'dustbin' by the Americans who ran it. It was set up for interrogating German industrialists and scientists, possibly involving some accused of atrocities and war crimes, chemical and biological warfare, grotesque experiments on concentration camp prisoners, and perhaps the mass extermination of Jews.

Rittner clearly shared the disgust of his party of nuclear physicists that they should be treated in such a way and that they should lose their privileges. He seemed to take it as a personal affront: 'The conditions were most unsatisfactory from my point of view as complete segregation was impossible and there was a great danger of undesirable contacts being made with the professors. In addition, only camp beds were provided and there was scarcely any other furniture. The food was the ordinary P.W. [prisoner of war] rations ... It was obviously impossible to carry out my mission in these surroundings but I was able to pacify the professors who accepted the situation with as good a grace as possible and I promised to do my best to get them moved as soon as possible.'[2]

In fact, the order to stop treating German captives as guests at a five-star-hotel came from Eisenhower himself after he was stung by press criticism that Goering was being treated like a VIP.

Ignoring the risks of rocking the boat, Rittner rang up Lieutenant Commander Welsh in London from the Dustbin to protest. It was Victory in Europe Day and he found it difficult to get through. He did nothing to conceal his frustration in his official report to Welsh and Perrin: '8 May. In spite of the general holiday atmosphere at SHAEF and in London consequent upon the declaration of VE Day, I managed to contact H.Q. (Lt. Cdr. Welsh) by telephone and explain the new situation.'

It is not difficult to imagine the irritation Rittner caused with his complaints. In London, vast crowds thronged the square and streets outside Parliament to hear Churchill announcing from a balcony in Whitehall the news that the war in Europe was over. Central London was given over to a huge street party that went on into the early hours of the next morning. Women and soldiers joined in the revels, dancing in the streets; in the darker corners of Green Park some couples celebrated VE Day with sex in the shrubbery; nearby, crowds waited for the king and queen to appear on the balcony of Buckingham Palace, and the princesses Elizabeth and Margaret joined the throng, dancing the conga through the doors of the Ritz and singing popular songs of the day, *Run Rabbit Run, Hang Out The Washing On The Siegfried Line, Roll Out The Barrel, Under The Spreading Chestnut Tree.*[3]

Welsh told Rittner to contact Major Furman in Paris and make other arrangements through him. Few shared Rittner's concern for the welfare of this privileged group of German scientists. The Allied advance had started to uncover the pure evil of some Nazi scientists at the concentration camps: Auschwitz had been uncovered by the Soviets in January 1945; Buchenwald by the Americans on 11 April; Bergen-Belsen by the British on 15 April; Dachau on 29 April – the same day Heisenberg saw the trainload of starving prisoners bound for the notorious concentration camp. One US colonel said that the sights and sounds and stenches they found at Dachau were 'horrible beyond belief, cruelties so enormous as to be incomprehensible to the normal mind …'[4] Ravensbrook, where Violette Szabo and hundreds of brave women died, was also uncovered that day.

Major Tony Calvert's film of 'Lightning A' arriving in Berlin underlines the anger felt towards Germany for the war. Shot from an Alsos Jeep on the way into the bombed-out city, it shows lines of German civilians, looking miserable and demoralised, wandering through the rubble of their once-great capital, selling their valuables at the shell-damaged Brandenburg Gate, trying to scratch out a living. The caption on the black and white film reads: 'Some of their own medicine.'

Rittner was a devout Catholic and his family had its roots in Germany; the Rittners were bankers who married into an old Frankfurt banking dynasty, the Heyder family. Thomas was born on 25 February 1906, the second son of George Herman Rittner, a wealthy barrister, and took his middle name from his mother, Dorothy Clara Hardwick. The Rittners must have been well off, for the 1911 census shows they had seven servants living at their large house in Roehampton.

Thomas's mother also was a deeply religious Catholic – she became a nun after she was widowed in 1923 – and Thomas was sent to Ampleforth, the Catholic boarding school; it is thought he met his German-born wife, Agnes, when studying at university in Bonn. Being married to a German must have caused considerable complications in the early months of the war, especially for an intelligence officer. Many German nationals were interned as enemy aliens behind barbed wire in seaside hotels on the Isle of Man.

'We were always told that he could not join the regular army because he was married to a German,' his nephew, Luke Rittner, chief executive of the Royal Academy of Dance in London, told me.[5]

Luke Rittner remembered Thomas Rittner as a 'stickler for etiquette and upright behaviour.' His father, Stephen, would invite Luke's uncle Thomas to share Christmas at their home in the West Country. 'He was a bit straight-laced. Underneath, there was a gentle humour there but it took a lot of searching to find it. He was always immaculately dressed,' Mr Rittner recalled.

Before the war, Thomas was a commercial traveller who sold cash telegraph systems to department stores, but he joined up soon after war was declared. T. H. Rittner – serial number 1234542 – appeared on the general list of commissioned officers in March 1940 as a Second Lieutenant. He transferred to the Intelligence Corps on 16 March 1943.[6]

Rittner's reports to Welsh and Perrin added wit and true insights to the surveillance operation on the scientists while they were in France. Heisenberg, who seemed the 'most sensible' of the professors, felt hard done by. Rittner reported that Heisenberg suspected their potential was being undervalued by what was in the documents found by Goudsmit at their institutions. 'He said that these did not give a true picture of the extent of their experiments which had advanced much further than would appear from these documents and maintained that they had advanced still further as a result of pooling information since their detention. He begged for an opportunity of discussing the whole matter with British and American scientists in order to acquaint them with their latest theories and work out a scheme for future cooperation.'

Welsh ignored Heisenberg's complaints. Events would show that Heisenberg was deluded. The extent to which the German scientists overestimated their own achievements in nuclear research became clear when Paul Harteck was interviewed by Sam Goudsmit in his office. Harteck admitted they had not succeeded in creating a sustained nuclear chain reaction, and told Goudsmit the process was very difficult to explain. Treating Goudsmit as a slow-witted student, he pointed to a metal cube on Goudsmit's desk that was being used as paperweight and said: 'Let us assume that represents uranium ...' When he picked it up, he realised it was far heavier than ordinary metal. 'But this is uranium!' Harteck exclaimed.

The truth suddenly dawned on Harteck: the innocent cube had come from the experimental atomic pile in Haigerloch; the Americans knew all about their research.

Major Furman told Major Rittner that he would try to get the German professors, who had been joined by Kurt Diebner and Werner Heisenberg, taken back to their more comfortable house at the Rue Gambetta in Reims. Rittner badgered the British authorities to get the German scientists transported to England, and after they were moved to a large house in Belgium, they eventually agreed. Goudsmit expressed surprise at the British move to have the German scientists evacuated to England, especially as he was convinced they knew far less than the Americans and the British about atomic energy.

Lieutenant Commander Welsh told R. V. Jones that he had heard that 'an American General had said the best way of dealing with the nuclear physics problem in post-war Germany was to shoot all their nuclear physicists'.[7] The alarm had been raised by the British scientist James Chadwick, who had established a close working relationship with Groves, and reported back to London that Groves had told him: 'The German scientists should all be shot as they were undoubtedly as great war criminals as anyone in Germany.'

Groves later confirmed Chadwick's reports in his unpublished notes: 'This view was not relished by Dr Chadwick although he understood the reason back of it.'[8] Groves's biographer Robert Norris said Groves would utter many a true word in jest – he sometimes would 'blurt out rough and raw words expressing his deeply felt opinions'.[9] It was difficult to tell whether in this case Groves was joking, but Welsh and Jones were taking no chances. Jones was suspicious of Welsh's motives – there was a power struggle going on between the two men over who was to gain the upper hand in post-war atomic intelligence which was won by Welsh – but Jones felt the danger had to be taken seriously. Jones therefore suggested to 'C', Sir Stewart Menzies, the head of MI6, that they might be accommodated in an MI6 safe house near Huntington called Farm Hall. Menzies agreed and before the physicists arrived, Jones arranged for the place to be bugged by Kendrick.

For Rittner, the move could not come quickly enough. He had tried to keep them happy – driving them to Versailles to see the former royal palace of Marie Antoinette, and providing them with a piano that the atomic scientists managed to tune – but despite his efforts, they had become more agitated about the fate of their families in Germany. It got worse after Furman let slip that Hechingen and Tailfingen had been occupied by French colonial troops from Morocco.

Welsh asked Rittner to fly to England to inspect Farm Hall. Rittner said: 'We arranged for Colonel Kendrick to transfer the necessary staff of technicians from CSDIC (Combined Services Detailed Interrogation Centre) to man the installation. We were fortunate also in obtaining the services of Captain Brodie from CSDIC (U.K.) to act as Administrative Officer.' Rittner returned to Belgium to collect his party and on 3 July they took off from Liege airport. They were transported from war-torn Europe to the peace and tranquillity of the country mansion among the water meadows of Huntingdonshire, where cows gently grazed. It was a quintessentially English scene – Rupert Brooke had distilled it all in his longing for the nearby Granchester meadows when he was in Berlin in 1912 in his poem 'The Old Vicarage.' It ended with the famous lines:

Oh! Yet stands the Church clock at ten to three?
And is there honey still for tea?'

Outside the walls of Farm Hall, few had honey for tea unless they had their own beehives. Had he returned to the water meadows of Cambridgeshire, Rupert Brooke would have found honey was rationed to four ounces a week. Weekly rations (if you had the money) were limited to four ounces of bacon, two ounces of tea, eight ounces of sugar, two ounces of butter, two ounces of lard, four ounces of margarine, two ounces of cheese, and two pints of milk. Fresh eggs were a luxury; you could get two eggs per month if you were lucky. You needed points to obtain clothes (seven points for a pair of shoes) or luxury items such as tinned stewed steak (twenty points) and you were allocated only twenty-four points to last for about four weeks. Soap, too, was rationed. You needed two coupons for a large bar of soap, and you were given only four coupons a month.[10]

Inside the walls of Farm Hall, there was more than honey for tea. Rittner's first report said 'ordinary army rations are drawn from the professors ... and these are prepared for all by the PW cooks'. He was being economical with the truth. Breakfast for Hitler's Uranium Club consisted of unlimited quantities of cornflakes, bacon and eggs, marmalade, toast and butter. For lunch or dinner, they had rump steak or ham and often chips. Otto Hahn commented: 'No wonder that we all rapidly gained weight.'

To try to keep active, they played volleyball – 'fist ball' – across a net on the back lawn of Farm Hall. Bonsey said it was an extraordinary spectacle to watch these men of truly great brainpower throwing a rubber ball about on the lawn and laughing like children as they chased it, or missed it when they tried to kick it.

Erich Bagge recalled the games of 'fist ball' across a makeshift net but said the only ball they could obtain was a rugby ball. They were not used to its oval shape and the wild mishits over the net increased their amusement. They also played bridge or a card game called Skat 'accompanied by beer which was available in any quantity'.

The daily regime was recorded by Bagge in his diary:

8 am wake up
9 am breakfast – porridge and bacon
9.45 am to 11 am work in their bedroom

11 am to 12.30 pm fist ball
12.30–1 pm washing, dressing
1 pm lunch, meat, vegetables, potatoes, dessert, cheese, bread, tea
2–4 pm in the room
4–4.45 pm coffee with pastries
4.45–7.45 pm in the room, colloquium, radio, concert
7.45–10.30 pm supper
10.30–12 midnight piano, Skat and Bridge.

Bagge was not satisfied with ball games or cards however. All the 'residents' of Farm Hall had given a parole in writing to Rittner that they would not escape, but Bagge did escape – and more than once – over the corner of the garden wall at the front of the house to go to a local pub in West Street (including the Nelson, now converted into a house) where he met some of the girls from Godmanchester over a few beers. He was so proud of his escapes, he showed the spot where he shinned up the wall to nights of freedom in the village to Professor Echenique, the owner of Farm Hall, in the 1980s when he revisited the place of his incarceration. Bagge also passed some of the time sketching; one of his pen and ink drawings of the hall and the gardens where they played fist ball survived their internment.

Entertainment and education were served by a rather good library, Bagge recalled. The library was in the large bow-windowed room next to the dining room on the ground floor of Farm Hall, which is used today by the current owner as his study and library. Major Rittner read Dickens to the professors in the afternoons to improve their English.

Heisenberg sometimes played Beethoven and Mozart sonatas on the piano in the library as he had done at the home of Niels Bohr in Copenhagen. Rittner again tried to keep them happy by taking them for drives in his Austin Shooting Brake into the country.

'One problem that arose with these chaps was that signposts were being put back,' recalled Bonsey. 'Not far from the house was one which denoted Cambridge 16 miles. Several of the scientists knew scientists at the Cavendish Laboratory in Cambridge from pre-war days and would want to rekindle old friendships, particularly if they knew how near to Cambridge they were. Such a meeting at the time was, of course, impossible as they were under a form of house arrest, so a subterfuge was adopted if they went for a drive in the countryside to distract their attention from the signpost if they happened to go in the vicinity of it. Apparently Major Rittner and Captain Brodie succeeded in this and so far as I know there was no clamour to go to Cambridge.'

Rittner sent in a report about once a fortnight of the most interesting conversations with a few notes of commentary to Welsh and Perrin at MI6, and a separate copy was sent to the military attaché at the American embassy who passed on the transcripts to Washington, where they were kept by General Groves.

Rittner updated his superiors on the relationships between the scientists:

Hahn – unpopular with the younger members of the party who consider him dictatorial. Heisenberg – has been accused by the younger members of the party of trying to keep information on his experiments to himself. Von Weizsäcker – told Wirtz that he has no objection to fraternising with pleasant Englishmen but felt a certain reluctance in doing so 'this year when so many of our women and children have been killed'. Diebner – is very worried about his future and told Bagge that he intends to send in a formal request to be reinstated as a civil servant. He hopes we will forget that he was a member of the Nazi Party. He says he only stayed in the Party as, if Germany had won the war, only Party members would have been given good jobs.[11]

Rittner said Max von Laue 'appears from monitored conversations to be disliked by his colleagues' but this was hotly disputed by von Laue himself after the war. It was not supported by Bonsey, who found von Laue a 'particularly amusing character'. Bonsey gave a more endearing picture of von Laue: 'Well over six feet tall, thin and clean shaven, he had wide-set German blue eyes, pointed nose and wide grin more often than not. He hugely enjoyed charging about on the lawn and if I happened to be around when an aircraft flew over, he came rushing over asking "Vass ist dat, vass ist dat?" I told him whatever it was – a Spitfire, a Mustang, a Mosquito, a Lancaster, to which he replied "Yah, yah", then ran off to join the ball game again.'[12]

There were splits in the group between the young and old, and Heisenberg emerged as their natural leader, being referred to as 'the chief'. Heisenberg conducted learned seminars on nuclear physics, all of which were dutifully recorded and transcribed by the listeners. Above all, they could not understand why their knowledge of atomic energy was not being exploited. Some looked forward to lucrative posts when they were released. In their bugged conversations, Heisenberg and his colleagues regarded their expertise as a highly saleable commodity and looked forward to the prospect of being paid large sums by Argentina – half a million pesetas was mentioned – for their secrets about unleashing nuclear energy after the war.

All their assumptions were blown apart by the news one hot summer's day on 6 August 1945 that the Americans had detonated a nuclear bomb at a place called Hiroshima.

Shortly before they sat down to dinner, Rittner went to Professor Hahn in his room on the first floor of Farm Hall, and told him that an announcement had been made by the BBC that an atomic bomb had been dropped on Japan by the Americans. The BBC report at 6 p.m. said: 'Scientists, British and American, have made an atomic bomb at last. The first one was dropped on a Japanese city this morning. It was designed for a detonation equivalent to twenty thousand tons of high explosive …'

Hahn – the great discoverer of nuclear fission in 1939 – was 'completely shattered by the news', Rittner reported. Hahn said he 'felt personally responsible for the deaths of hundreds of thousands of people, as it was his original discovery which had made the bomb possible.' Hahn later told Rittner that, from that moment, he contemplated suicide. Hahn said he realised the terrible potentialities of his discovery and felt that now these had been realised and he was to blame.

Rittner said he had to calm down Hahn with 'considerable alcoholic stimulant' – several stiff gins – and then they went down to dinner together for Hahn to break the news to the others around the dinner table.

'The guests were completely staggered by the news,' Rittner reported. 'At first they refused to believe it and felt that it was a bluff on our part, to induce the Japanese to surrender.'

Hahn said the Allies could only have done it if they had achieved uranium isotope separation. Gerlach, Hahn, Harteck and Laue speculated about how they had achieved it.

HAHN: If the Americans have a uranium bomb then you're all second-raters. Poor old Heisenberg!
VON LAUE: The innocent!

HEISENBERG: Did they use the word uranium in connection with this atomic bomb?

ALL: No.

HEISENBERG: Then it's got nothing to do with atoms ... But the equivalent of 20,000 tons of high explosive is terrific ... All I can suggest is that some dilettante in America who knows very little about it has bluffed them in saying: 'If you drop this it has the equivalent of 20,000 tons of high explosive' and in reality doesn't work at all.

HAHN At any rate, Heisenberg, you're just second-raters and you might as well pack up.

HEISENBERG: I quite agree ...

At length, the dinner guests moved from the dining room to the library next door, with its comfortable sofas and large wireless set by the bay window looking towards the rose garden and the kitchen garden at the side of the house. The debate raged on but at 9 p.m. they fell silent as the BBC news began. Major Rittner reported: 'All the guests assembled to hear the official announcement at 9 o'clock. They were completely stunned when they realised that the news was genuine. They were left alone on the assumption that they would discuss the position.'

Any lingering doubts nursed by Heisenberg were finally laid to rest by the extended report by the BBC Home Service:

Here is the news.

It's dominated by a tremendous achievement of Allied scientists – the production of the atomic bomb. One has already been dropped on a Japanese army base. It alone contained as much explosive power as 2,000 of our great ten-tonners. President Truman has told how the bombs were made in secret American factories, and has foreshadowed the enormous peace-time value of this harnessing of atomic energy. A statement by Mr Churchill (written before the change of Government) has described the early work on the project in this country and told the story of its development ...

At home, it's been a Bank Holiday of sunshine and thunderstorms; a record crowd at Lord's has seen Australia make 273 for five wickets ...'[13]

The announcer then reported that the US and British governments had each issued statements. Washington and Downing Street had carefully prepared for the world-shaking event they knew was coming. But there were two new world leaders to announce the news.

In the spring of 1945, the health of the much-loved 'FDR', Franklin D. Roosevelt, an invalid for most of his life as a result of polio, had suddenly worsened; on 12 April he died from a brain haemorrhage. Roosevelt had been replaced by his brash vice president, Harry S. Truman.

There also had been a totally unexpected political earthquake in Britain. Winston Churchill, the man who led Britain through all the vicissitudes of war to victory, had been voted out of office. On 26 July, when the result of the 1945 General Election was declared, the pipe-smoking Labour leader Clement Attlee emerged as the victor of the peace. The Whitehall expert and crossbench peer Lord Hennessey told me it was as if 'the lion' who gave Britain its roar in wartime had been 'replaced by a hamster'.[14]

Now it fell to these two new leaders, Truman and Attlee, to tell the world about the new superbomb.

Truman bluntly told his American audience: 'We have spent two billion dollars on the greatest scientific gamble in history – and won.' Sixteen hours earlier, an American airplane had dropped one bomb on Hiroshima 'and destroyed its usefulness to the enemy'.

It was the first time that many Americans had ever heard of Hiroshima and Truman left the impression that it was a military target, not a city that had been obliterated. Lest there be any concern for the fate of the victims of this new weapon, he added: 'The Japanese began the war from the air at Pearl Harbour. They have been repaid many fold ...'

In London, it was characteristic of Attlee, the most modest of men, that, rather than giving his own account, he read out the statement that had been prepared weeks earlier by Winston Churchill before leaving office.

Churchill's statement, which was more fully reported in the BBC bulletin than Truman's, described the history of the making of the Bomb, emphasising the leading role played by Britain from 1939 through 1941 – before America entered the war – including the creation of 'Tube Alloys' as cover for the British nuclear programme under Sir John Anderson.

Churchill's statement put the best possible gloss on the reason why he – despite Britain's lead in the field – surrendered the production of this new awesome means of destruction to America. It became clear in 1942, said Churchill, that the plants to build the atom bomb would have to be on a vast scale, which Britain at the time could not afford.

> Great Britain, at this period, was fully extended in war production and could not afford such grave interference with the current munitions programmes on which our war-like operations depended. Moreover, Great Britain was within easy range of German bombers ... By God's mercy British and American science out-paced all German efforts. These were on a considerable scale, but far behind. The possession of these powers by the Germans at any time might have altered the result of the war, and profound anxiety was felt by those who were informed.

Then Churchill broke the news about the clandestine efforts to stop Hitler's Nazi war machine acquiring an atomic bomb. Because of the secrecy surrounding the Tube Alloys project, wartime censorship had prevented the public from hearing about these operations before. They included the attack on the Norsk Hydro heavy water plant: 'Every effort was made by our Intelligence Service and by the Air Force to locate in Germany anything resembling the plants which were being created in the United States. In the winter of 1942/43 most gallant attacks were made in Norway on two occasions by small parties of volunteers from the British Commandos and the Norwegian forces, at very heavy loss of life, upon stores of what is called "heavy water", an element in one of the possible processes. The second of these two attacks was completely successful.'

He concluded by urging Japan to surrender and raised the hope that the terrible weapon would bring peace in the world:

> This revelation of the secrets of Nature, long mercifully withheld from man, should arouse the most solemn reflections in the minds and conscience of every human being capable of comprehension.
> We must indeed pray that these awful agencies will be made to conduce to peace among nations and that instead of wreaking measureless havoc upon the entire globe they may become a perennial fountain of world prosperity.[15]

The BBC reported the Americans had employed 125,000 people in the factories to build the bomb and 65,000 workers were still employed in the factories.

Compared to that, the German effort seemed pathetically small. Heisenberg had a handful of scientists cycling from Hechinghen to work on a crude pile in the pit of a cave in Haigerloch. The Americans had spent $2 billion on the Manhattan Project, dwarfing the German atomic budget.

In Farm Hall, the scientists debated the consequences of the first nuclear bomb attack until 1.30 a.m. the next morning, while casually playing cards as a show of their unconcern. Heisenberg wondered aloud: 'What would one want 60,000 men for?'

The answer was obvious – the Americans were producing more nuclear bombs on an industrial scale.

Over their game, Heisenberg and his co-detainees built their own house of cards; they reconstructed their own part in the unfolding history of the bomb. The transcript shows that before they retired to bed, Heisenberg and von Weizsäcker – the most politically attuned of the group at Farm Hall – begin polishing their version of events and staking out the moral high ground for themselves:

HEISENBERG: We wouldn't have had the moral courage to recommend to the government in the spring of 1942 that they should employ 120,000 men just for building the thing up.

VON WEIZSÄCKER: I believe the reason we didn't do it was because all the physicists didn't want to do it, on principle. If we had all wanted Germany to win the war, we would have succeeded.

HAHN: I don't believe that, but I am thankful we didn't succeed …

HEISENBERG: I would say that I was absolutely convinced of the possibility of our making a uranium engine but I never thought that we would make a bomb and at the bottom of my heart, I was really glad that it was to be an engine and not a bomb. I must admit that.

VON WEIZSÄCKER: If you had wanted to make a bomb we would probably have concentrated more on the separation of isotopes and less on heavy water.

HAHN leaves the room.

VON WEIZSÄCKER: If we had started this business soon enough we could have got somewhere. If they were able to complete it in the summer of 1945, we might have had the luck to complete it in the winter of 1944/45.

WIRTZ: The result would have been that we would have obliterated London but still would not have conquered the world, and then they would have dropped them on us.

VON WEIZSÄCKER: I don't think we ought to make excuses now because we did not succeed, but we must admit that we didn't want to succeed. If we had put the same energy into it as the Americans and had wanted it as they did, it is quite certain that we would not have succeeded as they would have smashed up the factories.

DIEBNER: Of course they were watching us all the time.

VON WEIZSÄCKER: One can say it might have been a much greater tragedy for the world if Germany had had the uranium bomb. Just imagine, if we had destroyed London with uranium bombs it would not have ended the war, and when the war did end, it is still doubtful whether it would have been a good thing ...

WIRTZ: I think it is characteristic that the Germans made the discovery and didn't use it, whereas the Americans have used it. I must say I didn't think the Americans would dare use it.

GERLACH: When we get back to Germany we will have a dreadful time. We will be looked upon as the ones who have sabotaged everything. We won't remain alive long there. You can be certain that there are many people in Germany who say that it is our fault ... Please leave me alone.

Gerlach leaves the room, and goes to his bedroom where he is heard sobbing by Kendrick's eavesdroppers listening with their headphones in the stables.

There were also fears for Hahn, the 'father' of atomic fission and, at sixty-six, the oldest member of the group, after he left the room. Von Weizsäcker says it has put Hahn into a 'frightful position' because he discovered fission, and the Germans had failed to take it as far as the Americans. Rittner draws Max von Laue, the next oldest of the group, to one side and asks him to make sure that Hahn does not do himself any harm. Von Laue says he does not fear Hahn will harm himself, but he thinks it would be wise to keep a check on Gerlach during the night. Heisenberg and Weizsäcker, who share a large bedroom like a dormitory with Gerlach, agree to keep a watch over him.

The listeners hear von Laue and Harteck enter Gerlach's room and try to comfort him.

In his report to MI6 and Washington, Rittner said Gerlach appeared to consider himself 'in the position of a defeated general, the only alternative open to whom is to shoot himself. Fortunately he had no weapon ...' Hahn then tries to console Gerlach.

HAHN: You are upset because we did not make the uranium bomb? I thank God on my bended knees that we did not make the uranium bomb. Or are you depressed because the Americans could do it better than we could?

GERLACH: Yes

HAHN: Surely you are not in favour of such an inhuman weapon as the uranium bomb?

GERLACH: No. We never worked on a bomb. I didn't believe it would go so quickly. But I did think that we should do everything to make the sources of energy and exploit the possibilities for the future ... I spoke to Speer's right-hand man, as Speer was not available at the time, an *Oberst* Geist, first and later Sauckel [the Gauleiter] at Weimar. He asked me: 'What do you want to do with these things?' I replied, 'In my opinion the politician who is in possession of such an engine can achieve anything he wants.' About ten days or a fortnight before the final capitulation, Geist replied, 'Unfortunately we have not got such a politician.'

HAHN: I am thankful that we were not the first to drop the uranium bomb.

GERLACH: You cannot prevent its development. I was afraid to think of the bomb, but I did think of it as a thing of the future, and that the man who could threaten the use of the bomb would be able to achieve anything.

Von Weizsäcker was alive to the political implications. The next day, 7 August, von Weizsäcker in private conversation with von Laue said: 'History will record that the Americans and the English made a bomb and that at the same time the Germans, under the Hitler regime produced a workable machine [reactor]. In other words, the peaceful development of the uranium [reactor] was made in Germany under the Hitler regime, whereas the Americans and the English developed this ghastly weapon of war.'

Shortly before 6 p.m. on 7 August, when Sir John Anderson made another broadcast on the BBC about the bomb, Heisenberg was also recorded in conversation with von Weizsäcker and Wirtz. Von Weizsäcker expressed horror at the use of the weapon. According to Rittner's summary, Heisenberg replied 'had they [the German scientists] dropped such a bomb they would certainly have been executed as war criminals having made "the most devilish thing imaginable".'

The anti-Nazi Max von Laue said it was the start of the *Lesart* (meaning their version or reading of the truth). Today, this would be called political 'spin'. It was the first great conspiracy at Farm Hall.

The scientist and author Arnold Kramish, Paul Rosbaud's biographer, accused Heisenberg and von Weizsäcker of hatching the 'conspiracy' to avoid the uncomfortable truth that they had signed up for the development of an Nazi bomb, when they joined the teams under the control of the German Army Ordnance Office.

Far from being totally innocent, Kramish wrote in a review for *Discovery* magazine of Robert Jungk's controversial book, Heisenberg had specifically referred to the development of a bomb of 'unimaginable power'. He added: 'The Germans knew in principle a bomb could be made; they had no idea how.'

There is also a possibility that Heisenberg and von Weizsäcker knew their conversations were being bugged by the time of the Hiroshima bomb, despite their apparent naivety that bugging was un-British when they first arrived. The British scientist Sir Charles Frank said this became apparent when he visited Farm Hall in November 1945 at the suggestion of Lieutenant Commander Eric Welsh, who was clearly interested to see if Frank could glean any more from the scientists. Frank was taken for a walk around the garden by Wirtz after lunch because Wirtz said they suspected their conversations were being bugged.[16]

Wirtz told him they had found wires in the back of a cupboard in the house and they assumed they were listened to. Wirtz felt more comfortable talking in the garden because he assumed they could speak privately.

This potentially casts the Farm Hall transcripts in a dramatically different light. It suggests Heisenberg, von Weizsäcker and the others were speaking for their wider audience, and that they were guilty of a huge deception against the Allies.

Sir Charles did not believe that was the case. Sir Charles said that after his conversation with Wirtz, he had read the transcripts again for any evidence of concerted deception and could find none.

But if they were not guilty of spin, was there some truth in the claims that they actively tried to avoid building the bomb for Hitler? Heisenberg later claimed he had 'sabotaged' the atomic bomb project. Hahn said: 'I must honestly say that I would have sabotaged the war if I had been in a position to do so.' Wirtz told

Sir Charles that, two months before they were captured, they had reached the point with their pile at Haigerloch where two more bricks of uranium oxide metal could have achieved a critical mass; more uranium oxide was available 200 miles away but they could not obtain it because of the bombing of the railways.

Goudsmit was contemptuous in his scepticism about the German experiments and upset with Heisenberg for claiming he chose not to develop the bomb. Goudsmit believed they wanted to build a bomb but failed to understand the science, as shown by a lecture given by Heisenberg on 14 August 1945 to the other 'guests' at Farm Hall on the construction of the American bombs. It contained so many unclear calculations that it has been widely held by Heisenberg's critics as further evidence that he still had failed to understand the fundamentals about achieving a chain reaction.

Little Boy and Fat Man

The core of the uranium bomb – code-named Little Boy after a character in the Hollywood movie *The Maltese Falcon* – had been entrusted by General Groves to Robert Furman to deliver to the tiny Pacific island of Tinian on board a fast heavy cruiser, USS *Indianapolis*. On 6 August it was carried in the B-29 Superfortress bomber, *Enola Gay*, named by the pilot Paul Tibbets with questionable taste after his mother. The bomb was dropped over Hiroshima at precisely 8.15 a.m. and it exploded forty-five seconds later at 1,820 feet over the city.

The bomb was 10 feet 8 inches long, 2 feet 4 inches in diameter and weighed about 4.3 tons. It contained about 64 kg of enriched uranium U-235 in two parts – using the 'gun' principle, a hollow uranium 'bullet' was fired into the target cylinder containing the remaining uranium, triggering the atomic explosion. Groves was not sure it would work, until the observers on the *Enola Gay* saw the flash and the mushroom cloud 30,000 feet below. Some of those on board said later they never saw the city intact – all they saw was a boiling muddy mess with fires breaking out on the periphery of the blast area.[17]

A second atomic bomb – code-named Fat Man after Kasper Gutman, a character played by Sydney Greenstreet in *The Maltese Falcon* – was dropped by another B-29 Superfortress, *Bockscar*, on the smaller city of Nagasaki three days later at about 11 a.m. on 9 August to demonstrate that the first, on Hiroshima, was not a 'one-off' and the Americans had the power to produce more atomic bombs. It was a different type of device, using a plutonium core and an implosion trigger.

The first the victims knew of the Hiroshima bomb was the flash of the searing light. A British expert group of scientists from the Home Office, including the polymath Jacob Bronowski, later renowned for his television series '*Civilisation*', spent the month of November 1945 sifting through the charred ruins of Hiroshima and Nagasaki. They were studying the effects of the two atomic bombs and the impact similar atomic bombs would have on British cities. Their report – *The Effects of the Atomic Bombs at Hiroshima and Nagasaki* – was published in 1946 as a public document by His Majesty's Stationery Office, London, priced at one shilling. A similar report was published in America at the same time. They discovered that the heat vaporised people in a split second. Shadows were left where people had sat on park benches, on steps, or leaned against walls. Shadows of leaves were cast on the ground before the leaves had time to shrivel.

In Hiroshima, around four square miles of the city were destroyed and 80,000 people were killed. In the smaller city of Nagasaki, one and a half square miles were destroyed and 40,000 were killed. This was greater than the 30,000 killed in London by air attack during the entire war and the 60,000 killed throughout Great Britain (including London).

'Eye-witnesses in Hiroshima were agreed they saw a blinding white flash in the sky, felt a rush of air, and heard a loud rumble of noise followed by the sound of the rending and falling of buildings.'

It was not like a conventional explosion. The temperature of the air was raised to the blinding heat of the sun, causing pressure that moved outward as a blast wave. Older buildings collapsed into rubble. More modern buildings, with steel frames, burned, but were left standing by the blast. Some in underground shelters survived but death for most was instantaneous.

95 per cent of those within a quarter of a mile of the epicentre died. That could have translated into around 1 million dead in central London if Hitler had dropped the bomb on London in 1945.

*

The debate that raged over the card table at Farm Hall continued long after the protagonists died. Heisenberg and von Weizsäcker are accused of being hypocrites and liars. Critics say Heisenberg demonstrated by his mistake in the key calculation of the amount of enriched uranium required to make a bomb – at one point, Heisenberg refers to needing 'ten tons of pure 235' – that the German scientists at Farm Hall really had no idea how an atomic bomb worked, and therefore their attempt to assume the moral high ground is an outrageous fraud. Goudsmit was infuriated by the implication by von Weizsäcker that the German scientists he helped to track down were somehow morally superior to the American scientists who produced the bomb. In his view, the Manhattan team were just better at science.

They traded blows and insults. Their weapons were books, speeches, and lectures. Heisenberg got permission by British authorities in 1946 to publish his account of the German atomic programme; Goudsmit fired his missiles in his book, *ALSOS*, in 1947. While the real Cold War was setting in, the propaganda war over the past war raged throughout the 1940s and 1950s. Elisabeth Heisenberg came to her husband's defence in her own book on the period. Heisenberg's account in Robert Jungk's book *Brighter than a Thousand Suns*, published in 1958, fuelled the animosity. It led to a lasting feud between Goudsmit and von Weizsäcker and, to a lesser extent, with his old friend Heisenberg. The American scientist and author Jeremy Bernstein, in his forensic study of the Farm Hall transcripts, concluded: 'If these scientists had simply pointed out that they had made these studies, found the bomb unfeasible and gone on trying to build a reactor, one might have felt differently about them. But to claim some high moral ground for what they did or did not do is what so many people found so distasteful.'[18]

R. V. Jones was dragged into the bitter war of words after the publication in 1978 of his bestselling book, *Most Secret War*. I discovered that the archive of Jones's papers at Churchill College, Cambridge is stuffed with angry letters and draft manuscripts from Heisenberg's sharpest critics seeking Jones's support for their own arguments against Heisenberg and von Weizsäcker. Jones was reluctant to give it.

In one handwritten letter to one of his correspondents in 1984, Jones was typically cautious about condemning Heisenberg. He quotes from a Gestapo summary dated May 1943, reproduced in Goudsmit's book *ALSOS*, saying there were two technical applications of uranium fission:

1. The Uranium Engine can be used as a motor if one succeeds in controlling the fission of atomic nuclei within certain limits

2. The Uranium Bomb can be realized if one succeeds in bombarding uranium nuclei suddenly with neutrons. The neutrons released in the fission should not be allowed to escape but their too-large initial speed must be slowed down sufficiently so that they will again produce further fissions. The process propagates itself like an avalanche.

Jones says this suggests the Germans thought they could make a bomb using slow neutrons with natural uranium and Goudsmit was right to say this would have been a 'squib' compared with a fast-fission bomb.

Jones leans towards Heisenberg's account: 'On balance I am inclined to conclude that: (1) The probability of fast fission bombs with U-235 and with plutonium was known to Heisenberg and/ or his colleagues; (2) The separation of U-235 appeared to them too great a task for World War ll.'[19] They did not make plutonium a priority, Jones adds, perhaps because they believed a graphite-moderator pile would not work and 'could not get enough heavy water to make a self-sustaining pile'. Jones concluded: 'I agree that my memories of the Farm Hall conversations suggest that there was some … confusion among the German physicists, though I do not know how much can be attributed to their state of shock.'

Confusion is an understatement. In his introduction to the publication of the Farm Hall transcripts in 1993, Sir Charles Frank accused Heisenberg and his colleagues of displaying 'a surprising degree of naivety, ignorance or reticence about plutonium' (the highly fissile by-product of the reactors that the Americans used to make the Fat Man bomb) by claiming that in pursuing a reactor they were pursuing a purely peaceful use of atomic energy.[20]

The argument turned on the bizarre symbol of a pineapple. Heisenberg claimed he told the German high command (see Chapter Eight) that it would only require about 10 kg of U-235 with a core 'about the size of a pineapple' to make a bomb. The size of the core was roughly in line with the landmark predictions made in England by the refugee theoretical scientist Rudolf Peierls, Heisenberg's former pupil in Leipzig. It is also evidence that Heisenberg correctly understood the requirements for the bomb, though that has been challenged by some of Heisenberg's critics who were keen to prove he did not choose to avoid building a bomb. His son, Jochen, also a scientist, insists his father did compare the critical mass required for a bomb to a pineapple.

'My father told us that he had informed the people in the government that a bomb would require a critical mass roughly the size of a pineapple. Some people want to believe he mistakenly thought it would take several tons. I am biased but I checked Diebner's official report of the so-called Uranium Club to the Army Ordnance Ministry. I read that the estimate was of 10 to 100 kg U-235 for a nuclear bomb, which translates to just about the size of a pineapple, confirming his truthfulness. This was known at the time my father went to Copenhagen.'[21]

Heisenberg's former colleagues support his claims. The evidence that Heisenberg correctly estimated it would need between 10 kg and 100 kg of the material to make a bomb is quoted by Erich Bagge, Kurt Diebner and Kenneth Jay in their book on the development of the British reactor at Calder Hall (now Sellafield) to produce weapons-grade plutonium for the British nuclear deterrent.[22] They quote in full the official report for the poorly attended conference at the *Kaiser-Wilhelm Institut für Physik* held between 26 and 28 February 1942. Heisenberg stated that the operation of a *Uranmaschine* – a reactor – would produce element 94, plutonium, which could be used to make a bomb.

In a conversation with Hahn the day after the news of Hiroshima, Heisenberg speculated that one way to make the bomb with a much smaller amount of enriched uranium would be to make it in two halves, each one of which would be too small to produce an explosion, but the two halves could be joined together at the moment of dropping the bomb to turn back the fast neutrons, intensifying the power of the reaction. 'They have probably done something like that.' Heisenberg was correct. That is what the Americans did.

The man who owns Farm Hall, Professor Marcial Echenique, is convinced the truth is that Heisenberg did understand that he could produce a bomb with a small amount of plutonium; he just never got to that stage. Professor Echenique questioned several of the scientists who were held at Farm Hall. They included Bagge and von Weizsäcker, and Karl Wirtz. Bagge told him on his visit back to Farm Hall that the uranium 'machine' was for producing electricity but the by-product was plutonium. 'They nearly were there,' Professor Echenique told me. 'The British copied their work in Calder Hall and that was the British system for making the bomb.'[23]

We walk along the corridor to the dimly lit dining room where the news was broken to Heisenberg and his colleagues – the dining room is now a snooker room; the dining table has been replaced by a huge snooker table. Then we step next door to the comfortable ground-floor drawing room where they read books, Heisenberg played the piano, and the great debate was held into the early hours of 7 August 1945. The room is now Professor Echenique's library and study, lined with books on architecture. He points to the corner near the window where he believes the wireless was. We look around the room where history was played out.

I ask Professor Echenique whether Bagge had told him they had sufficient technology to make the bomb. 'Of course,' said Professor Echenique. 'Everything to me fits. They were building this engine. They got up to critical mass that is the moment of nuclear reaction. They didn't succeed in doing it because the war ended, but according to Bagge the British used their technology at Calder Hall because the Americans wouldn't share the secret of the nuclear bomb.'

So how close did Heisenberg and Hitler's scientists come to exploding a nuclear bomb?

Rumours still persist today that Nazi scientists tested a nuclear bomb in vast underground caverns made with slave labour. In 2013 a German filmmaker claimed to have uncovered a 1944 American intelligence document showing interest in a vast bunker near the town of Sankt Georgen an der Gusen in Austria. The *Daily Mail* in London reported: 'A labyrinth of secret underground tunnels believed to have been used by the Nazis to develop a nuclear bomb has been uncovered ... Documentary-maker Andreas Sulzer, who is leading the excavations, said the site is "most likely the biggest secret weapons facility of the Third Reich".' It was explored by the Allies and Russia after the war, but they had missed the tunnels, which had been newly found, because the Nazis appeared to have gone to greater lengths to conceal them. The *Daily Mail* added: 'The probe was triggered by a research documentary by Mr Sulzer on Hitler's quest to build an atomic bomb. In it, he referenced diary entries from a physicist called up to work for the Nazis. There is other evidence of scientists working for a secret project managed by SS General Hans Kammler.'[26]

There were rumours the tunnels had been used to test a nuclear device, and talk of traces of radiation being found. Film of the network showed overgrown bunkers and deep tunnels. However, the evidence was as elusive as Hitler's bomb. A similar scare was caused in Washington in 1945 after Major Furman of the Alsos mission was asked to take samples of water from the Rhine to see if it contained traces of radiation. In addition to the water from the Rhine, he sent a sample of German wine back to Washington as a joke. The Pentagon's scientists found the Rhine water had no traces of radiation, but the wine did. It caused some excitement until American scientists decided it was in the vineyard soil naturally.

German historian Rainer Karlsch claimed in his 2005 book *Hitlers Bombe* that Hitler's scientists and the military carried out three nuclear tests, one on the Baltic island of Ruegen in 1944 and two in Thuringia in March 1945. He quoted a KGB report of 'two large explosions in Thuringia' in March 1945, destroying an area of 500 square metres and killing hundreds of prisoners in a concentration camp. But the evidence was met with deep scepticism from other historians, which continues today. I could find no references to evidence of the tests in the private papers of Goudsmit and Pash who led the hunt, and would be expected to have found some clues if they existed.

Most of the rumours have turned out to be phantoms or mad Nazi nightmares, some deliberately spread by Joseph Goebbels, Hitler's propaganda chief, to sow doubt in the minds of the Allied invaders. In September 2015, there were global reports that a Nazi armoured train had been located in a secret tunnel in Poland. It was rumoured to be laden with Nazi gold and treasure. So far, the train remains hidden with its fabulous cargo.[27] But not all stories are fantasies.

There were stories at the end of the war of Nazi gold being brought to the mountain region where Heisenberg had gone into hiding, with it being dumped into the deep mountain lakes or secretly buried at night. There were reports that Nazi gold had been buried on a remote forested track in the Bavarian Alps. It had been carried at night by a mule train led by a ghostly white mule and buried by Nazi soldiers in the snow. It sounded like a fantastical ghost story; in fact, it turned out to be true: the Americans investigated and recovered dozens of gold bars hidden in the ground among the trees.[28]

The Farm Hall transcripts would normally have been released under the 'thirty-year rule' in 1975 – the height of the Cold War. They were not declassified until after forty-seven years in 1992 when they were simultaneously released by the Tory Government of John Major through the National Archives and the US archives in Washington. Some suggested that the transcripts were kept Top Secret for so long because of the embarrassment they may have caused to the post-war German government: Carl Friedrich von Weizsäcker's brother, Richard, was a rising politician in the Christian Democratic Union party in the new Federal Republic of West Germany, later becoming the West German president in 1984.

Having spent thirty years covering politics at Westminster as a lobby journalist, it seemed to me that this was unconvincing nonsense. Richard von Weizsäcker had no objections to the Farm Hall transcripts being released, according to a letter from the author and scientist Arnold Kramish that I found among the papers of R. V. Jones at Churchill College, Cambridge library archives. The British and American governments would have been more worried about the impact of the transcripts nearer to home at the height of the Cold War, with 'Ban the Bomb' marches being organised by the Campaign for Nuclear Disarmament and East German secret services fomenting civil unrest at the siting of American nuclear weapons as part of the NATO commitment in West Germany. I believe the Farm Hall transcripts were supressed because they contained the claim by Heisenberg and his colleagues that Churchill and Truman, Groves and the Manhattan Project team were guilty of committing a war crime at Hiroshima and repeating it at Nagasaki.

The Farm Hall transcripts were only declassified and released after a powerful campaign was mounted in the UK. It was supported by Sir Charles Frank, R. V. Jones, Professor Margaret Gowing, who wrote the definitive history of the birth of the British nuclear bomb, Rudolf Peierls, who first realised that a bomb could be made with as little as 1 kg of enriched uranium, and the President of the Royal Society, Sir Michael Atiyah. They were reinforced by an army of the so-called Great and Good: Lord Bullock, Lord Blake, Lord Dacre, Sir Sam Edwards, Lord Flowers, Lord Zuckerman, Professor Nicholas Kurti, and Anthony King, President of the British Academy. They all signed a joint letter to the Lord Chancellor in the Major Government, Lord Mackay of Clashfern. They said the historical interest in the transcripts 'arises in part because there still is controversy about the role of the scientists in the German atomic-energy project. Some historians and some journalists claim that moral scruples prevented the German scientists from completing a nuclear weapon.'

I contacted Lord Mackay and he told me: 'I believe the reason was ... the sensitivity on the morality aspect of the matter.'[24]

Fear in 1942 drove the Manhattan Project scientists forward because they were afraid that the Germans would beat them to the bomb. Fear had the opposite effect in 1942 in Hitler's Reich. Fear of Hitler made Speer reluctant to galvanise the German war machine to creating a bomb as Groves had done. Goudsmit was convinced, as early as November 1944, that the Germans did not possess the wherewithal to build an atomic bomb.

So why were the German scientists rounded up and transported to Farm Hall?

Operation Big – the final lap in the race to capture the German atomic reactor and Heisenberg's team – was the second great conspiracy to be revealed at Farm Hall.

It was a sham. As the German scientists fretted about their continued detention at their five-star jail in the Cambridgeshire countryside, the truth began to dawn on them: the Americans had mounted their audacious plan to seize them from their laboratories in Germany not for what they knew, but to stop them falling into the hands of the Russians (or the French, come to that). Lieutenant General Groves later said: 'Generally, our principal concern at this point was to keep information and atomic scientists from falling into the hands of the Russians.'

Jochen Heisenberg told me: 'The Americans knew that Germany was not attempting to build a nuclear bomb, in the same way as later they knew Saddam Hussein did not have WMDs. Collecting the German Scientists was to make sure they were not captured by the Russians.'[25]

Groves was desperate to stop atomic secrets falling into the hands of the advancing Red Army in Germany. The problem, however, was in his own backyard. Soviet spies inside the Manhattan Project had leaked the key secrets about the building of the atomic bomb at Los Alamos to Josef Stalin and the Soviet leadership, despite all Groves's attempts to counter Soviet espionage. They were led by Klaus Fuchs, a gifted scientist who had been recruited to the Manhattan Project through Britain, and the Cambridge spies, Guy Burgess, Donald Maclean and Kim Philby. They also included John Cairncross who worked at Bletchley Park.

After six months in detention, Heisenberg and his fellow detainees were taken out of Farm Hall and flown back to Germany. Heisenberg returned to academic life and was given honours, including being made a fellow of the Royal Society in London.

Hitler's Uranium Club had nothing to teach the Americans. Farm Hall was not merely the setting for the final scene of Hitler's Uranium Club in the Second World War. The mansion house deep in the bucolic countryside of England was the backdrop for the opening scene in the next conflict, the Cold War.

15

The Dirty Secret

As a post-war Baby Boomer, I was brought up to believe the world's first atomic bombs were dropped on Hiroshima and Nagasaki in order to bring about the end of the Second World War.

Every child of my age knew about the horrors of the Japanese, and the US war in the Pacific, not least from the John Wayne epic 1949 movie, *The Sands of Iwo Jima*. In early 1945, American troops were still engaged in bloody fighting against fanatical Japanese troops in the Philippines. More than a million US troops were waiting for the order to invade the Japanese mainland. British troops were fighting in Burma to free Rangoon.

Harry S. Truman inherited the plan to drop the bomb on Japan when he assumed the presidency on Roosevelt's death on 12 April 1945. Truman had no knowledge the Americans were almost ready with the nuclear bomb until he was briefed on 25 April by Secretary of War Henry Stimson and General Groves, the head of the Manhattan Project.

The day before, Stimson stressed the importance of the A-bomb to America's position in the world, rather than ending the war, when he asked for the meeting with Truman to brief the President on the new weapon. 'It is very important I should have a talk with you as soon as possible on a highly secret matter,' said Stimson. 'It has such a bearing on our present foreign relations and has such an important effect upon all my thinking in this field that I think you ought to know about it without much further delay.' Truman scrawled across it: 'Tomorrow Wed 25 HST.'[1]

They met in the White House at noon. Stimson noted in his diary Groves had to go through underground passages to a room near the President and wait there to be called in to see Truman to avoid the press getting wind of the historic briefing. Having heard about the A-bomb, Truman told Stimson he now understood why, when he was chairing the Truman committee, Stimson had steered him away from probing too deeply into the Manhattan Project.

They need have had no fears about the new commander-in-chief. Truman had no doubts about its use. Stimson said the Japanese were likely to stage a 'last ditch defence' against an invading army as they had at Iwo Jima and Okinawa; he estimated it would cost the Americans up to 1 million lives.

On 9 August, after the plutonium bomb 'Fat Man' was dropped on Nagasaki, President Truman said: 'We have used it in order to shorten the agony of war, in order to save the lives of thousands and thousands of young Americans. We shall continue to use it until we completely destroy Japan's power to make war.'

His point needed no further explanation back home in the United States. On 29 July, a Japanese submarine had sunk the USS *Indianapolis,* the same warship that a few days earlier had carried Robert Furman and the small cylindrical container containing uranium for the Hiroshima bomb; it went down with the loss of 881 crewmen. She went down so fast that no Mayday signal could be sent, and survivors were adrift in shark-infested waters for two days.

The Japanese finally agreed to an unconditional surrender on 15 August. British families greeted the news with relief too, because it meant husbands and brothers, who had been held as prisoners of war by the Japanese in unimaginable conditions, could come home. They included Harry, the brother of Ray Berry, the boy from the East End of London who was evacuated to Farm Hall at the outbreak of the war. Harry Berry, who spent his brief one-night honeymoon with his new wife Gwen at Farm Hall, had spent three years in a Japanese prisoner-of-war camp in Tokyo, along with thousands of British servicemen after their capture at the fall of Singapore. 'Harry and Gwen were only reunited after Japan capitulated to the Allies with the dropping of the atomic bomb that had so stunned those Farm Hall physicists,' said Ray.[2]

The detonation of the atomic bombs truly caused shock and awe around the globe. It also came as a shock to British intelligence, as they were aware that the Japanese were putting out diplomatic feelers to surrender. R. V. Jones, the chief scientist at SIS, revealed: 'We were awestruck, not so much at the power of the bomb, for this we had expected, but because the Americans had used it with so little notice.'[3]

Jones knew some dissidents within the Japanese government had approached the Russians to sound out the possibilities of an end to hostilities, if the Allies would drop their demand for an 'unconditional' surrender. On 13 July, intelligence services in Washington decoded an intercepted cable from the Japanese Foreign Minister Shigenori Togo to his Ambassador in Moscow stating: 'Unconditional surrender is the only obstacle to peace.' Secretary of State for the Navy, James Forrestal noted in his diary: 'The first real evidence of a Japanese desire to get out of the war came today through the intercepted messages from Togo, to Sato, Jap Ambassador in Moscow.'

Jones's unease was shared by many of the scientists who had helped to produce the bomb. Farrington Daniels, director of the Met Lab at the University of Chicago, reckoned a majority of scientists were in favour of a demonstration explosion to show the power of the bomb to the Japanese, before it was dropped on them.

On the eve of the Potsdam conference on 17 July 1945, when the Big Three – Truman, Churchill and Stalin – stepped on to the world stage for the last time to discuss the problem of Japan, a petition was gathered by Leo Szilard and signed by sixty-eight scientists from the Manhattan Project to urge the President not to use the bomb:

> We, the undersigned scientists, have been working in the field of atomic power. Until recently, we have had to fear that the United States might be attacked by atomic bombs during this war and that her only defense might lie in a counterattack by the same means. Today, with the defeat of Germany, this danger is averted and feel impelled to say what follows.
>
> The war has to be brought speedily to a successful conclusion and attacks by atomic bombs may very well be an effective method of warfare. We feel, however, that such attacks on Japan could not be justified.

Szilard was directed by Truman to see his Secretary of State, James Byrnes, a hawk on the bomb, at his home in Spartanburg. Szilard went with Harold Urey, who had won the Nobel Prize for the discovery of heavy water. Szilard said: 'Byrnes was concerned about Russia's having taken over Poland, Rumania and Hungary and so was I. Byrnes thought that the possession of the bomb by America would render the Russians more manageable in Europe.'[4]

Truman did not read their petition before he reached the outskirts of Berlin known as Potsdam, where he received news of the first test of the nuclear weapon at Alamogordo, New Mexico.

Churchill was acutely aware of the moral arguments. After the firestorm at Dresden caused by RAF carpet bombing on the city, Churchill circulated the British War Cabinet with a memorandum on 28 March 1945 calling into question the 'bombing of German cities simply for the sake of increasing the terror ... The destruction of Dresden remains a serious query against the conduct of Allied bombing.'[5]

For tactical reasons, however, Churchill was firmly against issuing any precise advance warning to the Japanese about the Allies dropping an atomic bomb on them. Truman's chief advisers, too, were worried that if they gave a demonstration on some barren island, as some of the Manhattan Project scientists wanted, it would still not convince the Japanese – or the Russians – that they had cracked the code of the atomic problem, and had the bomb. There was a secondary worry that if they told the Japanese in advance which of their cities was to be destroyed by the new bomb, they would put American and British prisoners of war into the target zone to blackmail the Allies not to use it.

A warning was issued on 26 July from the Potsdam conference but it was given in general terms threatening destruction, unless Japan surrendered; two days later, Japan announced its intention to carry on the war.

Szilard's petition, however, raised a more fundamental strategic point: he accused the US of changing the goal of the atomic bomb project for which they had worked so strenuously. It was no longer being used as a deterrent against Hitler's Nazis from whom many of them had fled. By dropping the atomic bomb on Japan, who did not possess it, the A-bomb was not being used as a deterrent, but instead as a first-strike weapon.

'If you are making an atomic bomb to stop Hitler, well, who could argue with that? But if you are making a bomb to use it against a non-nuclear power, to use it as a military weapon and not a deterrent, then things start to get problematic,' said the science historian Professor Alex Wellerstein.[6]

The bomb was so powerful it had its own political momentum that proved unstoppable. Sam Goudsmit was shocked by his 'mysterious major', Robert Furman, in November 1944 when Goudsmit said to him, 'Isn't it wonderful that the Germans have no atom bomb ... Now we won't have to use ours?' Furman replied: 'Of course you understand Sam ... if we have such a weapon, we are going to use it.'

The escalating cost of the Manhattan Project to nearly $2 billion dollars was a further factor in its use. James Byrnes, Roosevelt's Director of War Mobilization, warned FDR in the spring of 1945 that the Democrats would be vulnerable to attack in the next presidential elections for spending so much on the bomb if it was not used successfully.

> SECRET March 3, 1945
> MEMORANDUM FOR THE PRESIDENT
> FROM: JAMES F. BYRNES
> I understand that the expenditures for the Manhattan project are approaching two billion dollars with no definite assurance yet of production.
> We have succeeded to date in obtaining the cooperation of Congressional Committees in secret meetings. Perhaps we can continue to do so while the war lasts.
> However, if the project proves a failure, it will be subjected to relentless criticism ...

Hungarian-born Szilard feared there was also an overriding diplomatic imperative to using the atomic bomb: to show the Soviets that America was the world's superpower and was unassailable, just as Adolf Hitler had threatened in his Danzig speech at the start of the war. Russia had been threatening to invade Japan through Manchuria, thus enlarging its sphere of influence even further. The Japanese capitulation after the bombs at Hiroshima and Nagasaki had curtailed the move, but far more worrying for Churchill and Truman was that, in the rush to defeat Hitler, Soviet Russia had already stolen a march on the West through large swathes of Eastern Europe. They had taken Poland, for whom Britain went to war in the first place, and through Communist leaders such as Tito imposed their hegemony on Yugoslavia and the Balkans and East Germany.

Churchill famously warned on 5 March 1946: 'From Stettin in the Baltic to Trieste in the Adriatic, an iron curtain has descended across the continent.' However the ageing Churchill and the ailing Roosevelt had failed to stop the iron curtain being lowered. If Truman was to use the bomb as leverage to loosen Stalin's grip on Russia's neighbours, he needed to have a monopoly on the new weapon.

On 14 May 1945, Stimson recorded in his diary that he told the US Army Chief of Staff, George Marshall, that the best way of dealing with the Russians was to 'keep our mouths shut and let our actions speak for words. The Russians will understand them better than anything else. It is a case where we have got to regain the lead and perhaps do it in a pretty rough and realistic way ... I told him this was a place where we really held all the cards. I called it a royal straight flush and we mustn't be a fool about the way we play it.'[7]

The moment came to play the 'royal straight flush' at the Potsdam conference when it reconvened after Roosevelt's death and Churchill's defeat in the British general election of 1945. Truman wanted to go armed with the results of the test. Some historians deny the Potsdam meeting was delayed for the test, but Stimson confided in his diary: 'He [Truman] did not want to meet until July. He had his budget on his hands (the atomic bomb – he told me then of the atomic bomb experiment in Nevada. Charged me with utmost secrecy). He also told me of another reason, etc. The test was set for June, but had been postponed until July ...'

This seems to me clear evidence that Truman and Stimson used the atomic bomb against Japan partly as a 'trump card' against the Soviet Union. This is the 'dirty secret' that emerges from Operation Big and its aftermath. Stimson's record of a White House conference with the president on 6 June confirms that they did discuss dealing with the Russian gains in Eastern Europe in the same breath as the bomb. They began by discussing how they should deal with the occupation of Italy by French troops, and the French leader, de Gaulle, whom Stimson described as 'psychopathic'. Truman cut off military aid to France to force its withdrawal from Italy.

The conversation then turned to the bomb and a possible pact with the Russians over arms control. 'The greatest complication was what might happen at the meeting of the Big Three. He told me he had postponed that until 15 July on purpose to give us more time ... [He] mentioned the same things that I was thinking of, namely the settlement of the Polish, Rumanian, Yugoslavian and Manchurian problems.'

Stimson then made the most breath-taking admission of all about his secret briefing with the President. Stimson told Truman he was worried that Japan would be too 'bombed out' to demonstrate the power of the new superbomb. He records telling Truman he had been trying to hold the USAF to precision bombing against Japan 'first, because I did not want to have the United States get the reputation of outdoing Hitler in atrocities; and second, I was a little fearful that before we could get ready the Air Force might have Japan so thoroughly bombed out that the new weapon would not have a fair background to show its strength. He laughed and said he understood.'

On 16 July, as he prepared for the Potsdam conference, Truman was told the test in Alamogordo had been a success. Groves said later the light was 'equal to several suns in midday' and was clearly seen in Albuquerque about 180 miles away, while the noise was heard 100 miles away. Truman used biblical terms in his diary. He said it was the 'most terrible bomb in the history of the world – it may be the fire destruction prophesied in the Euphrates valley era, after Noah and his fabulous Ark ...'

The president, however, seemed not to have fully understood its indiscriminate effects:

> I have told the Secretary of State of War, Mr Stimson to use it so that military objectives and soldiers are the target and not women and children. Even if the Japs are savages, ruthless, merciless and fanatic, we as the leader of the world for the common welfare cannot drop this terrible bomb on the old capital or the new. [Groves had strongly argued for it to be dropped on Kyoto]. He and I are in accord ... It is certainly a good thing for the world that Hitler's crowd or Stalin's did not discover this atomic bomb.

The scene was set for the big reveal on 24 July 1945: the moment when Truman would tell Stalin that the Americans had the bomb. If they were expecting Stalin to wave a metaphorical white flag, they were disappointed.

The Soviet leader smiled.

Stalin fooled Churchill, who said the Soviet leader looked 'delighted ... I was sure that he had no idea of the significance of what he was being told ... His face remained gay and genial and the talk between these two potentates soon came to an end. As we were waiting for our car I found myself near Truman. "How did it go?" I asked. "He never asked a question," he replied.'[8]

Truman wrote on the back of a photograph of Stalin shaking hands with James Byrnes: 'In which I tell Stalin we expect to drop the most powerful explosive ever made on the Japanese. He smiled and said he appreciated my telling him – but he did not know that I was talking about the Atomic Bomb!'[9]

Truman could not have been more wrong. Stalin had known for three years, long before Truman was let in on the secret, about the American bomb, thanks to the treachery of a series of Soviet spies, some at the heart of the Manhattan Project. Chief among them was Klaus Fuchs, a German refugee from the Nazis, who had worked in Britain before being cleared in a perfunctory security check by MI5 to join Oppenheimer's team in the Theoretical Division at Los Alamos.

British intelligence failed to uncover the fact that Fuchs had been a committed, hard-line member of the Communist Party in Germany before he fled to Britain in 1933 as a student and continued his studies at Bristol and Edinburgh universities. He became an outstanding theoretical physicist but lost none of his commitment to the Communist Party. Despite his Communist past, and being interned on the Isle of Man and in Canada as an enemy alien, Fuchs secured security clearance to return to Britain to work for Rudolf Peierls on the Maud Committee report and on Tube Alloys, the British bomb programme. For three years, unknown to British intelligence, Fuchs was handing atomic secrets to a handler from the Soviet embassy in London. It is estimated that between 1941 and 1943, Fuchs passed 570 papers – mostly mathematical calculations – from Britain's TA programme, amounting to an almost complete record of the British research into the atomic bomb. It had spurred Stalin to order the development of a Soviet nuclear bomb.[10] Fuchs continued his supply of secrets to Moscow after he joined the Manhattan Project at Los Alamos through his work with Peierls.

Stalin's atomic spy helped design the bomb Oppenheimer called 'the gadget', and witnessed its detonation at the Top Secret Trinity Test. Fuchs had been responsible for the implosion calculations that made sure that the plutonium core detonated properly. Had he miscalculated, an embarrassing squib would have been a shattering blow to the confidence of the Truman administration.

The device – an implosion bomb using plutonium at its core – was a metal sphere about 1.5 metres in diameter surrounded by a mass of wires. An initiator of polonium and beryllium was placed inside two hemispheres of the plutonium core. The core was then seated inside a uranium tamper plug and air gaps were filled with gold foil. The two halves of the plug were then held together with uranium screws. High explosives were detonated, compressing the mass of the plutonium, and triggering fission.

The gadget was placed in a small corrugated-iron hut at the top of a tower in the rough desert scrub of Alamogordo, New Mexico,

200 miles south of the mountains of Los Alamos. Most observers were kept fifteen miles from the blast.

The countdown began at 5.10 a.m. and lasted twenty minutes. The counting stopped at 5.30 a.m., before the sun had gone up. It was still dark when the high explosive charges fired into the plutonium heart of the bomb. A flash of white light split the black sky and then rose like a new sun, lighting up the horizon. It was a strange sun that shocked most of those who witnessed it, including Fuchs. Some said it was like an alien sun; as it rose in the sky, it radiated flashes of fire, turning yellow, green and violet and purple, and then erupted in a withering wind from the blast wave that was strong enough to knock observers off their feet. 'The strong sustained awesome roar which warned of doomsday and made us feel that we puny things were blasphemous to dare tamper with the forces heretofore reserved to the Almighty,' recalled General Farrell, a staunch Catholic.

They knew now they had succeeded in unleashing something truly terrible; everyone was shocked into stunned silence as the mushroom cloud rose to over seven miles high.

Stalin may have showed no outward sign of surprise at Truman's news, but he ordered the production of the first Soviet plutonium bomb, code-named JOE-1 by the CIA, to be accelerated, using Fuch's calculations. The US monopoly lasted just four years.

Soviet scientists used German ore and some of their expertise to manufacture their own plutonium device. Stalin's scientists had managed to grab vital uranium ore and scientific expertise from the ruins of Berlin. Red Army troops overran Heisenberg's laboratory in the Dahlem suburbs of Berlin on 25 April, three days after Pash had reached Haigerloch. Firing katyusha rockets and supported by battle tanks, they swept through the tree-lined roads around the *Kaiser-Wilhelm Institut für Physik* and pressed on to the centre of the capital.

The ordinary Soviet troops knew little of the institute's importance, but they were followed within forty-eight hours by a large force of Lavrentiy Palovich Beria's feared NKVD (the People's Commissariat of Internal Affairs), the Soviet secret police, under the direction of General Khrulev, commander of the Red Army rear sector.

They were, in effect, the Soviet Alsos mission, and their prime target was the atomic laboratory at the institute, which they knew was to be part of the sector of Berlin allocated to the forces of the West. Their mission was to clear out the most important equipment and material and evacuate it to Moscow before the Allies got near Dahlem.

Colonel General Makhnev, in charge of the NKVD mission on the ground, was, in effect, the Soviet Boris T. Pash, while the Soviet Sam Goudsmit was General Avraani Zavenyagin, the chief metallurgist of the NKVD. They failed to capture their key targets – Heisenberg and Hitler's Uranium Club – but they did take some leading German scientists to Moscow including Professor Baron von Ardenne, who volunteered to work for the Soviet Union, Professor Peter Thiessen and Doctor Ludwig Bewilogua.

Above all, they wanted uranium. Zavenyagin conducted the search with a team of scientists who quickly set about dismantling the laboratories. Like the US Alsos team, they struck 'pay dirt'. In his sweeping history of the battle for Berlin, the historian Antony Beevor says Makhnev reported to Beria and Stalin that they found '250 kilograms of metallic uranium, three tons of uranium oxide, and twenty litres of heavy water'.[11] Makhnev's orders from the State Committee for Defence were clear: 'Taking into account the extreme importance for the Soviet Union of all the above-mentioned equipment, we request your decision ... to evacuate to the Soviet Union to Laboratory No. 2 of the Academy of Sciences and Special Metal Department of the NKVD all the equipment and materials and archive of the Kaiser Wilhelm Institute in Berlin.'

The uranium seized in Berlin was used in the development of the Soviet atomic bomb. The first successful test came almost exactly four years after the Hiroshima bomb, on 29 August 1949, which totally shocked the Americans. Soviet Russia became the world's third nuclear state that day, if you counted Britain. The Soviet atomic scientists would have got there without Fuchs but he eased the way; his calculations overcame the difficulties experienced at Los Alamos in triggering the implosion device, and sped up its delivery.

The Soviets had succeeded in detonating an atomic bomb without any official help from the Americans or the British. Joseph Rotblat, the only scientist to resign in protest from the Manhattan Project at that time, claimed he overheard Groves telling a dinner party: 'You realise of course that all this effort is really intended to subdue the Russkies.'[12] It triggered the post-war arms race.

Szilard and the scientists said in their memorandum to Truman:

If no efficient international agreement is achieved, the race of nuclear armaments will be on in earnest not later than the morning after our first demonstration of the existence of nuclear weapons.

Stimson secretly shared their concern and in a remarkably prescient memorandum to the president in September 1945 he urged Truman to reach an international nuclear weapon treaty with the Russians and the UK for arms control, including the impounding of existing stocks of atomic bombs if necessary:

> Unless the Soviets are voluntarily invited into the partnership upon a basis of cooperation and trust, we are going to maintain the Anglo-Saxon bloc over the Soviet Union in the possession of this weapon. Such a condition will almost certainly stimulate feverish activity on the part of the Soviet Union towards the development of this bomb in what will in effect be a secret armament race of a rather desperate character.[13]

Stimson could not stop the arms race that Szilard, Niels Bohr and others who had signed the letter in 1944 had feared. Only now, the scientists on both sides of the Cold War had embarked on a new more devastating weapon than the atomic bomb: the hydrogen bomb.

Sir William Penney from the Aldermaston facility where Britain's warheads were made told an expert British committee that the H-Bomb involved a series of chain reactions that, at the last stage, produced very fast neutrons. It was reckoned the H-bomb was 1,500 times more powerful than the A-bomb, but in theory there was no limit to the size of explosion that could be produced by a bomb of this type.

Penney estimated that an H-bomb dropped on London would produce a crater three-quarters of a mile across and 150 feet deep, and a fireball two and a quarter miles in diameter. The blast would crush the Admiralty Citadel, a Second World War reinforced concrete bunker on the corner of Horse Guards Parade in Whitehall, from a mile away. Suburban houses would be wrecked at a distance of three miles from the explosion, and they would be badly damaged by the blast at a distance of seven miles. All homes would catch fire over a circle of two miles radius from the air burst.

Cold War America was seized by an anti-communist fever that led to the McCarthyite purges of communists from politics and the arts, including, notoriously, Hollywood, in which Colonel Boris T. Pash and General Groves would play a part. Even J. Robert Oppenheimer was caught in the McCarthyite witch-hunt for Communists and Pash became a witch-finder general. Pash and Groves testified in the Oppenheimer security hearings, which resulted in the scientist who led the Manhattan Project having his security clearance revoked. His supporters claim he was punished because he argued against America's move to the much more powerful generation of H-bombs.

It coincided in a rift between America and its oldest ally, fuelled by American alarm at British spies such as Alan Nunn May working for the Russians, which resulted in the McMahon Act banning America from supplying 'restricted data' about nuclear weapons to Britain or Canada. It was lifted in 1958 but the decade-long rift officially led to Britain 'going it alone' with its nuclear deterrent.

The Labour Prime Minister, Clement Attlee, who took over from Churchill at Potsdam, faced a split in his Cabinet between the left-wingers including Hugh Dalton, the Chancellor, and Sir Stafford Cripps, who wanted Britain to abandon the nuclear bomb because of the development costs, and the Foreign Secretary, Ernest Bevin, who said: 'We've got to have this thing over here, whatever it costs. We've got to have the bloody Union Jack on top of it.'[14]

The Attlee Government decided that Britain had to go on with its own nuclear deterrent, although critics today insist it is neither independent nor a deterrent to the modern threat of terrorism.

Post-war baby boomers lived with the daily fear of nuclear bombs. Like tinnitus, it was always in the background. One morning in October 1962, I woke up wondering if we were going to survive to the next day. It was the height of the Cuban missile crisis and President Kennedy had given an ultimatum to the irascible Soviet leader, Nikita Khrushchev, to remove Soviet nuclear missiles targeted at the United States from Cuba. The next day, both sides backed off, and the world breathed a collective sigh of relief.

There were other, less publicised, nuclear stand-offs. A former senior RAF officer has told me how close he came to delivering a British nuclear bomb to stop a Soviet tank attack across West Germany at a time of crisis: he had to sit in the cockpit of his Vulcan bomber on the runway of a British base with the engines running with a three-minute warning to take off. It was not a training exercise; his nuclear bombs were armed and ready to go.

The Aldermaston 'Ban the Bomb' marches that were a feature of Britain in the 1960s and early 1970s were revived in the 1980s when there were protests about the siting of US Cruise missiles in Britain. The Imperial War Museum staged an exhibition in January 2016 of the artwork it spawned, including a photomontage by Peter Kennard of Constable's' Hay Wain' with two Cruise missiles in the cart. So far, the doctrine of Mutually Assured Destruction – MAD – has held, but given such close calls in the past, many wondered: for how long?

The fear of nuclear Armageddon between the world's superpowers has given way to a general fear about terrorism, but the argument about the bomb refuses to go away. It has its echo in today's Labour Party under Jeremy Corbyn who supports unilateral nuclear disarmament. Since the Attlee government wrestled with the problem, however, nuclear weapons have proliferated; the nuclear states now include China, Israel, Pakistan, India, South Africa, North Korea; Iran has put on hold its nuclear ambitions.

And it is not only seen as an insurance policy against nuclear attack. Winston Churchill and Ernest Bevin correctly anticipated that ownership of the nuclear weapon would become a guarantee of a nation's international status. When confronted with the argument in 1954, Churchill had no doubt: 'We must do it. It's the price we pay to sit at the top table.'[15]

The five permanent members of the U.N. Security Council – the United States, the United Kingdom, France, China and Russia – all have nuclear weapons. If Britain gave up its nuclear weapon, it would come under pressure to give up its permanent seat on the Security Council. The continued possession of a nuclear weapon for the British is therefore a much greater issue than the bomb itself – it is about whether we are willing to continue playing the role of a world power.

Since Heisenberg and Hitler's *Uranverein* claimed the moral high ground at Farm Hall, Britain is still struggling to come to terms with the loss of its imperial past. Germany, meanwhile, is the economic powerhouse of the European Union. Germany could develop nuclear weapons, but under the Nuclear Non-Proliferation Treaty, has decided not to do so.

Britain's need to replace the ageing Trident missile system has rekindled the arguments for a new generation, who are learning to come to grips with the extraordinary facts about the British 'independent' nuclear deterrent: there are four submarines, one of which is at sea every hour of every day, travelling the earth's oceans 24/7, waiting for the Doomsday order from the prime minister. Each of the missiles carries multiple, independently-targetable warheads; the number is still Top Secret but it is enough to swamp the most sophisticated defensive systems in the world and crack 'hardened' targets, such as Moscow or Beijing. The replacement for

Trident has to be yet more powerful and the cost has escalated to an estimated £100 billion. Is Britain still prepared to pay the price for staying at the top table?

On 16 November 1945 – three months after the atomic bombs on Hiroshima and Nagasaki – the detainees read a report in the *Daily Telegraph* that Otto Hahn had been awarded the 1944 Nobel Prize for Chemistry for the discovery of fission. The inmates of Farm Hall decided to throw a celebration party for Hahn, which was duly recorded in one of his last intelligence reports by Major Tom Rittner. Under the Top Secret stamp, he reported that the detainees had enjoyed a comic speech by Bagge and then joined in a song specially composed for the Nobel Prize winner:

> Detained since more than half a year
> Are Hahn and we in Farm Hall here
> If you ask who bears the blame
> Otto Hahn's the culprit's name.
>
> (refrain)
> The real reason by the by
> Is we worked on nuclei

Hahn was denied permission to go to Stockholm to receive the Nobel Prize and the detainees spent a restless Christmas 1945 demanding to be released. Their demands were finally met on 3 January 1946 when the ten German scientists were flown to Lubeck in the British occupation zone in Northern Germany and released to return to academic and research careers in Germany. It was exactly six months after they arrived at the manor house in Godmanchester. Farm Hall finally closed its doors on the secret war and the race to stop Hitler gaining the atomic bomb.

Postscript

Colonel Boris T. Pash joined the CIA after the war and became a Cold War warrior. He ran a controversial black-ops unit, PB/7, tasked with counter-espionage of the Soviet Union and its satellites. It was alleged that this included kidnapping of people of value to the Soviets from behind the Iron Curtain and assassinations, 'wet ops'. Pash vehemently denied the claims made by E. Howard Hunt while Hunt was in prison for his part in the Watergate affair. But Pash admitted PB/7 had a wide remit, covering tasks not covered by the other six CIA units with a PB/ prefix. He died in 1995 at the age of ninety-four.

Major General Leslie R. Groves was promoted to Lieutenant General before leaving the army in 1948; the promotion was backdated to 16 July 1945, the day of the Trinity Test. He went on to become vice president of the electronics giant, Sperry Rand. He died in 1970 aged seventy-three.

Werner Heisenberg became a leading figure in science policy in West Germany. He returned to Germany as director of the institute for physics in Göttingen in 1946 and later in Munich. He died in 1976, aged seventy-four.

Otto Hahn was awarded the Nobel Prize in Chemistry for 1944. He died in 1968 aged eighty-nine.

Carl Friedrich von Weizsäcker worked with Heisenberg at Göttingen after the war and became a respected professor of philosophy at the University of Hamburg. He died in 2007 aged ninety-four.

Lieutenant Commander Eric Welsh was awarded a CMG – a Foreign Office honour for MI6 officers – in the 1952 Honours

List. He died suddenly of a heart attack on 21 November 1954 when years of heavy drinking caught up with him. He was aged fifty-seven. Special Branch are said to have searched his home at 48 Addison Road, among the upmarket white-stucco mansions of Holland Park, West London, in search of his 'little black book' in which he kept a secret diary, but if it existed, they did not find it.

Wing Commander Bruce Bonsey left the SIS in December 1945 to join British Air Forces of Occupation (BAFO) headquarters in the German town of Bad Eilsen with 'Flash Harry Humphrys' as his boss. He confided to R. V. Jones: 'I was completely adrift and hated it, except that I enjoyed the location. It was a horribly harsh adjustment to make, being "one of a mob" when, since August '43, I had been running Farm Hall after Cautley handed over to me ...' He married Phyllis Gabell in Kensington in 1957 when he was fifty-one. He retired to the Algarve, Portugal, where he died in 1989 aged eighty.

Major Tom Rittner took sick leave from Farm Hall and left the Intelligence Corps in 1946. His daughter, Rosemarie, told me he had an operation for a slipped disc at that time. He never spoke about what made him give up his commission in the armed forces less than a year later, but it may also have been the stress of reporting on the reaction of Hitler's nuclear scientists when they heard the Allies had detonated the world's first atomic bomb. 'I would not have thought it unlikely that as the moral dimension to it became clear, he would have wanted to wash his hands of the whole thing,' said Luke Rittner. Major Rittner devoted the rest of his life to his faith. His mother died on 1 December 1947 in the Convent of Mary Reparatrix in Edinburgh and the probate records show that at that time, the Major Rittner was making a living again as a commercial traveller. However, his passion was the Catholic Church. He became general secretary of the Catholic Truth Society, edited a history of the Catholic Church in England and Wales, and published a new version of the Catholic Bible for which he was personally honoured with a papal knighthood by Pope Pius XII. He died in 1975, aged sixty-nine. His obituary in *The Tablet* in March 1975 said: 'With his habitual calm and subdued elegance in appearance, Tom Rittner looked rather as if he had stepped out of Whitehall than from his large headquarters in Eccleston Square. He was always courteous even in disagreement and he was deeply devout but never self-righteous.'[7]

Notes

1 – The House of Secrets

1. Professor Echenique interview with the author
2. Ray Berry, *We're at War Boys*, WW2 People's War, BBC, www.bbc.co.uk/history/ww2peopleswar/

2 – The Führer's Superweapon

1. Foot, M. R. D., Obituary of R. V. Jones, the *Independent*, 21 September 2011
2. Jones, R. V., *Most Secret War* (London: Hamish Hamilton, 1978), p. 92
3. http://ww2news.com/europe/joyous-crowds-greet-hitler-in-danzig/
4. http://www.hitler.org/speeches/09-13-39.html
5. Jones, R. V., report to Lord Cherwell, G535/2 Cherwell Archive, Nuffield College, Oxford
6. Jones, R. V., *An Improved Scientific Intelligence Service*, AIR 40/2857 National Archives, Kew
7. Jones, R. V., *Most Secret War* (London: Hamish Hamilton, 1978), p. 117

3 – Hitler's Uranium Club

1. *Hitler's Atomic Bomb*, Horizon 1992
2. Szilard, Leo, *His Version of the Facts: Selected Recollections and Correspondence* (Cambridge Massachusetts: MIT Press, 1980), p. 17
3. Bronowski, J., *Ascent of Man* (London: BBC Publications, 1973) p. 370
4. Rife, Patricia, *Lise Meitner and the Dawn of the Nuclear Age* (Boston, US: Birkhauser, 1999), p. 166
5. Cornwell, John, *Hitler's Scientists, Science War and the Devil's Pacts* (London: Penguin, 2004), p. 216
6. Cornwell, p. 217

7. Einstein, Letter to F. D. Roosevelt, Box 5, Franklin D. Roosevelt Presidential Library and Museum, New York, 2 August 1939

8. Szilard, Leo, Memorandum, Box 5, FDR Presidential Library and Museum, New York.

9. Rosbaud correspondence and manuscripts, Box 28, Folder 42, Samuel A. Goudsmit papers 1921–79, Series IV Alsos Mission, Niels Bohr Library and Archives, American Institute of Physics, p. 9

10. Rhodes, Richard, *The Making of the Atomic Bomb* (London: Simon and Schuster, 2012) p. 290

11. Heisenberg, Werner, *Professor in Leipzig*, American Institute of Physics, online: www.aip.org/history/heisenberg

12. Rosbaud, Paul, Box 28, Folder 42, Samuel A. Goudsmit papers, 1921–79, Niels Bohr Library and Archives, American Institute of Physics, p. 8

13. Heisenberg, Werner, *Research in Germany on the Technical Application of Atomic Energy* (America: Nature, 16 August 1947)

14. Hahn, Otto, *My Life* (London: MacDonald, 1970)

15. Armin, Hermann, *The New Physics: The Route into the Atomic Age* (Munich: Heinz Moos Verlag, 1979), p. 47

16. Von Weizsäcker, Carl Friedrich, *Hitler's Atomic Bomb* (Horizon, 1992)

17. Rosbaud, Paul, Correspondence and manuscripts, Box 28, Folder 42, Samuel A. Goudsmit papers 1921–79, Series IV Alsos Mission, Niels Bohr Library and Archives, American Institute of Physics, p. 9

4 – Heavy Water and the French Connection

1. Kowarski, Lew Interview by Charles Weiner on 20 October 1969, session III, Niels Bohr Library & Archives, American Institute of Physics (AIP), College Park, Maryland, USA: www.aip.org/history-programs/niels-bohr-library/oral-histories/4717-3

2. Kowarski, AIP session II

3. Kowarski, AIP session III

4. History of BNP Paribas, website: http://history.bnpparibas/document/jacques-allier-banker-in-the-secret-war/

5. Clark, W. Ronald, *The Birth of the Bomb* (London: Phoenix House Ltd, 1961), p. 71

6. Clark, p. 72

7. Clark, p. 141

8. Kowarski, AIP III

5 – The Crown Jewels

1. Freeman, Kerin, *The Civilian Bomb Disposing Earl: Jack Howard and Bomb Disposal in WW2* (London: Casemate Publishers, 2014), p. 96

2. Kowarski, Lew interview by Charles Weiner on 1969 October 20, session III, Niels Bohr Library & Archives, American Institute of Physics, College Park, Maryland, USA. AIP Online: aip.org/history-programs/niels-bohr-library/oral-histories/4717-3

3. AVIA 22-2288A National Archives, Kew, Obituary of the Earl of Suffolk, *The Times*, 21 May 1941

4. Nicolle, Marguerite, *Diary*, posted by Ian Golding, son of Major Golding, with Suffolk-Golding mission documents: www.ww2talk.com

5. ibid.

6. Spears, Major General Sir Edward, *Assignment to Catastrophe*, Volume 1 (London: Heinemann, 1954). p318-9

7. AVIA 22/3201 Report of Suffolk-Golding mission to France 1940, National Archives, Kew

8. Kowarski AIP III www.aip.org/history-programs/niels-bohr-library/oral-histories/4717-3

9. ibid.

10. ibid.

11. BT 389/5/203 Log of SS *Broompark*, the National Archives, Kew

12. CUST 106/854, the National Archives, Kew

13. Macmillan, Harold, *Blast of War* (London: Harper and Row, 1968), p. 79

14. Martin, Roy V. *The Suffolk Golding Mission: A Considerable Service* (UK: Brook House Books, 2014)

15. AVIA 22-2288A, the Suffolk-Golding Mission, the National Archives, Kew

16. Morshead, O.F., letter AVIA22-2288A, the National Archives, Kew

17. *The Ranger, The Queen's Castle*, Episode 3/3, BBC TV, 2005

6 – Catastrophe

1. Jones, R. V. *Most Secret War* (London: Hamish Hamilton, 1978), p. 269

2. Jones, p. 269

3. Jones, p. 270

4. Jones, p. 59

5. '*Nuclear reactor secrets revealed*', BBC News report 1 June 2007

6. Heisenberg, Werner, transcript, Box 27, Folder 40, Miscellaneous Papers, Samuel A. Goudsmit papers, 1921–79, Niels Bohr Library and Archives, American Institute of Physics

7. Jeffrey, Keith, *MI6: The History of the Secret Intelligence Service 1909–1949* (London: Bloomsbury Press, 2010), p. 375

8. Churchill, Winston, *Their Finest Hour*, Volume 2 (London: Cassell, 1949), p. 412

9. O'Connor, Bernard, *RAF Tempsford, Churchill's Most Secret Airfield* (Stroud: Amberley 2010)

10. Olsen, Oluf Reed, *Two Eggs on My Plate* (London: George Allen and Unwin Ltd, 1952), p. 96

11. WO 331/16-18, War Office records, War Crimes, the National Archives, Kew

7 – The Real Heroes of Telemark

1. Haukelid, Knut, *Skis Against the Atom* (North Dakota: North American Heritage Press, 1989)

2. *Last Hero of Telemark: The Man Who Helped Stop Hitler's A-Bomb*, Gordon Corera, 25 April BBC, 2013: www.bbc.co.uk/news/uk-22298739

3. Helm, Sarah, *A Life in Secrets – The Story of Vera Atkins and the Lost Agents of SOE* (London: Little Brown, 2005), p. 8

4. Dahl, Per F., *Heavy Water and the Wartime Race for Nuclear Energy* (London: Institute of Physics Publishing, 1999), p. 198

5. Haukelid, p. 74

6. 'WWII Hero Credits Luck and Chance in Foiling Hitler's Nuclear Ambitions', Andrew Higgins, *New York Times*, 20 November 2015

7. Haukelid, p. 75

8. O'Connor, Bernard, *RAF Tempsford, Churchill's Most Secret Airfield* (Stroud: Amberley 2010)

9. Haukelid, p. 76

10. Olsen, Oluf Reed, *Two Eggs on My Plate* (London: George Allen and Unwin Ltd, 1952), p. 96

11. *Memories of a Sutton Girl*, Mrs Park, WW2 People's War, BBC Online: www. bbc.co.uk/history/ww2peopleswar/stories/66/a4055366. html

12. Charrot, John, WW2 People's War, BBC TV 2005

13. ibid.

14. *The Telemark Sabotage*, Stormbird, forum: www.ww2talk.com

15. 'WWII Hero credits luck and chance in foiling Hitler's nuclear ambitions', Andrew Higgins, *New York Times*, 20 November 2015

16. 'A New Mission for the Hero of Telemark', Paul Kendall, *Daily Telegraph*, 2 May 2010

17. Rønneberg, Joachim, Lecture to the International Conference on Nuclear Technology and Politics Rjukan 16–18 June 1993

18. Foot, M. R. D., *SOE The Special Operations Executive 1940–45* (London: BBC 1984), p. 211

19. Wilkinson, Peter and Joan Bright Astley, *Gubbins and SOE* (Barnsley, UK: Pen and Sword, 2010), p. 120

20. Gubbins, Sir Colin, Lecture at the Royal United Services Institute (RUSI) 1948

21. Biography of Charles Jocelyn Hambro, The Cobbold Trust: http://family-tree. cobboldfht.com/people/view/453

22. Dalton, Hugh, *The Political Diary of Hugh Dalton*, edited by Ben Pimlott (London: Jonathan Cape, 1987), p.428

23. Krause, Carolyn, *Historically Speaking* column *The Oak Ridger*, 10 December 2012

24. *A Tentative Decision to Build the Bomb*, US Department of Energy: www. osti.gov/opennet/manhattan-project-history/Events/1939-1942/tentative_ decision_build.htm

8 – The Bomb and the Carlsberg Brewery

1. Irving, David, *The Virus House* (London: William Kimber, 1967), p. 109

2. Schaaf, Michael, *Heisenberg, Hitler und die Bombe: Gespräche mit Zeitzeugen* (Berlin: Diepholz, 2001)

3. Speer, Albert, *Inside the Third Reich* (New York: Macmillan, 1970), p. 317

4. ibid.
5. Letter, Arthur Compton to Vannevar Bush, 22 June 1942, RG227, Bush-Conant File, Development of the Atomic Bomb, Records of the Office of Scientific Research and Development National Archives and Records Administration, Washington, DC
6. Gowing, Margaret, *Britain and Atomic Energy 1939–1945* (London: Macmillan and Co, 1964), p. 247
7. *Who Was Werner Heisenberg*, family website: http://werner-heisenberg.unh.edu/
8. *Hitler's Atomic Bomb*, Horizon, 1992
9. Niels Bohr Archive: www.nba.nbi.dk/papers/docs/cover.html
10. *The Difficult Years*, American Institute of Physics and David Cassidy, 1998–2015: www.aip.org/history/heisenberg/p11.htm
11. Kramish, Arnold, *The Griffin* (Boston: Houghton Mifflin, 1986), p. 203
12. *The World in a Briefcase* by Angela Hind, BBC News, BBC Radio 4, 5 February 2007
13. Gowing, Margaret, Minute from Sir John Anderson to Prime Minister, 30.7.42 Appendix Three, *Britain and Atomic Energy 1939–1945* (London: Macmillan and Co, 1964)
14. Norris, Robert S., *Racing for the Bomb, the True Story of General Leslie R. Groves* (New York: Skyhorse Publishing, 2014)
15. Prime Minister's Personal Minute Prem 3/139.11A M662/4, National Archives, Kew
16. Aide-memoire of conversation between the president and the prime minister, Hyde Park, 18 September 1944, Prem 3/139/11A, National Archives, Kew
17. Prem 3/139/11A, National Archives, Kew

9 – The Bastard Mission

1. ARC 61137, National Archives, Washington, US
2. Pash, Colonel Boris T., *The Alsos Mission* (New York: Charter, 1969), p. 19
3. Pash, p. 36
4. Dorril, Stephen, *MI6: Inside the Convert World of HM SIS* (London: Simon and Schuster, 2000), p. 133
5. Goodman, Michael S., *Spying on the Nuclear Bear* (Stanford California: Stanford University Press, 2007)
6. Goodman, p. 12
7. Groves, General Leslie, *Now It Can Be Told: The Story of the Manhattan Project* (Boston: De Capo Press, 2009), p. 199
8. Tube Alloys, Prime Minister's Papers Prem 3/139/11A 26/4, National Archives, Kew
9. ibid.
10. Brown, Colin, *Real Britannia, Our Ten Proudest Years – the Glory and the Spin* (London: Oneworld Publications, 2012), p201

11. Groves, General Leslie, memorandum to Dill, Correspondence of the Manhattan Engineer District 1942–46, microfilm publication M1109, Roll 5, Target 8, Folder
12. Groves, p. 199
13. Groves, p. 206
14. POW Conversations, Message to Major R. R. Furman, 22 June 1944, Collection Robert S. Norris, Box 36, Folder RG227 OSRD, Hoover Institution Archives, Stanford, California

10 – The Wild Bunch

1. Pash, Boris T., Papers, Box 2, Folder 1, Hoover Institution Library and Archives, Stanford, California
2. Tompkins, T. P., Boris T. Pash, Papers, Box 2, Folder 3–4, Hoover Institution Archives, Stanford, California
3. ibid.: First draft of official history of ALSOS Mission
4. Weart, Spencer R., *Scientists in Power – France and the Origins of Nuclear Energy, 1900–1950*, Bulletin of the Atomic Scientists, March 1979
5. Joliot, Frederic, interrogation, Boris T. Pash, papers, Box 2, Folder 1, Hoover Institution Archives, Stanford, California
6. Pash, p. 87
7. Johnson, Paul, *Churchill* (London: Viking, 2009), p. 136
8. Furman, Robert, interview, *Voices of the Manhattan Project*, Atomic Heritage Foundation, Washington, 20 February 2008: www.manhattanprojectvoices.org/oral-histories/robert-furmans-interview
9. Goudsmit, p. 69
10. 'New Book Says US Plotted to Kill Top Nazi Scientist', by William J. Broad, *New York Times*, 28 February 1993
11. Pash, p. 162

11 – Operation Big

1. Heisenberg, Werner, diary, http://werner-heisenberg.unh.edu/
2. Bagge, Erich, Interview, Hitler's Atomic Bomb, Horizon 1992
3. Rosbaud, Paul, correspondence and manuscripts 1945, p. 12, Box 28, Folder 42, Samuel A. Goudsmit Papers 1921–79 Niels Bohr Library and Archives
4. Groves, p. 234
5. Groves, p. 239
6. Prem 3/139/12 Prime Minister's papers, National Archives, Kew
7. Goudsmit, p. 88
8. Atomkeller-Museum, Haigerloch
9. Beck, Hans, *Historical Witnesses from Haigerloch*, Atomkeller-Museum, Haigerloch
10. Guide, Marquard, *Historical Witnesses from Haigerloch*, leaflet Atomkeller-Museum, Haigerloch

11. Beck, Hans, *Historical witnesses from Haigerloch*, Atomkeller-Museum, Haigerloch
12. Pash, p. 206
13. Pash, p. 207
14. Atomkeller-Museum, Haigerloch
15. Guide, Marquard, *Historical Witnesses from Haigerloch*, leaflet Atomkeller-Museum, Haigerloch
16. Wing Commander Rupert Cecil, *Obituary, Daily Telegraph*, 14 July 2004.
17. Fechter, Egidius, guide and expert on the Atom-Keller, interview with the author, September, 2015

12 – The Jackpot

1. Speer, p. 626
2. Pash, p. 211
3. Pash, Boris T., Papers, Box 2, Folder 1, Hoover Institution Library and Archives, Stanford, California
4. Pash, Boris T., Alsos Mission, 1 of 4 films, Hoover Institution Library Archives, Stanford, California
5. Interrogation Reports, Freedom of Information release, p. 81, CIA, USA http://www.foia.cia.gov/

13 – Farm Hall at War

1. Bonsey, Wing Commander Bruce, Letter to R. V. Jones, Jones papers, Section B 95-8-00/B322, Churchill Library Archives Centre, Churchill College, Cambridge
2. Document 6609, Private Papers of Wing Commander Bonsey, Imperial War Museum, London
3. ibid.
4. ibid.
5. ibid.
6. Margaret Thatcher interview, *The Downing Street Years*, Fine Art Productions, www.awesomestories.com/asset/view/Iron-Lady-Treachery-with-a-Smile-on-Its-Face
7. *Group Captain P.C. 'Pick' Pickard*, Chris Hobbs: www.chrishobbs.com
8. *Operation Jericho*, documentary by Martin Shaw, BBC TV, 2011
9. Olsen, Oluf Reed, *Two Eggs on My Plate* (London: George Allen and Unwin, 1952)
10. Helm, Sarah, *A Life in Secrets, The Story of Vera Atkins and the Lost Agents of SOE* (London: Brown Little, 2005)
11. 'WWII heroine Violet Szabo's George Cross fetches £260k', *Daily Telegraph*, 22 July 2015
12. 'On the Run Again', Angus Nasmyth-Shaw, interview with Jeff Barbee, *The Guardian*, 9 April 2005

14 – Operation Epsilon

1. Fry, Helen, author of *The M Room* (London: Marranos Press, 2012), email to the author
2. Rittner, Major T. H., P5 report to Lt Col. M. W. Perrin and Lt Comdr E. Welsh, Farm Hall Transcripts, WO 208/5019 National Archives, Kew
3. 'The Princesses' Big Night Out', *Daily Express*, 2 May 2015
4. *Holocaust: The Events and Their Impact on Real People*, p. 146 (London: DK Publishing, 2007)
5. Rittner, Luke, interview with the author, 10 November 2015
6. Records of Intelligence Corps supplied by A. F. Judge, Intelligence Corps Museum, Chicksands, Bedfordshire
7. Jones, p. 604
8. Groves, General Leslie, notes on discussion with Dr Chadwick, Friday 1 June 1945, Folder 001, Meetings, Box 33, Entry 5, RG77, National Archives and Records Administration, USA
9. Norris, Robert, *Racing for the Bomb: The True Story of General Leslie R. Groves* (New York: Skyhorse Publishing, 2014)
10. Hill, Ralph W., *Rationing and shortages*, WW2 People's War, BBC online: http://www.bbc.co.uk/history/ww2peopleswar/stories/84/a4537884.shtml
11. WO 208/5019 National Archives, Kew
12. Bonsey, Wing Commander B., private papers, 6609 Imperial War Museum, London
13. BBC News broadcast, 9 p.m. on 6 August 1945, BBC Written Archives
14. Brown, Colin, *Glory and B*llocks – the Truth Behind 10 Defining Events in British History*, (London: Oneworld, 2013), p. 242
15. BBC News broadcast, 9 p.m. on 6 August 1945, BBC Written Archives
16. Frank, Sir Charles, Introduction, *Hitler's Uranium Club: The Secret Recordings at Farm Hall* (New York: Copernicus Books, 2001)
17. Norris, Robert S., *Racing for the Bomb, the True Story of General Leslie R. Groves* (New York: Skyhorse Publishing, 2014).
18. Bernstein, Jeremy, *Hitler's Uranium Club: The Secret Recordings at Farm Hall* (New York: Copernicus Books, 2001), p. 334
19. Jones, R. V., *Most Secret War* (London: Hamish Hamilton, 1978)
20. Frank, Sir Charles, *Introduction, Operation Epsilon, the Farm Hall Transcripts* (Berkeley: University of California Press, 1993)
21. Heisenberg, Jochen: werner-heisenberg.unh.edu/mit-jochen.htm
22. Bagge, Diebner and Jay, *Von der Uranspaltung bis Calder Hall* (Hamburg: Rowohlt, 1957)
23. Echenique, Marcial, interview with the author, Farm Hall, October 2013
24. Mackay, Lord, email to the author, 1 November 2015
25. Heisenberg, Jochen, email to the author, 2015
26. 'Found, Hitler's Secret Nuke Plant: Vast underground complex where the Nazis worked on developing weapons is discovered in Austria', *Daily Mail*, 28 December 2014
27. 'Men tell Polish TV they have 'irrefutable proof' Nazi gold train exists', *Guardian*, 4 September 2015.
28. *Gold of the Nazi Underground*, documentary, National Geographic, 2014

15 – The Dirty Secret

1. Stimson, Henry, letter to Truman, 24 April 1945, Harry S. Truman Library
2. Berry, Ray, *We're at War, Boys*, Part4, BBC People's War: http://www.bbc.co.uk/history/ww2peopleswar/stories/25/a6390425.shtml
3. Jones, p. 605
4. Szilard, Leo, interview, US News and World Report, 15 August 1960
5. CAB 120/303, National Archives, Kew
6. Wellerstein, Alex, *When did the Allies know there wasn't a German bomb?* The Nuclear Secrecy Blog, 13 November 2015: www.nuclearsecrecy.com
7. Stimson, Henry, Diary, Henry Stimson Papers, Manuscripts and Archives, Yale University Library
8. Churchill, Winston, *Triumph and Tragedy* (Boston: Houghton-Mifflin, 1953), p. 669–70
9. Potsdam Note, *The Manhattan Project – an Interactive History*, US Department of Energy
10. Rossiter, Mike, *The Spy Who Changed the World* (London: Headline, 2014)
11. Beevor, Antony, *Berlin, the Downfall 1945* (London: Penguin Books, 2007), p. 326
12. Stone, Oliver, 'America Always Wins', *Guardian*, 5 April 2013
13. Stimson, Henry, letter to President Harry S. Truman, Confidential File, Truman Papers, Truman Library
14. Hennessy Peter, interview with Lord Plowden, *A Bloody Union Jack on Top of It*, BBC Radio 4, 5–12 May 1988
15. Hennessy, Peter, *The Secret State, Whitehall and the Cold War* (London: Penguin Press, 2002), p. 55

Select Bibliography

Beevor, Antony, *Berlin – The Downfall 1945* (London: Penguin Books, 2007)

Bernstein, Jeremy, *Hitler's Uranium Club*, Appendix A (New York: Copernicus Books, 2001)

Cornwell, John, *Hitler's Scientists, Science War and the Devil's Pacts* (London: Penguin, 2004)

Clark, Ronald W., *The Birth of the Bomb* (London: Phoenix House, 1961)

Foot, M. R. D., *SOE The Special Operations Executive 1940-45* (London: BBC 1984)

Freeman, Kerin, *The Civilian Bomb Disposing Earl* (Barnsley, UK: Pen and Sword Books, 2015)

Fry, Helen, *The M Room: Secret Listeners who Bugged the Nazis* (London: Marronos Press, 2012)

Goudsmit, Samuel A., *ALSOS* (New York: American Institute of Physics, 1996)

Gowing, Margaret, *Britain and Atomic Energy 1939–1945* (London: Macmillan and Co, 1964)

Groves, General Leslie, *Now It Can Be Told, the Story of the Manhattan Project* (Boston: De Capo Press, 2009)

Haukelid, Knut, *Skis Against the Atom* (North Dakota: North American Heritage Press, 1989)

Helm, Sarah, *A Life in Secrets – The Story of Vera Atkins and the Lost Agents of SOE* (London: Little Brown, 2005)

Hennessy, Peter, *The Secret State, Whitehall and the Cold War* (London: Penguin Press, 2002)

Jeffrey, Keith, *MI6: The History of the Secret Intelligence Service 1909–1949* (London: Bloomsbury Press, 2010)

Jones, R. V., *Most Secret War* (London: Hamish Hamilton, 1978)

Irving, David, *The Virus House* (London: William Kimber, 1967)

Kramish, Arnold, *The Griffin* (Boston: Houghton Mifflin, 1986)

Norris, Robert S., *Racing for the Bomb, the True Story of General Leslie R. Groves* (New York: Skyhorse Publishing, 2014)

Martin, Roy V. *The Suffolk-Golding Mission: A Considerable Service* (UK: Brook House Books, 2014)

O'Connor, Bernard *RAF Tempsford, Churchill's Most Secret Airfield* (Stroud: Amberley, 2010)

Olsen, Oluf Reed, *Two Eggs on My Plate* (London: George Allen and Unwin Ltd, 1952)

Richelson, Jeffrey T., *Spying on the Bomb* (New York: W. W. Norton and Company, 2006)

Rose, Paul Lawrence, *Heisenberg and the Nazi Atomic Bomb Project* (Berkeley: University of California Press, 1998)

Speer, Albert, *Inside the Third Reich* (London: Weidenfeld and Nicholson, 1970)

Pash, Colonel Boris T., *The Alsos Mission* (New York: Charter, 1969)

Walker, Mark, *German National Socialism and the Quest for Nuclear Power. 1939–1949* (Cambridge: Cambridge University Press, 1989)

Wilkinson, Peter and Joan Bright Astley, *Gubbins and SOE* (Barnsley, UK: Pen and Sword, 2010)

Acknowledgements

I owe a debt of gratitude to many including: Professor Marcial Echenique, the owner of Farm Hall; Carol A. Leadenham, assistant archivist for reference at the Hoover Institution Archives Stanford for tireless access to the papers of Boris T. Pash; Joe Anderson, Director of the Niels Bohr Library and Archives at the American Institute of Physics; Gerry Taggart for help with research on Major Thomas Hardwick Rittner; Luke Rittner for his assistance on his uncle, Major Rittner; Adam Ganz for his assistance on his late father and the team of 'listeners' at Farm Hall; Jane Koropsak at the Brookhaven National Laboratory, USA; Maria Payne, assistant curator at the Imperial War Museum; Paul Johnson at the National Archives, Kew; Angus Shaw for assistance on his father, Cautley Nasmyth-Shaw; Al Larson for permission to quote from Knut Haukelid's *Skis Against the Atom*; Jochen Heisenberg for the use of his father's diary; Sarah Helm for her expertise on SOE women; Fred Judge, senior researcher at the Intelligence Museum; Owen Pagano at the Atomic Heritage Foundation in the US for permission to use extracts of the Major Robert Furman interview; Kerin Freeman for her generosity in sharing information on the Suffolk-Golding mission; David Denholm of J. and J. Denholm for supplying the image of his company's ship, SS *Broompark*; Ian Golding for sharing the gems of memorabilia from the Suffolk-Golding mission; Clare Kavanagh, assistant librarian of the Nuffield College Library, Oxford; Roy Martin for his assistance on the Suffolk-Golding mission; Graeme Hill for expertise in drawing the maps; Professor Christian Baumgart of Wurzburg for assistance with translation of German texts; Hannah Ratford of the BBC Written Archives Centre; my editor Shaun Barrington for his support; but most of all to my indefatigable researcher in America, Dr Camilla Lindan, and in London, my wife, Amanda Brown.

List of Illustrations

18. The Maud Report found that atomic bombs could be made with just 11 kg of uranium. (Author's collection)

19. Alsos Council of War at Hechingen: back row (left to right) Major David Gattiker, Lieutenant Commander Eric Welsh, Dave Griggs, Captain Reg Augustine, Wing Commander Rupert Cecil; seated (left to right) Lieutenant Colonel Percy Rothwell, Sir Charles Hambro, Dr Carl Bauman, Fred Wardenberg, Lieutenant Colonel John Lansdale, Michael Perrin, James Lane and Colonel Boris T. Pash. (Courtesy of Brookhaven National, AIP Emilio Segre Visual Archives, Goudsmit Collection)

20. Robert Oppenheimer led the Manhattan Project team but had his security clearance withdrawn. (Author's collection)

21. General Leslie R. Groves, known as the 'biggest son-of-a-bitch', ran the Manhattan Project. (Author's collection)

22. The Big Three at Potsdam: Churchill, Truman and Stalin. (Courtesy of the US National Archives and Records Administration)

23. The Alsos team reviewing documents seized at Walter Gerlach's lab at Thuringen. From left to right: Sam Goudsmit, Fred Wardenberg, Eric Welsh and Rupert Cecil. (Courtesy of Brookhaven National Laboratory, AIP Emilio Segre Visual Archives, Goudsmit Collection)

24. Sam Goudsmit (right) and Lieutenant Toepel driving a military jeep during the Alsos Mission in Stadtilm 16 April 1945. (Photograph by Malcolm Thurgood, reproduced courtesy AIP Emilio Segre Visual Archives)

25. Colonel Boris T. Pash (left) on Operation Big in Hechingen with Sergeant Holt (middle) and Corporal Brown (right). (Courtesy of the Brookhaven National Laboratory, AIP Emilio Segre Visual Archives, Goudsmit Collection)

26. The Jackpot, the message from SHAEF to Marshall and Eisenhower saying Pash has 'hit the jackpot'. (Courtesy of the Boris Pash Collection, Box 2, Folder 1, Hoover Institute Archives)

27. The cave at Hagierloch, where the Alsos team found the German atomic reactor. It now houses the Atomkeller Museum. (Author's collection)

28. American trucks assembled outside the Haigerloch cave. (Author's collection)

29. The Alsos team dismantling the German atomic pile at Haigerloch – portly Lieutenant Commander Eric Welsh stands on the rim handing out graphite blocks. Wing Commander Rupert Cecil is in the foreground. (Author's collection)

30. Hagierloch. The cave where the Alsos team found the German atomic reactor.

31. A reconstruction of the German atomic pile in the Atomkeller Museum at Haigerloch. (Author's collection)

32. Members of the Alsos team digging up uranium cubes buried near Haigerloch. (Courtesy of AIP Emilio Segrè Visual Archives, gift of Michaele Thurgood Haynes and Terry Thurgood, Thurgood Collection)

About the Author

Colin Brown is the former Deputy Political Editor of the *Independent* and Political Editor of the *Sunday Telegraph* and the *Independent on Sunday*. He worked for thirty years as a lobby journalist at Westminster and is the author of five books, including *Whitehall: The Street That Shaped a Nation* (Simon and Schuster).